Robert Vashon Rogers

Wrongs and Rights of a Traveller

By boat-by stage-by rail

Robert Vashon Rogers

Wrongs and Rights of a Traveller
By boat-by stage-by rail

ISBN/EAN: 9783337413071

Printed in Europe, USA, Canada, Australia, Japan

Cover: Foto ©Lupo / pixelio.de

More available books at **www.hansebooks.com**

WRONGS AND RIGHTS

OF

A TRAVELLER,

BY BOAT—BY STAGE—BY RAIL.

BY
A BARRISTER-AT-LAW,
OF OSGOODE HALL.

TORONTO:
PUBLISHED BY R. CARSWELL.
1875.

TO

HIS FELLOWS OF THE LEGAL FRATERNITY,

THE TRAVELLING PUBLIC,

AND

ALL OTHERS WHO MAY CARE TO READ THEREIN,

THIS BOOK IS

Respectfully Dedicated

BY

THE AUTHOR.

PREFACE.

THIS little work does not aspire to compete with the learned productions of Redfield, Chitty or Story, but merely to supply a want, felt by many to exist in this age of perpetual motion, of a plain and brief summary of the rights and liabilities of carriers and passengers by land and by water.

An attempt is made in the following pages to combine instruction with entertainment, information with amusement, and to impart knowledge while beguiling a few hours in a railway carriage, or on a steamboat. Whilst it is hoped that the general public will peruse with interest the text, containing elegant extracts from ponderous legal tomes—gems from the rich mines of legal lore—and where in many cases the law is laid down in the very words of learned judges of England, Canada and the United States; the notes—a cloud of authorities—the index and the list of cases are inserted for the special delectation of the professional reader.

Though written in Ontario, the book will be found applicable to all parts of the Dominion, as well as to the United States and England.

The Author, even if the style is deemed novel, does not seek the praise of originality for the substance of the following chapters, as the greater portion of the text, and well nigh all the notes, have been taken from the works of others, to whom all due thanks are now rendered.

How far the book is likely to be of use to the seeker after knowledge, or of assistance to those desiring to kill time, is for others to determine. If mistakes be discovered it is hoped that the reader—professional or otherwise—will bear with them, "for if the work be found of sufficient merit to require another edition, they will probably be corrected, and if no such demand is made the book has received as much labour as it deserves."

The Author is very "'umble, coming of an 'umble family," like the celebrated Uriah—not the Hittite, but he of the Heap tribe—and he will be quite content and satisfied if every reader, after having perused this work, says of him as Lord Thurlow said of Mansfield: "A surprising man; ninety-nine times out of a hundred he is right in his opinions and decisions, and when once in a hundred times he is wrong, ninety-nine men out of a hundred would not discover it."

CONTENTS.

BOOK FIRST.—BY RAIL.

CHAPTER I.

DRIVING.

                                                                                              PAGE

New Year's Day—Collision with Old Bolus—Must I pay for my servant's deeds—Deaf man run over—Effects of an Avalanche—Housemaid injured by Coachman—Wives, snakes or eels—Driver and Driven—Right side or wrong—Look out—Erskine and Kenyon   1

CHAPTER II.

INSURANCE.

What's an accident ?—Major vis—Exposure and death—Wholly disabled—What can be recovered—Heavy weights — Stumbling — Pitchforked—Change of business—Lost beneath the dancing waves—A man not a private conveyance—Carelessness   8

CHAPTER III.

STATIONS AND STARTING.

Meditations on crossings—Bell or whistle—Access to stations—Slippery ice—Checks on trunks—Notice of arrivals and departures—Trains late as usual—Must keep time—Damages, damages—Proof—Ill fared Welfare—Waiting rooms not smoke-houses—Charge of the iron horse—Tripped up   14

CHAPTER IV.

TICKETS.

Man and wife double as to baggage—Money in trunk—Authority of American decisions—Annual tickets—Badge of officers—Legislature outwitted—"Tickets, sir"—"Good for this day only"—"Good for this trip"—Stepping off—Lose a ticket, and pay again—The Acts   26

CHAPTER V.

PRODUCING TICKETS, OR EVICTION.

Carried past—Jumping off—Junctions—Cave canem—Conductors refusing change—Fighting in the cars—Turned out in the dark—No seats—Coloured persons—Tickets lost and found too late—Conductor's conduct—Damages for wrongful ejectment—Go quietly—Companies heavily mulcted—By law as to producing Tickets—A lover, his mark—Getting off for a moment 35

CHAPTER VI.

PLATFORMS AND ALIGHTING.

Right to safe ingress, egress and regress—Defective platforms—The Englishman and the C'rum cat'or—Getting out of cars—Train not at platform—Calling out name; is it an invitation to alight? Ladies jumping—Must have safe place to alight—Leaving train in motion............. 47

CHAPTER VII.

BAGGAGE.

Gone—Company liable for lost baggage—Carelessness of owner—Checking—What is baggage?—Papers—Spring horse—Household goods going west—Luggage left in cloak room—Limitation of liability—Taking change—Railroad police—Beauties of checks—Fall of a window—Legs and arms outside—Officials squeezing fingers—Stern Boreas. 57

CHAPTER VIII.

DUE CARE.

Snowed up—Pacific Railway—Passenger carriers not insurers—Company must use due care—Defective machinery—Broken axle—Company must account for accident—Difference between goods and men—What is due care? Latent defects in cars—English rule—Rule in New York—Moralizing 69

CHAPTER IX.

ACCIDENTS TO TRAVELLERS.

Standing on platforms of cars—Room and seats to be furnished—Riding in express cars—In caboose car—Rule in Illinois—Walking through the train—Innocent blood—Damages to infants and juveniles—Child's fare unpaid—$1,800 for a baby's leg and hand—Negligence of a nurse—Travelling on free pass—Conditional liability—Company exempt—Pat and Sambo—Home again from a foreign shore 77

CHAPTER X.

INJURIES TO PASSENGERS AND EMPLOYEES.

Inefficient line—Passengers hurt—Employees killed—Lord Campbell's Act—Compensation for death—Solatium for wounded feelings—Scotch law—American law—Hen-pecked husband's will—The rule in Massachusetts—in Pennsylvania—in Maryland—in Canada—Hard to decide—Annuity tables—Bad or diseased—Insured—Children injured.—Parents compensated—Amounts obtained.—A leg at $24,700—For what compensated—Chances of matrimony— Servants injured — Fellow servants—Different companies—Which one to sue—Strangers' acts—Greedy ruminant 88

CHAPTER XI.

BAGGAGE AGAIN.

Epistolary model—Dog lost—Quitting a moving car—When liability for luggage commences—Goods of third party—Left in the car—Baggage lost—English rule—Limited liability—Personal luggage, what it is—Watch—Rings—Pistol—Railroad porter—Hotel 'bus—Tools and pocket pistols—Fiddles and merchandize—Farewell........ 107

CHAPTER XII.

TELEGRAMS AND FIRE.

Assault—Authority of officials—A dear kiss—Arresting passengers—Telegraphic messages—Interesting examples—Who can sue for mistake—Fire-fiend's pranks—Train arrives, liability ceases—Trunks in warehouse—Baggage left at station—Dissolving domestic view.................... 11

BOOK SECOND.—BY STAGE.

CHAPTER I.

EVERYTHING MUST BE SOUND, AND EVERYONE CAREFUL.

The reason why—Literature of stages—Off on wheels—Soundness warranted—Seats taken—Fare paid, either first or last—Damage to trunks—Involuntary aeronautics—Passengers injured—Negligence of passengers, or of drivers—Carrier liable for smallest fault—Not insurers—Genuine accidents—Horses left standing—Driving and upsetting a friend—Pleasures of the weed and rural life 124

CHAPTER II.

NEARLY DRIVEN TO DEATH, AND HOW TO PASS.

Narrow escape—Look out for the locomotive when the bell rings—Railway not liable when driver in fault—On the wrong side—The laws of the road—Fatal indecision—Lien on trunks—Reflections on lawyers................. 135

CHAPTER III.

DINING, RAINING, LOSING AND ENDING.

Must wait at stopping places—Place booked taken at any time—Falling in ascending—Drenched with rain—Coachmen are common carriers and liable as such—Loss of money—Loss of luggage—Dangerous short cut—Safe arrival. 141

BOOK THIRD.—BY BOAT.

CHAPTER I.

HOTEL EXPERIENCES.

A common inn-keeper and his duties—Choice of rooms—Limitation of liability—Act of Parliament—The view—The tea—Mine host responsible for losses—Kicking horses—Ferries and ferrymen—Lien on travellers—A midnight hunt—Entomological—A man pummelled 147

CONTENTS. xi

CHAPTER II.

LIFE ON THE ROLLING DEEP.

Primitive steamers—Hole in the wharf—Passenger injured—Curiosity hunters hurt—Breaking of fender—A grievous case—Steamboats must carry all—Unless disreputable, disobedient or disgusting—Not up to time—Time the essence of contract—Behaviour at table—Ungentlemanly conduct—Sea sickness 161

CHAPTER III.

THE AUTOCRAT ON BOARD SHIP.

Calm after storm—Disreputable people on board—Landing passengers *nolens volens*—Carriers responsible for effects of gravitation—Protection against fellow travellers—Lost by fire, Imperial, American and Dominion statutes—Rocks and snags—Running on anchor — Authority of captain—Imprisonment — Compelling passengers to fight or work — Too far—The Devil's Invincibles—Charge—Tennysonian stanzas 172

CHAPTER IV.

LOST! AND LAST!

Petty larcenies—Statutory exceptions to liability—Valuables—American rule—Lien on luggage—None on person—Pranks of rats and mice—Acts of God, of the Queen's enemies—No fare for newly born babes—Dead men must pay—Horse overboard—Vessel overladen—Trunk given to wrong man—Owner retaining possession of baggage—Limiting liability of carrier—Delivery to passenger—Proof of age—Pedestrians—Colliding—Telegrams after missing baggage—The King's town—The resting place........ 182

TABLE OF CASES.

A.

	PAGE
Abraham v. Reynolds	103
Accidental Death Ass. Co. v. Hooper	9
Aimes v. Stevens	178
Alden v. N. Y. Central Railway	74, 75
Aldworth v. Stewart	179
Alexander v. Toronto & Nipissing Railw.	86
Allen v. London & S. W. Railway	64
Anderson v. North Eastern Railway	62
Armistead v. White	154
Armsworth v. South Eastern Railw.	91, 94
Ashby v. White	138
Aston v. Heaven	70, 131, 132
Austin v. Grand Trunk Railway	82, 85
Ayles v. South Eastern Railway	105

B.

Baird v. Pettit	103
Baltimore & Ohio Rail. v. Breing	136
" " " v. State	42, 71, 93, 95
Bancroft v. Boston & Worcester Railw.	93
Barnard v. Poor	99
Barrett v. Malden & Melrose Railw.	37
" v. Midland Railway	15
Barrow v. Baltimore & Ohio Railw.	42
Bartholemew v. St. Louis, Jacksonville, &c., Railway	121
Bartonshill Coal Co. v. Reid	3, 101
Batchelor v. Buffalo & Brantford Railw.	98
Bayley v. Lancaster Railway	63
" v. Manchester, &c., Railw.	116, 117
Beecher v. Great Eastern Railway	109
Belfast, B. L., &c., Rail. v. Keys	114
Bennett v. Mellor	155
" v. Peninsula and Oriental Steamboat Co.	164
Benson v. New Jersey Railway	21
Bernstein v. Baxendall	183
Bilbee v. London & Brighton Railw.	15, 136
Birkett v. Whitehaven Junction Railway	95, 105
Birney v. New York and Washington Telegraph Co.	120
Blackman v. London B. & S. C. Railw.	24
Blake v. Midland Railway	90, 91, 96
Boggs v. Great Western Railway	14, 135
Boice v. Hudson River Railway	31
Bonner v. Maxwell	111
Boss v. Litton	3
Boston & Lowell Railw. v. Proctor	32
Bowie v. Buffalo, Brantford & G. Railw.	121

	PAGE
Bowman v. Teall	177
Boyce v. Bayliffe	179, 180
Bradley v. Waterhouse	28
Brand v. Troy & Syracuse Railway	16
Bramhill v. Lee	96
Bremner v. Williams	126
Briddon v. Great Northern Railway	68
Bridges v. North London, &c., Railway	17, 40, 54
Brien v. Bennett	142
Briggs v. Grand Trunk Railw.	22, 31
Brind v. Dale	112
Bristol & Exeter Railw. v. Collins	110
Brissell v. New York Central	85
Brooke v. Pickwick	111, 145
" v. Grand Trunk Railway	31
Brown v. Maxwell	101
" v. Railway Pass. Accident Co.	13
Bruty v. Grand Trunk Railw.	111, 113, 114
Bryant v. American Telegraph Co.	120
" v. Rich	170
Butcher v. London & S. W. Railw.	112
Burgess v, Clements	153, 154
" v. Great Western Railway	49
Burwell v. New York Central	121
Butler v. Basing	144
Butterfield v. Forrester	78
Butterworth v. Brownlow	28
Buxton v. North Eastern Railway	106, 163

C.

Cahill v. London and North Western Railway	114
Camden v. Great Southern and Western Railway	97
Camden and Amboy Railway v. Baldauf	28
" " " v. Belknap	108
Camp v Western Union Tel. Co.	120
Campbell v. Caledonian Railway	109
" v. Grand Trunk Railway	122
" v. Great Western Railway	99
Canning v. Williamstown	92
Carpenter v. Taylor	153
Carpue v. London and Brighton Railway	71, 72
Carr v. Lancashire and York Railw.	111
Carrol v. New York and New Hampshire Railway	79
Carter v. Hobbs	155
Cashill v. Wright	154

TABLE OF CASES.

	PAGE.
Caswell v. Boston and Worcester Railway	24
Cayle's case	153, 159
Chaffee v. Boston and Lowell Railw.	16
Chamberlain v. West. Trans. Co.	176
Champlin v. Traveller's Pass. Ins. Co.	12
Chaplin v. Haines	6, 138
Cheney v. Boston and Maine Railway	31, 173
Chicago and Alton Railw. v. Roberts	44
" and Aurora Railw. v. Thompson	27
" and North' Western Railw v. Jackson	103
" " " v. Williams	39
" B. and Q. Railw. v. Hazzard	80
Chilton v. London and Croydon Railw.	45
Christie v. Griggs	73, 130, 131
Cincinnati Col. & Co. Railw. v. Bartram	31
" & Co. Railw. v. Rontius	110
City of Chicago v. Major	95
Clapp v. Hudson River	98
Clark v. Gray	143
Clay v. Willan	28
" v. Wood	6, 139
Cleveland v. Terry	85
Cockle v. London and South-Eastern Railw.	50, 55
Coggs v. Bernard	84
Cohen v. Frost	188
" v. Hume	156
Colegrove v. New York and N. H. Railw.	78
" v. New York and Harlem Railw.	130
Coleman v. Southwick	99
" v. South-Eastern Railw.	67
Collett v. London and N.-W. Railw.	71, 85
Collins v. Albany and Schn. Railw.	98
" v. Boston and Maine Railw.	114
Colorado and Ind. Railw. v. Farrel	52
Colt v. McMeachan	178
Commonwealth v. Power	143, 173
Converse v. Brainard	177
Coon v. Syracuse and Utica Railw.	103
Copley v. Burton	148
Coppin v. Braithwaite	173, 178
Cotton v. Wood	14
Corbin v. Leader	168, 189
Cornwall v. Eastern Counties Railw.	24
Crafter v. Metropolitan Railw.	17, 25
Craig v. Great Western Railw.	32
Cranston v. Marshall	167
Crocker v. New London, Will. and Pat. Railw.	42, 44
Croft v. Allison	2
Crofts v. Waterhouse	126, 131
Crosby v. Fitch	177
Cross v. Andrews	155
Crouch v. London and N. Western Railw.	28
Cunningham v. Grand Trunk Railw.	105
Curtis v. Drinkwater	133
" v. Grand Trunk Railw.	34, 41
" v. Rochester and Syracuse Railw.	99, 105

D.

Dale v. Hall	185
Dalton v. South-Eastern Railway	97
Damont v. New Orleans and Carolton Railway	35, 36
Dascomb v. Buffalo and State Line Railway	136
Davey v. Chamberlain	6
Davis v. Grand Trunk Railway	43
Davis v. Talcot	21
Dawson v. Manchester, S. and L. Railw.	71, 72
" v. Chauncey	152, 156
Dearden v. Townsend	44
Deedes v. Graham	27
Denton v. Great Northern Railway	20
Derby v. Philadelphia and Reading Railway	117
Detouches v. Peck	127
Dexter v. S. B. and N. Y. Railway	113
Dickenson v. Winchester	113
Dietrich v. Penn. A. Railway	31, 32
Dibble v. Brown	114
Dill v. Railway Co.	17
Doe v. Laming	148
Downs v. N. Y. and N. H. Railway	29
Duckworth v. Johnson	97
Dudley v. Smith	129
Duffy v. Thompson	27, 58, 111
Duke v. Great Western Railway	30, 34
Dunlop v. International Steam Co.	183
Dunn v. Grand Trunk Railway	80
Dwight v. Brewster	143, 144

E.

Eaton v. Delaware, Lacka. & W. Railw.	80
Edgerton v. New York & Harlem Railw.	79
Edwards v. London & N. W. Railw.	118
Eldridge v. Long Is. Railw.	36
Ellis v. American Telegraph Co.	120
" v. Grand Trunk Railw.	135
Ellsworth v. Tartt	104
Ernst v. Hudson River Railw.	136
Ewbank v. Nutting	177

F.

Fairchild v. California Stage Co.	92
Farewell v. Boston & Worcester Railw.	101, 103
" v. Grand Trunk Railw.	30, 35
Farmers & Mechanics' Bank v. Champlain Transportation Co.	110

TABLE OF CASES.

	PAGE.
Farnsworth v. Parckard	154
Farnworth v. Packwood	154
Farrish v. Reigle	131
Faulkner v. Erie Railway	103
Faulkner v. Wright	177
Feaver v. Montreal Telegraph Co.	119
Fell v. Knight	148, 150
Feltham v. England	103
Ferrie v. Great Western Railw.	96
Fisher v. Clisbee	188
Filton v. Accidental Death Ins. Co.	11
Fitzpatrick v. Great Western Railw.	100
Flint v. Norwich & N. Y. Transp. Co.	174
Ford v. London & South Western Railw.	71
" v. Monroe	100
Fordham v. London, Brighton & South Coast Railw.	67
Forshaw v. Chabert	177
Forsyth v. Boston, &c., Railw.	24
Forward v. Pittard	176
Foy & Wife v. London B. & S. C. Railw.	52
Franklin v. South Eastern Railw.	97
Frazer v. Pennsylvania Railw.	101
Frink v. Potter	70, 129, 130
Frost v. Grand Trunk Railw.	47
Fuller v. Talbot	75
Fulton v. Grand Trunk Railw.	38, 40

G.

Galena & Chicago Union Railw. v. Loomis	15, 136
Galena & Chicago Railw. v. Yarwood	80
Gamble v. Great Western Railw.	58, 59
Gibbon v. Paynton	28
Gibbons v. Pepper	4
Gilbert v. Bertenshaw	99
Giles v. Fauntleroy	114
" v. Taff Vale Railw.	117
Gillenwater v. Madison & Indian. Railw.	85
Gillshannon v. Stony Brook Railw.	103
Gillivard v. Lancaster & Yorkshire Railw.	91
Glover v. London & South Western Railw.	43
Godderd v. Railway	170
Goff v. Northern Railw.	117
Goldey v. Pennsylvania Railw.	105
Goodman v. Taylor	132
Gough v. Bryan	128
Grace v. Morgan	99
Grant v. Newton	27
Great Northern Railw. v. Harrison	85
" v. Shepherd	26, 110, 112, 114
Great Western Railw. v. Blake	104, 105, 163
" v. Fawcett	89
" v. Braid	89
Great Western of Canada v. Brand	84
Great Western Railw. v. Goodman	58

	PAGE.
Greenland v. Champlain	137
" v. Chaplin	174
Grieve v. Ontario & St. Lawrence Steam Co.	163
Grimston v. Innkeeper	155
Grippen v. New York Central Railw.	136

H.

Hageman v. Western Railw.	72
Hall v. Power	173
Hamlin v. Great Northern Railw.	21
Hammond v. White	71
Hankel v. Pape	119
Hanover Railw. v. Coyle	100
Harold v. Great Western Railw.	54
Harris v. Costar	130
" v. Rand	177
Harrow v. White	4
Hart v. Windsor	159
" v. Rensselaer & Saratoga Railw.	65, 110
Havens v. Erie Railw.	136
Hawcroft v. Great Northern Railw.	39
Hawkins v. Hoffman	58, 112, 113
Hawthorn v. Hammond	148
Hearle v. Ross	176
Hearn v. London & South-Western	185, 188
Heirn v. McCaughan	20, 166
Hewlett v. Cruch	99
Hickox v. Nangatuck Railw.	108
Hicks v. Newport, A. & H. Railw.	96
Higgins v. New York & Harlem Railw.	78
Hodsall v. Stallebras	99
Hogan v. Providence & W. Railw.	42
Holbrook v. Utica & Sch. Railw.	66
Hollenbeck v. Berkshire Railw.	93
Holly v. Boston Gas Light Co.	83
Holmes v. Clark	101
" v. Doane	42
Hood v. New York & N. Ham. Railw.	104
Hooper v. Accidental Death Ins. Co.	10, 12
Horner v. Wood	21
Hopkins v. Atlantic & St. Lawrence Railw.	99
Hopkins v. Westcott	114
Howell v. Jackson	148
Howland v. Brig Lavinia	127
Hudston v. Midland Railw.	60
Hunter v. McGowan	175
Huntsman v. Great Western Railw.	43
Hurd v. Vermont & Canada Railw.	101, 103
Hurton v. Dibbin	183
Hutchinson v. York, &c., Railw.	101
Hurst v. Great Western Railw.	21, 38
Hutton v. Bolton	143
Hyde v. Trent & Mersey Navig. Co.	176

I.

Illinois Central Railw. v. Abell	35
" v. Read	85

TABLE OF CASES.

	PAGE.
Indiana Central Railw. v. Mundy	85
Indianapolis & Cincinnati Railw. v. Rutherford	66
Indemaur v. James	162
Ingalls v. Bills	36, 75, 126, 129, 130
Inman v. Buffalo & Lake Huron Railw.	121

J.

James v. Great Western Railw.	15
Jencks v. Coleman	143, 165
Jenkins v. Biddulph	99
Jennings v. Great Northern Railw.	29, 44
Joel v. Morrison	2
John v. Bacon	104, 162
Johnston v. Northern Railw.	135, 136
Jones v. Boyce	126, 129
" v. Voorhes,	111, 143
Jordan v. Fall River Railw.	27

K.

Kay v. Wheeler	184
Keegan v. Western Railw.	101
Keith v. Pinkman	130
Kenvard v. Benton	138, 139
Kent v. Midland Railw.	111
" v. Shuckard	154
Ker v. Mountain	126, 141
King v. Franklin	179
Knight v. Ponchartrain Railw.	55
" v. P. S. & P. Railw.	104

L.

Lackawanna v. Cheneworth	130
Laing v. Calder	66, 71
Lamb v. Palk	2
Lambeth v. N. Carolina Railw.	56
Latch v. Rimmer Railw.	105
Laugher v. Forester	6
Lawrenceburgh and Upper Miss. Railw. v. Montgomery	80
LeCouteur v. London & South-Western Railw.	58, 109
Leslie v. Canadian Inland Navigation Co.	175, 176
Lewis & Wife v. London, C. & D. Railw.	55
Limpus v. London Omnibus Co.	2
Lockwood v. Ind. Line of Tel. Co.	119
Loker v. Inhabitants of Brookline	18
Long v. Home	126
Longmore v. Great Western Railw.	16
Louisville & N. Railw. v. Collins	103
Lovett v. Hobbs.	143
Lucas v. New York Central Railw.	91
" v. Taunton & New Bedford Railw.	36, 108
Lygo v. Newbold	142
Lynch v. Smith	83
Lynn v. Mills	177

M.

	PAGE.
Macon & Western Railw. v. Johnson	95
Macrow v. Great Western Railw.	61, 111, 113, 114
Mallory v. Travellers' Insurance Co.	9, 11
Manser v. Eastern Counties Railw.	72
Marshall v. York, N. & B. Railw.	108
Martin v. Great Northern Railw.	49
Martin v. Travellers' Insurance Co.	10
Mayor v. Humphries	128
Meir v. Pennsylvania Railway	75
Memphis &c., Railway v. Whitfield	55
Mershon v. Hobensack	176
Michael v. Alistree	4
Miles v. Cottle	144
" v. James	155
Minor v. Chicago & North Western Railway	122
Mississippi Central Railw. v. Kennedy	111
Mitchell v. Cressweller	2
Mobile & Chicago Railw. v. Hopkins	108
Moffatt v. Bateman	133
" v. East India Co.	186
Moore v. Auburn & Syracuse Railw.	92
" v. Metropolitan Railway	117
Morel v. Mississ. Valley Ins. Co.	12
Morgan v. Ravey	153, 156
" v. Vale of Neath Railway	102
Morley v. Great Western Railway	97
Morrison v. European & N. American Railway	191
Mote v. Chicago & North Western Railway	121
Mouse's case	187
Murray v. Metropolitan District Railw.	65
Muschamp v. Lancaster & Preston Junction Railway	110
Mutton v. Midland Railway	114
Mytton v. " "	105
McAndrew v. Electric Telegr. Co.	118, 120
McCawley v. Furness Railway	86
McCormick v. Hudson River Railw.	104, 111
McDonald v. Chicago and North Western Railway	23, 47, 49
McGill v. Roward	111
McIntyre v. New York Central Railw.	80
McKay v. " " "	136
McLure v. Philadelphia, Will. and Balt. Railway	31
McManus v. Crickett	2
McPadden v. New York Central Railway	71, 73, 75

N.

New Jersey Railw. v. Kennard	66
New Orleans, &c., Railw. v. Hurls	166
New York & Wash. Printing Tel. Co v. Dryburgh	118, 120
Newman v. Walters	179
Nicholls v. Great Western Railw.	135, 137
Nicholson v. Lancashire & York Railw.	49

TABLE OF CASES. xvii

	PAGE.
Nolton v. Western Railway	85
North America Insurance Co. v. Burroughs	11
North Pennsylvania Railw. v. Mahoney	83
Noyes v. Rutland & Burlington Railw.	117

O.

Oakley v. Portsmouth & Ryde Steam Packet Co.	177
Ohio and Mississippi Railw. v. Muhling	84
" " v. Schiebe	35
Oliver v. North Western Railway	16
O'Neil v. Great Western Railway	121
Oppenheim v. White Lion Hotel Co.	154
Orange Co. Bank v. Brown	27
Ormond v. Holland	101
Osborn v. Gillett	27
Ouimet v. Henshaw	61, 122
Oxlade, in re	20

P.

Pack v. Mayor of New York	99
Pardee v. Drew	60, 114
Parker v. Adams	136, 139
" v. Flagg	132
" v. Flint	147
Parsons v. Hardy	177
Paterson v. Wallace	3
Pennewell v. Cullen	177
Peixotti v. McLaughlin	112
Pennsylvania Railway v. Adams	96
" " v. Beale	135
" " v. Books	84
" " v. Kilgrove	36
" " v. McClosky	93
" " v. Vandiver	42
Penton v. Grand Trunk Railway	122
People v. Tillson	38
Peoria Br. Ass. Co. v. Loomis	85
Phelps v. London & North Western Railway	59, 114
Philadelphia & Reading Railway v. Derby	85, 117
Philleo v. Landford	143
Pier v. Friel	31
Pittsburgh A. & M. Railw. v. Pearson	83
" Fort Wayne, &c. Railw. v. Hinds	39
" Fort Wayne, &c. Railw. v. Maurer	105
" & H. W. Railw. v. Dunn	136
Plant v. Midland Railway	54
" v. Grand Trunk Railway	102
Playford v. United Kingdom Telegraph Co.	119
Pluckwell v. Wilson	6, 138
Porter v. Hildebrand	113
Porterfield v. Humphreys	186
Poulton v. London & South Western Railw.	118

	PAGE.
Powell v. Mills	157
Praeger v. Bristol & Exeter Railw.	51, 54
Prendergast v. Compton	170
Priestly v. Fowler	101, 102
Providence Life Ins. & Inv. Co. v. Fennel	11
Providence Life Ins. & Fire Co. v. Martin	9, 11, 12
Pym v. Great Northern Railw.	91, 96, 97
P. & C. Railway v. McClurg	66

Q.

Queen, The, v. Frere	44
Quarman v. Burnett	6

R.

Railway Company v. Aspell	36
" v. Barrow	95, 105
Ranch v. Lloyd	82
Read v. Great Eastern Railw.	96
Readhead v. Midland Railw.	74
Redpath v. Vaughan	177
Reid v. Great Northern Railw.	72
Rex v. Jones	148, 149
Richards v. London, Brighton & S. C. Railw.	58, 109
Richardson v. Metropolitan Railw.	67
" v. North Eastern Railw.	108, 186
Richmond v. Smith	154
Rigby v. Hewitt	137
Ringland v. Corporation of Toronto	18
Ripley v. Railway Passengers Assur. Co.	12
Ripsley v. Railw. Pass. Ass. Co.	9
Rittenhouse v. Independent Line of Tel. Co.	119
Robertson v. New York & E. Railw.	79
Robinson v. Bletcher	132
" v. Cone	78
" v. Fitzburgh & Worcester Railw.	78
" v. Dunmore	143, 145
" v. Great Western Railw.	21
Rock Island & Pacific Railw. v. Fairclough	121
Roe v. Birkenhead, &c. Railw.	2
Ross v. Hill	112
Roth v. Buffalo & State Line Railw.	122
Rowley v. London & North Western Railw.	95

S.

Sanback v. Thomas	99
Sawyer v. United States Casualty Co.	10
Schiefflen v. Harvey	188
Schneider v. Prov. Life Ins. Co.	12
Secord v. Great Western Railw.	94, 97
Seilers v. Western Union Tel. Co.	120

B

TABLE OF CASES.

	PAGE.
Senecal v. Richelieu Nav. Co.	187
Seymour v. Greenwood	2
Sharp v. Gray	126, 130, 178
Shaw v. Boston & Worcester Railw.	99
" v. Grand Trunk Railw.	114
Shedd v. Troy & Boston Railw.	32
Shepherd v. Bristol and Exeter Railw.	121
" v. Midland Railw.	18
Simmons v. New Bedfordshire, &c. Stage Co.	174
Sinclair v. Maritime Pass. Ass. Co.	8
Siner v. Great Western Railw.	23, 53, 55
Singleton v. Eastern Counties Railw.	83
Skelton v. London & North Western Railw.	14, 136
Skinner v. London, Brighton and S. C. Railw.	72, 73, 85
Sleath v. Wilson	2
Smith v. Accidental Ins. Co.	11, 12
" v. Dearlove	157
" v. Great Eastern Railw.	37
" v. Marrable	158
" v. New York and Harlem Railw.	95
Smyrl v. Molin	177
Snow v. Housatonic Railw.	103
Southard v. Railway Pass. Ass. Co.	10
Southern Express Co. v. Shea	110
Southern Railw. v. Kendrick	56
Sprague v. Smith	104, 105
Springett v. Ball	97
Stallard v. Great Western Railw.	62
Stanton v. Weller	131
Stapley v. London, Brighton and S. C. Railw.	15, 16
St. John v. Pardee	178
State v. Baltimore & Ohio Railw.	96
State v. Campbell	31
" v. Gould	44
" v. Grand Trunk Railw.	46
" v. Overton	31
Steves v. Oswego & Syracuse Railway	16
Stokes v. Cardiff Steam Navigation Co.	37
" v. Saltonstall	36, 126, 129, 131
Story v. New York & Harlem Railw.	21
Stout v. S. C. & P. Railway	83
Stove v. United States Casualty Co.	11
Stuart v. Crawley	107, 186
Stubley v. London & North Western Railway	15, 136, 137
Sunbolf v. Alford	140, 157
Sutherland v. Great Western Railway	86
Sutton v. Temple	159
Sweetland v. Illinois &c. Tel. Co.	120

T.

Talley v. Great Western Railway	58
Tarrant v. Webb	101
Taylor v. Humphries	148
Tebbutt v. Bristol & Exeter Railway	37
Teirniery v. Peppinger	105
Thatch v. Great Western Railway	73

	PAGE.
Thayer v. St. Louis &c. Railway	105
Theobald v. Railway Pass. Ass. Co.	9, 10, 11
Thomas v. Rhymney Railway	104
Thorogood v. Bryan	137
Tilley v. Hudson River Railway	91
Toland v. " " "	40
Toledo & Wabash Railway v. Hammond	114
Tooley v. Railway Pass. Ass. Co.	12
Toomey v. London, Brighton & S. C. Railway	25
Torrance v. Smith	176
Tower v. Utica & Schenectady Railw.	58, 110, 145
Treadwin v. Great Eastern Railway	183
Trent Navigation Co. v. Wood	177
Trew v. Railway Pass. Ass. Co.	11, 12
True v. International Telegraph Co.	120
Tunney v. Midland Railway	102
Tyler v. Western Union Tel. Co.	120
Tyson v. Grand Trunk Railway	136
Two Friends, The ——	179

U.

United States Telegraph Co. v. Gildersleeve	120

V.

Vanhorn v. Kerniet	108
Van Lantvoord v. St. John	110
Van Toll v. South Eastern Railway	62
Venton v. Middlesex &c. Railway	39

W.

Wakeman v. Robinson	4
Walker v. Great Western Railway	49
" v. Jackson	28, 143, 127
Wann v. Western Union Tel. Co.	118, 120
Wanless v. North Eastern Railway	16
Warner v. Erie Railway	103
Warren v. Fitchburg Railway	48
Watbrooke v. Griffith	155
Watson v. Ambergate &c. Railway	110
" v. Northern Railway	79
Wayde v. Carr	138
Webb v. Sage	143
Weed v. Saratoga & Sch. Railway	27
Weeds v. Saratoga Railway	105
Weems v. Mathieson	101
Weld v. Hudson River Railway	16
Welfare v. London & Brighton Railw.	17, 22
Weller v. London Brighton & S. C. Railway	55
Welles v. New York Central Railw.	85, 86
Westchester Railway v. Miles	39

TABLE OF CASES.

	PAGE.
Western Union Telegraph Co. v. Carew	120
Wheatley v. Patrick	6
Whitaker v. Manchester & S. Railway	52, 54
White v. Bolton	143
" v. North Eastern Railway	83
" v. Winniesinick Co.	156
Whitney v. Clarendon	99
Wiggett v. Fox	101
Willetts v. New York & Erie Railw.	90
Williams v. Richards	7, 14
" v. Grant	177
" v. Great Western Railway	58
Williamson v. Grand Trunk Railway	41
Willis v. Long Island Railway	78, 79
Willoughby v. Horridge	156
Wilton v. Atlantic Royal Mail Steam Nav. Co.	188
Wilsons v. Hamilton	156
Winckler v. Great Western Railway	136, 137
Wolf v. Summers	140, 184
Woodward v. Eastern Counties Railw.	29
Woods v. Devon	113
Woodruff v. Great Western Railway	86
Woolley v. Sewell	3
Wordsworth v. Willan	6
Worley v. Cincinnati, H. & D. Railw.	91
Wright v. Caldwell	187
" v. Midland Railway	105
" v. Malden & M. Railway	83
" v. New York Central Railw.	101, 103
Wyld v. Pickford	185

Y.

Yarborough v. Bank of England	117
Yates v. Duff	166
Young v. Fewson	168
" v. Smith	189

Z.

Zemp v. W. & M. Railway	78
Zung v. South-Eastern Railway.	110

WRONGS AND RIGHTS OF A TRAVELLER.

BOOK FIRST.—BY RAIL.

CHAPTER I.

DRIVING.

New Year's Day—Collision with Old Bolus—Must I pay for my servant's deeds—Deaf man run over—Effects of an Avalanche—Housemaid injured by Coachman —Wives, snakes or eels—Driver and Driven—Right side or wrong—Look out—Erskine and Kenyon.

MY life, so far as the readers of this sketch are concerned, may be taken to have commenced on the New Year's morning after I had married a wife, and set up a trap with the necessary accompaniments of a horse and a man.

It was my intention, pursuant to the time-honoured custom, to go out in the afternoon with a friend to call upon my extensive circle of lady acquaintances. At ten a.m. Mrs. Lawyer came into my library frantic and breathless; the palpitations of her heart having somewhat subsided, and her heaving bosom sunk to rest, she exclaimed:

"O Eldon, that horrid John must be drunk! He took out the horse and sleigh this morning, and when driving down Main Street, he ran into Dr. Bolus' cutter and knocked it all to pieces."

"Ah, my dear Elizabeth, calm your troubled mind;" I coolly replied, "John, without my knowledge, and wrongfully, took my horse and sleigh for some purpose or other of his own and ran into old Bolus' turn-out, you say: well, the law is perfectly clear that I am not responsible for the injury, as I did not intrust my servant with the sleigh.[1] I may tell you for your edification that the general rule is that a master is not liable for the tortious act of his servant, unless that act be done either by an authority, express or implied, given him for that purpose by the master;[2] or as Mr. Baron Parke puts it, if a servant is going on a frolic of his own, without being at all on his master's business, the master will not be liable."[3]

"Oh, but dear Don, I forgot to tell you that I sent him to the confectioner's for some cakes; but I told him to drive along West Street."

"Confound it, that's a different matter. The Doctor will rush off to friend Erskine, and I will have to pony up for the damage; because, as that rascal John was driving on his master's business, it matters not that he disobeyed his express orders in going out of his way, or made a detour to please himself."[4]

"Yes, but Eldon dear," continued my wife; "it was not on his master's business, it was on mine."

"Stupid, what difference does that make?" replied I, impatiently; and then, seeing that my wife did not like the adjective, I added more feelingly, but rather vaguely: "Don't you see, I'm his master, you are mine, and so must be his also."

"Heigh-ho!" sighed the wife of my bosom. "But I have not told you all. After the collision the horse ran against an old

---

1. *McManus* v. *Crickett*, 1 East, 106; *Croft* v. *Alison*, 4 B. & Ald, 590; *Sleath* v. *Wilson*, 9 C. & P. 607, qualified by *Seymour* v. *Greenwood*, 6 H. & N., 359, 7, 355; *Lamb* v. *Palk*, 9 C. & P., 631.
2. *Roe* v. *Birkenhead &c. R. W. Co.*, 7 Ex. 36.
3. *Joel* v. *Morrison*, 6 C. & P., 501.
4. *Limpus* v. *London Omn. Co.*, 1 H. & C., 526; *Joel* v. *Morrison*, supra; *Mitchell* v. *Cresweller*, 13 C. B., 237; *Seymour* v. *Greenwood*, 7 H. & N., 356.

man who was walking along the street, knocked him down and hurt him : but, of course, he had no right to be on the road, when there was a good sidewalk for him."

"Of course he *had* a right to be on the road : just as much right there as the horse and sleigh had, even though he were sick and infirm : and it was John's business to take care where he was going !"[1]

"Yet John says he told the man to get out of the way, and he wouldn't do it ;" pleaded my wife.

"That does not matter.[2] I hope no more damage was done ?" I queried. "Yes : the horse shied and upset the sleigh ; and John says that all his—I mean John's—ribs are broken, and that he is kilt entirely : and he swears that he'll make you pay for it —that he'll sue you."

"Let him sue away and be hanged ; he'll get nothing for his pains but the pleasure of spending his earnings : he is my servant and has to run the risk of being hurt in my employment."[3]

"But then, Eliza Jane, the housemaid, was with him, was thrown out too and had all the skin taken off her face ; and she says she'll sue too."

"Oh, I'm sorry for that : I like her, and then she was so pretty."

"Eldon ! how dare you say so—to your wife too !"

"I—I—only meant that I would have to pay for the damage to her, and that if I did not do it willingly any jury would be persuaded by her pretty face to give a heavy sum against me for the injury done to her by my servant.[4] Well, 'tis a pretty how-do-ye-do for a New Year's gift. I'll go down and see the wretch."

Off I went glad to get out of Elizabeth's sight : she had grown a little jealous because I had shown a few trifling civilities to pretty Eliza Jane—very trifling they were, I assure you : besides

---

1. *Boss* v. *Litton*, 5 C. & P., 407.
2. *Woolley* v. *Scovell*, 3 M. & Ry, 105.
3. *Paterson* v. *Wallace*, 1 Macq. 751.
4. Lord Cranworth, *Bartonshell Coal Co.* v. *Reid*, 3 Macq., 294-307.

I wanted to vent my rage on the man John. In a very short time some words and phrases were used in the yard to which, doubtless, Moses would have objected, if he had the first table of stone in his hand: my ire, however, cooled down in time when I found that the man was "all serene," and that all the trouble had been caused by the horse having taken fright at the fall of a lot of snow and ice off a house-top—a circumstance over which, of course, I had not the slightest control; and therefore I was not liable to Dr Bolus, the old man, nor to pretty Eliza Jane.[1] But to make matters all straight I gave my man a couple of dollars, and meeting E. J. on the back-stairs as I went in I chucked her under her dimpled chin, and told her that crying would make her pretty eyes look red and swollen; and then retiring to my library read up all the cases bearing on the subject, beginning with the old case of *Michael v. Alistree*[2] where the defendants "in Lincoln's Inn Fields, a place where people are always going to and fro about their business, brought a coach with two ungovernable horses, *et ex improvide, incaute et absque consideratione inaptitudinis loci*, there drove them, &c., and the horses, because of their ferocity, being not to be managed, ran into the plaintiff, and hurt and grievously wounded him," and the plaintiff got damages as well as damaged.

At the appointed hour my friend and young brother-in-the-law, Tom Jones, arrived. As he sank into one of the softest of our drawing-room chairs, and gazed around, he exclaimed.

"By Jove, Eldon, you look so snug and cosy here that I am half inclined to follow suit, quit our bachelor's hall, marry a nice little girl I wot of and settle down."

"Do so at once," said my wife.

"Ah! I cannot forget the words of that good old judge, Sir John Moore;" he replied with a sigh.

---

1. *Wakeman* v. *Robinson*, 1 Bing., 213; *Harrow* v. *White*, 11 C.B., N.S., 588; *Gibbons* v. *Pepper*, 1 Ld. Raym., 38.
2. 2 Sev., 172; 1 Ventr. 295.

"Oh, you are as bad as Eldon, always quoting some fusty old judge. But what did he say?" queried my wife.

"He said that he would compare the multitude of women who are to be chosen for wives unto a bag full of snakes, having among them a single eel. Now, if a man should put his hand into this bag, he might chance to light on the eel, but it is one hundred to one he would be stung by a snake," returned Jones.

"The horrid old wretch. I am sure I was neither a snake nor an eel: was I Eldon? I hate both."

"Oh, no, my dear," I replied. "But Tom, that surely is only an *obiter dictum*, not a decision of that worthy judge."

"Of course," replied Jones; "but all the dicta of judges are entitled to weight." Tom had just been called to the bar.

"Here's the sleigh at the door; and you two horrid men may go now," said Mrs. L. "Is your life insured against accidents, Mr. Jones?" she added; "for you are sure to be run away with and upset."

"Only against railway accidents," he said.

"That's stupid," I remarked, "for it is well settled that hardly seven per cent. of accidental claims arise from accidents in travelling by rail or water, while those arising from horse or carriage injuries exceed in number those from all other causes combined."

"A pleasant idea wherewith to start for an afternoon's drive:" quoth Tom.

And off we went, bells jingling, horse prancing, dog barking, all joyous with the exhilarating influences of frost and sunshine.

"Look here, old fellow," said Tom, "your horse seems pretty skittish to-day: let us settle the law as to our mutual liability for damages before we run into anything. Who will have to pay? you don't seem very much accustomed to driving."

"Never mind that. The law is clear; as you are merely a passenger in my sleigh, you are not responsible for any misconduct of which I may be guilty while driving—you have nothing to do with the concern.[1] Even if I had only borrowed the turn-out, and kindly let you take the ribbons, I still would be the party responsible for negligence."[2]

"That's satisfactory," returned my friend. "But would it not be different if we had both hired the horse and cutter?"

"Quite correct Mr. T. J.: your store of legal lore is rapidly accumulating. In the case you put, both of us would be equally answerable for any accident arising from the misconduct of either whilst it was under our joint care,[3] and if we had hired the horses to draw my sleigh and had likewise obtained the services of a driver, then we would not be liable for the negligence or carelessness of that driver."[4]

"Look out, you had better keep on your own side of the road," said Jones.

"Never mind I can go on either side, I'll only have to keep my eye a little wider open to avoid collisions;[5] besides there is plenty of room for any person to pass, so he would have only himself to blame in case of accidents."[6]

"A person approaching you might think there was not sufficient space."

"If an accident happens it will be a matter of evidence whether I have left ample room or not,[7] so you can look about you and see."

"But suppose some fiery steed was to run into yours?" urged Thomas.

"My being on the wrong side would not prevent my recovering against a negligent driver, as long as there is room for him to pass without inconvenience.[8] Whoa, old fellow," I cried, just as I

---

1. *Davey* v. *Chamberlain*, 4 Esp., 229.
2. *Wheatley* v. *Patrick*, 2 M. & W., 650.
3. *Davey* v. *Chamberlain*, 4 Esp., 229.
4. *Laugher* v. *Forister*, 5 B. & C., 547; *Quarman* v. *Burnett*, 6 M. & W., 499.
5. *Pluckwell* v. *Wilson*, 5 C. & P., 375.
6. *Chaplin* v. *Hawes*, 3 C. & P., 554.
7. *Wordsworth* v. *Willan*, 5 Esp., 273.
8. *Clay* v. *Wood*, 5 Esp., 44.

was on the point of running over a philosopher who was walking slowly over a crossing gazing up at the azure vault of heaven. "What a stupid donkey; it is as much his business to be watchful and cautious that he does not get under my sleigh, as it is mine that my sleigh does not get over him!"

"By the way," said Jones, "have you seen that anecdote told by Erskine about Lord Kenyon, and which has recently been brought to light?"

"No. Has it anything to do with driving?"

"Everything. Kenyon was trying a case at the Guildhall and seemed disposed to leave it to the jury to say whether the plaintiff might not have saved himself from being run into by the defendant by going on to the wrong side of the road, where—according to the witnesses—was ample room; so Lord Erskine in addressing the jury said: 'Gentlemen,—If the noble and learned judge, in giving you hereafter his advice, shall depart from the only principle of safety (unless where collisions are selfish and malicious), and you shall act upon it, I can only say that I shall feel the same confidence in his lordship's general learning and justice, and shall continue to delight, as I always do, in attending his administration of justice: *but I pray God that I may never meet him on the road!*' Lord Kenyon laughed, and so did the jury, and in summing up the judge told them that he believed it to be the best course *stare super antiquas vias.*"

"Not so bad!"

On and on we drove, the very air seemed alive with the tintinnabulation that so musically wells from the jingling and the tinkling of the bells in the icy air of winter.

---

1. *Williams* v. *Richard* 3 C. & K., 81.

CHAPTER II.

INSURANCE.

What's an accident ?—Major vis—Exposure and death—Wholly disabled—What can be recovered — Heavy weights — Stumbling— Pitchforked — Change of business—Lost beneath the dancing waves—A man not a private conveyance—Carelessness.

SHORTLY after the events related in my last chapter, business called me away from home. Accidents by rail—explosions, collisions, over-turnings, exploits of the fire-fiend—had become so much the reverse of angel's visits that though some said I had the hanging mark upon me, I determined to make assurance doubly sure and take a bond of fate in the shape of an "accident ticket;" not that hope told a flattering tale, or that vain expectations of making anything by the transaction filled my soul, but as a preventive rather than a cure, for accidents seldom happen when one is prepared, as showers seldom descend when one is armed *cap-a-pie* with umbrella and thick boots.

Ere spending my twenty cents, however, I determined to find out what an accident, within the meaning of the ticket, really might be; but I discovered that no satisfactory definition of the word had ever been given by the courts. Cockburn, C. J., says that it means some violence, casualty, or *vis major*; and that disease or death generated by exposure to heat, cold, damp, the vicissitudes of climate or atmospheric influences, cannot be called accidental; unless, perhaps, where the exposure is actually brought about by circumstances which might give it the character of accident—as a shipwrecked mariner dying from exposure to cold and wet in a small boat upon the roaring, raging ocean.[1] This

---

1. *Sinclair* v. *Maritime Pass. Ass. Co.*, 3 El. & E., 478.

decision settled that I could recover nothing if my nose or my toes were frozen off; nor if my early demise was brought about by croup, measles, or small-pox, caught in the cars, could my family recover any remuneration for the loss of the house-band. If, like the good Samaritan's friend, I should chance to fall among thieves, who should strip me of my raiment, wound me and depart leaving me dead, that, probably, would be considered a death by violent and accidental means, for Judge Withey, of Michigan, has laid it down that an accident is any event which takes place without the foresight or expectation of the person acted upon or affected by the event.[1] In Maryland it has been defined as an unusual and unexpected result attending the performance of a usual and necessary act; and there it has been decided that every injury caused by accident, save those specially excepted by the policy, are covered by it.[2] And in New York an accident is said to be something which takes place without any intelligent or apparent cause, without design and out of course.[3]

I was pleased to find that I might recover for a "railway accident," if anything happened to me while travelling by the cars, although nothing happened to the train, for instance if while getting out after the cars had stopped I should slip, fall and injure myself, not through any negligence of my own, but because the steps were slippery.[4] Where compensation to the insured is granted " in case of bodily injury of so serious a nature as wholly to disable the assured from following his usual business, occupation or pursuits," I would be entitled to pay if so disabled that I could not get to my office to work, although I were well enough to transact business in my own bedroom, or clad in a *robe de nuit* instead of a professional toga.[5] For total disability from

---

1. *Ripsley* v. *Rw. Pas. Ass. Co*,, 2 Bigelow, Ins. Cases, 738.
2. *Provi. Life Ins. Co.* v. *Martin*, 32 Maryland, 310.
3. *Mallory* v. *Travellers Ins. Co.*, 47 N.Y., 52.
4. *Theobald* v. *Rw. Pass. Ass. Co.*, 10 Ex., 45.
5. *Accidental Death Ass. Co.* v. *Hooper*, 5 H. & N., 546; affirmed on Appeal, 5 H. & N., 557.

the prosecution of one's usual employment means inability to follow one's usual occupation, business or pursuits in the usual way :[1] *i.e.-e.g.*, a farmer who can do nothing but milk, and a merchant who can only keep his books, are totally disabled within the meaning of such a provision as the above.[2] To be wholly or *quite disabled* is to be unable to do what one is called upon to do in the ordinary course of business, and this is by no means the same thing as being " unable to do any part of one's business."

The decided cases made it clear that I could recover only for the personal expense and pain occasioned by the accident, and not damage for loss of time or of profit occasioned thereby : and also, that if I insured my life for only $1000, it could not be assumed that my life was worth only that and nothing more, and an injury sustained estimated at a proportionate sum.[4]

I also as a result of my researches learnt the following. If a policy provided that the company would be responsible for accidents operating from external causes, I would get something if I injured my spinal marrow by lifting my trunk :[5] but it would appear that rupture caused by jumping from the cars while in motion and afterwards running to accomplish certain business, done voluntarily and in the ordinary way, and without any necessity therefor, and with no unforseen or involuntary movement of the body, such as stumbling, or slipping, or falling, is not caused by violent or accidental means. Though it might be otherwise if in jumping I should lose my balance and fall, or strike some unseen object, or in running should stumble or slip.[6] If, while on my travels, I should take to amateur farming (not the most likely thing in the world, bucolic desires not filling my soul and the thermometer being down below nothing,) and while pitching

1. May on Insurance, p. 644.
2. *Sawyer* v. *United States Casualty Co.*, 8 Law Reg., N.S., 233.
3. Per Wilde, B., *Hooper* v. *Accidental Death Ins. Co.*, 5 H. & N., 546.
4. *Theobald* v. *Rw. Travellers Ins. Co,*, 10 Ex. 45.
5. *Martin* v. *Travellers Ins. Co.*, 1 F. & F., 505.
6. *Southard* v. *Rw. Pass. Ass. Co.*, 34 Conn., 574.

hay let the handle of the pitchfork slip and pitch into my bowels, producing thereby peritoneal inflammation, whereof I should die, that would be an accidental death!¹ Nor would the casual change of occupation from the pursuits of the forum to that of the field, forfeit my right to recover.² Where an accident produced hernia, which caused death, it was held that the death was not within the exception of the policy which provided that the company did not insure against death or disability arising from rheumatism, gout, hernia, &c.³ If I should go in bathing and die from the action of the water causing asphyxia, that, too, would be a death by external violence within the meaning of the policy, whether I swam out too far, struck my head against a rock in diving, or—unskilled in the natatorial art—got out of my depth; but if I succumbed to an attack of apoplexy while taking the bath, that would not be a death from accident.⁴ A provision that no claim is to be made under a policy, except in respect of an injury caused by some "outward and visible means," applies only to non-fatal injuries.⁵

I found also, that it was legally correct—however paradoxical it may appear—to say that I was travelling in a carriage when in fact I was actually alighting therefrom :⁶ and that I would be " travelling in a carriage provided for the transportation of passengers," if, while in the prosecution of my journey, I walked on foot, as passengers are wont to do from one station to another. The courts, ever ready to interpret a policy in the way most ad-

1. *N. American Ins. Co.* v. *Burroughs*, 69 Penn. St., 43.
2. *Admins. of Stone* v. *U. S. Casualty Co.*, 34 N.J., 371 ; *N. A. Insurance Co.* v. *Burroughs*, supra ; *Provident Life Ins. Co.* v. *Fennel*, 49 Ill., 180 ; *Pro. Life Ins. & Inv. Co.* v. *Martin*, 32 Ind., 310.
3. *Fitton* v. *Acc. Death Ins. Co.*, 17 C.B., N.S., 122 ; but see *Smith* v. *Acc. Ins. Co.*, 22 L. J., 861, a case of erysipelas.
4. *Trew* v. *Railway Pass. Ins. Co.*, 5 H. & N., 211, affirmed on Appeal, 6 H. & N., 839.
5. *Mallory* v. *Travellers Ins. Co.*, Ct. of Appeals, 47 N.Y., 52.
6. *Theobald* v. *Rw. Pass. Ass. Co.*, 10 Ex., 44.

vantageous to the insured,[1] will not allow "travelling in a public conveyance" to be construed literally, and if an accident happens while one is getting off or on a train, or attempting to do so for any reasonable purpose, it comes within the terms of a policy insuring against accidents while travelling by public conveyance.[2] Mr. John Wilder May (who has written a large book on Insurance,) thinks that, perhaps, in a reasonable and substantially accurate sense a man may be said to be travelling by public conveyance, when he is prosecuting a journey by rail or boat, whether he is sitting still in a motionless car, or standing serenely on the station-platform, or walking to and fro thereon waiting for a start, or going into a station for prog, or returning therefrom after having grubbed,[3] although Chase, C. J., held that a man who had performed the greater part of a journey by steamboat and, there being no public conveyance, proceeded on foot to his house some miles distant from the port, could not exactly be said to be a private conveyance to himself while walking.[4]

A poor fellow away down in Kentucky inadvertently and needlessly put his arm out of a car window and had it injured by being bumped against a post, and the court held the injury not accidental, being attributable to the person's own negligence.[5] But as this case stands alone it will scarcely answer to point a *moral* or adorn a tale, and the better opinion seems to be that contributory negligence is no defence, as the liability rests upon contract, one of the chief objects of which is to protect a man against his own carelessness or negligence.[6] But one must

---

1. *Hooper* v. *Accid. Death Ins. Co.*, 5 H. & N, 545; 6 *ib.*, 839; *Smith* v. *Acc. Ins. Co.*, per Kelly, C.B., supra.
2. *Tooley* v. *Rw. Pass. Acc. Ins. Co.*, 2 Ins. L. J., 275.
3. May on Insurance, p. 661.
4. *Ripley* v. *Rw. Pass. Ass. Co.*, 15 Wall (U.S.), 580.
5. *Morel* v. *Mississippi Valley Life Ins. Co.*, 4 Bush (Ky.), 535.
6. *Providence Life Ins. Co.* v. *Martin*, 32 Md., 310 ; *Trew* v. *Rw. Pass. Ins. Co.*, 6 H. & N., 839 ; *Schneider* v. *Providence Life Ins. Co.*, 24 Wis., 28 ; *Champlin* v. *Travellers Pass. Ins. Co.*, 6 Lansing (N.Y.), 71.

not be guilty of wilful and wanton exposure of himself to unnecessary danger, for instance he must not ride on the engine[1] or attempt to cross the track when an approaching train is within fifty feet.[2]

I was now assured that to be insured was sure to bring contentment if not riches.

1. *Brown* v. *Rw. Pass. Ass. Co.*, 45 Mo., 221; May p. 657.
2. May on Insurance, p. 667.

CHAPTER III.

STATIONS AND STARTING.

Meditations on crossings—Bell or whistle—Access to stations—Slippery ice—Checks on trunks—Notice of arrivals and departures—Trains late as usual—Must keep time—Damages, damages—Proof—Ill fared Welfare—Waiting rooms not smoke-houses—Charge of the iron horse—Tripped up.

HAVING settled the insurance question to my own satisfaction, and purchased both a railway and an accident ticket, as the proper hour for the departure of my train approached, I started bag in hand, being minded to go afoot to the station. "As I walked by myself, I talked to myself and myself replied to me, and the questions myself then put to myself with the answers, I give thee," my would-be-wise reader.

Coming upon the railroad where it ran close to a house which hid the line on one side completely from view, I was rather startled by a freight train dashing past within a few feet of my nose, and I asked myself: "Should not a bell have been rung?" and I replied: "Yes, wherever a train crosses a highway there the bell should be rung or the whistle sounded; and no engine should have gone at such a speed." "Should not the company place a watchman at a crossing to warn pedestrians of the approach of trains?" the answer that came was, "I fancy not, for *prima facie*, a foot passenger crossing a railway is bound to look out for his own safety;[1] just as it is his duty to use due care and caution in crossing a street, so as not recklessly to get among the carriages."[2] There is, it appears, no general duty devolving upon railway

---

1. *Skelton* v. *L. & N. W. Rw.*, L.R. 2 C.P., 631; *Boggs* v. *Great Western Rw.*, 23 (U. C.), C.P., 573.
2. *Williams* v. *Richards*, 3 C. & K., 82; *Cotton* v. *Wood*, 3 C.B., N.S., 571.

companies to place watchmen at such places, but it depends upon the particular circumstances of each individual case as to whether the omission of such a precaution amounts to negligence or not.[1]

But then this crossing is peculiarly dangerous, the line being hid as it is ? In such a case the mere occurrence of an accident to one crossing, would be evidence of negligence.[2] I remember that once on a certain foggy morning in the land of fogs, a man took the trouble to look up the line and to look down the line, but owing to the dimness of the light failed to see a train coming, the engine never whistled, the man was injured and the company was found guilty of negligence.[3] Where persons are in the habit of crossing a line at a particular place, though there is no right of way there, still the responsibility of taking reasonable precautions in their use of such place is thrown upon the company.[4]

Every locomotive should be furnished with a bell and a steam-whistle, and the one should be sounded or the other rung at the distance of eighty rods from every place where the railway crosses a highway, and be kept ringing or sounding at short intervals, until the engine has crossed the road, under a penalty of eight dollars for every neglect, to be paid by the company, who will also be liable for all damages arising from such neglect.[5] The omission to give the required signal constitutes a *prima facie* case of negligence : still, to make the company liable for damages, the injury must be the result of the want of the signal, and the onus of showing this will not be upon the company, but upon the plaintiff.[6]

When a carriageway crossed a line on a level, and the gates on the down side of the line being open, young Wanless, with some

---

1. *Stubley* v. *London & N. W. Rw.*, L.R., 1 Ex. 13.
2. *Bilbee* v. *London & B. Rw.*, 54 L.J., 182 ; 18 C.B. (N.S.), 584 ; see also, *Stubley* v *L. & N. W.*, L.R., 1 Ex., 13 ; *Stapley* v. *L. B. & S. C. Rw.*, L.R., 1 Ex. 21.
3. *James* v. *Gt. W. R. C.*, L. R., 2 C.P., 634 n.
4. *Barrett* v. *Midland Rw. Co.*, 1 F. & F. 361.
5. Railway Act, 1868, s. 20, ss. 9, 10. (Canada,)
6. *Galena & Chicago Union Rw.* v. *Loomis*, 13 Illin., 548.

other boys, entered on the railway at the time when a train on the up side was passing, intending to cross as soon as the train had passed: meanwhile another train, on the down side, which he could have seen if he had looked, knocked him down and injured him. The Court of Queen's Bench and the House of Lords both held that the company were guilty of negligence.[1]

A railway company is not bound to use the same amount of care towards strangers who voluntarily and wilfully go on their track, as they owe towards their passengers. This, Mr. Brand found out after he had his legs cut off while walking on the track through the city.[2]

When on the point of crossing a track about the time a train is due one should not bundle up his head, so as to impair the sense of hearing, and then go straight ahead without looking out for the cars. If a man does so and is made mince-meat of, he has only himself to blame, even though neither bell nor whistle sounded.[3] A company is bound so to lay their line at a crossing that no injury will be done by reason of the rails being above the level of the road.[4]

Near the station and forming one way of access thereto is a bridge, said to be in a dangerous state, and across this I saw several persons hurrying, but I preferred to go round by a longer way, for although it has been decided that a company is liable for the death of a passenger through the faulty construction of a bridge, erected by them for the more convenient access to the station, when there is a safe one about one hundred yards further off, which the unfortunate deceased might have used,[5] still I considered discretion the better part of valour and chose keeping sound

---

1. *Wanless* v. *North Eastern Rw.*, L.R., 6 Q. B., 481; affirmed on appeal, W. N., Ap. 25, 1874; *Stapley* v. *London & B. Rw.*, L.R., 1 Ex. 21.
2. *Brand* v. *Troy & Syr. Rw.*, 8 Bart, 368.
3. *Steves* v. *Oswego & Syr.*, 18 N.Y., 422; *Weld* v. *Hudson River Rw.*, 24 N.Y., 430; but see *Chaffee* v. *Boston & Lowell Rw.*, 104 Mass, 108.
4. *Oliver* v. *North Western Rw.*, L. R., 9 Q.B., 409.
5. *Longmore* v. *G. W. Rw. Co.*, 19 C.B., N.S., 183.

bones in a whole skin, to my wife enjoying plenty and prosperity out of my life insurances. Besides, I recollected that Mr. Justice Clesby had once said, that where a passenger having full knowledge of the fact, still preferred using a dangerous way, and in consequence was injured, it would seem that such a foolish body would have no ground of complaint, on the principle of the old maxim *volenti non fit injuria*.[1] What risks men will run to save a few minutes or a few steps, verily well saith the poet—

> " Of all the creatures that fly in the air
> Swim in the sea, or tread earth so fair,
> From Paris and Rome to Peru and Japan,
> The most foolish beast, as I think, is man."

On entering the station-yard I found engines puffing and snorting, backing and switching on every side, and really it was at considerable danger of my journey being summarily put an end to ere well commenced, that I made my way to the platform. This rather annoyed me and ruffled the habitual serenity of my temper (and the serenity of the most serene would be tried by a locomotive spirting and squirting out a jet of steam at one's nether garments), for it is the duty of railway companies to take all reasonable care to keep their premises in such a state that those whom they invite there (and they invite all who may desire to be carried to any place whither the line runs) will not be unduly exposed to danger.[2] But they need not go so far as to put a handrail upon a stairway for unsteady folks to steady themselves with, where the stair is protected on either side by walls: and they may put brass on the steps instead of lead, although it is more slippery.[3]

I had scarcely stepped on to the platform when one foot slipped from under me, and down with a whack I descended upon the back of my head; my carpet bag, too, fell with a crash telling of

---

1. *Bridges* v. *N. London &c.*, L.R., 6 Q.B., 377.
2. *Welfare* v. *London & Brighton Rw.*, L.R., 4 Q.B., 693.
3. *Crafter* v. *Metropolitan Rw.*, I.R., 1 C.P., 300.

ruin to some valuable therein contained. Up rose I in wrath and found that a strip of ice had been the cause of my discomfiture, and I registered an oath on high that the company should answer to me in solid gold for the damages I had sustained; for I knew of one Shepherd, who having fallen on a slippery place, while he tramped up and down the platform waiting for a train, recovered a goodly sum from the company; and Martin, B., said, railway servants ought to be alert during cold weather to see whether there is ice upon the platform, and to remove it, or make it safe by sanding it, or otherwise, if it is there.[1] (Still, where Mr. Ringland, while walking along a side walk in Toronto, on a frosty day in mid-winter, stept on some ice, slipt, fell and broke his collarbone, it was held that the corporation was not liable as for neglect to keep the sidewalk in good repair, for the existence of the piece of ice was no evidence of actionable negligence, considering our climate.[2])

On I strode in ire—for I saw some girls snickering at me—to where the baggage-master was checking the luggage.

"Check this," I exclaimed.

"Take it into the car with you:" he replied.

"I won't; you must check it: there's a handle," I returned.

"I won't: handle be hanged; you must take it," he retorted.

"All right," I answered, inwardly resolving that, as a check had been refused me when demanded, the company should pay me the penalty of eight dollars, as well as the costs of the action which I should bring against them for it, and that I would insist upon the conductor in charge of the train refunding me the fare that I had paid for my ticket.[3] I was sorry now that I had bought the ticket in advance, for under the circumstances they

---

1. *Shepherd* v. *Midland Rw. Co.*, 20 W.R., 705.

2. *Ringland* v. *Corporation of Toronto*, 23 U.C., C.P., 93. But see as to the liabilities of corporations for defects and obstructions caused by snow; *Loker* v. *Inhabitants of Brookline*; Dillon on Municipal Corp., p. 754, sec. 789; and cases under heading "Snow and Ice."

3. Railway Act, 1868, s. 20, s.s. 5 and 6 (Can.).

would have had no right to collect or receive from me any toll or fare.[1]

I was determined to teach railway companies their duties, and baggage-masters are far too fond of refusing to check small parcels or bags; and at way stations, in their wisdom, even decline sometimes to check large trunks—although the law of this Canada of ours says, " checks shall be affixed by an agent or servant to every parcel of baggage having a handle, loop or fixture of any kind thereupon (though what may be included in the latter term goodness only knows), and a duplicate shall be given to the passenger delivering the same."[2]

It was not many minutes before I found cause of action number *three* against the respectable railway company to whose tender mercies I was about to commit my precious self. The law directs that " the trains shall be started and run at regular hours to be fixed by public notice,"[3] but most locomotives—their drivers and conductors—treat that clause with a contempt truly philosophical. The train by which I desired to embark was overdue for half-an-hour, according to the time-table which hung mockingly on the wall, so I looked about me to see if there had been " put up on the outside of the station-house over the platform of the station in some conspicuous place, a written or printed notice signed by the station master, stating to the best of his knowledge and belief the time when such over-due train might be expected to reach the station" as it was the duty of the company to do. Of course, no such notice was visible, such enactments being too often deemed effete from the very day they appear on the statute book, so I still further comforted and consoled my wounded feelings by the thought that for this neglect or omission they were liable to an action at my suit, in which full costs might be recovered[4] (the latter was an object of importance just now).

1. Railway Act, 1868, s. 20, s.s. 5 and 6.
2. *Ibid.*, s. 20., s.s. 5.
3. *Ibid.* s. 20., s.s. 2.
4. 34 Vict., c. 43, s. 6 (Can.).

I now retired into the waiting-room to ponder over the business that had thus unexpectedly turned up. I knew that few men were bold enough to fight a great railway company on any question, and especially one involving a small amount, and that as a result of this, railways have been virtually exempt from the penalties attaching to many breaches of duty and of contract which they are daily committing; but I determined to sacrifice myself for the good of my fellows—I was eager, too, to see my name figuring in the reports.

I also now began to reflect that if the train was much later I would miss my appointments, and then cause of action number *four* would accrue. For it is as clear as daylight that if a railway company publishes or authorizes the publication of a time-table, representing that a train will start at a particular hour for a particular place, or arrive at a particular hour, and no train is prepared or arrives, the company is responsible in damages to all persons who have acted upon the faith of the representation, and have been deceived and put to expense, and have sustained damage thereby;[1] but if they give proper notice they will not be liable for any necessary delay.[2] The company make a continuous representation whilst they continue to hold out printed or written papers as being their time-tables, and they thereby make a public profession and representation that they will exercise their vocation of common carriers, and despatch passengers or goods, as the case may be, to certain specified places at or about the time named in such tables: and if they fail to do so they commit a breach of their duty as common carriers, and are guilty of a fraudulent representation, which may be the foundation of an action for deceit by any one who, relying on the representation, tenders himself or his goods for conveyance at the appointed time, and finds there is no train about to start.[3] I also ran the risk of miss-

---

1. Addison on Torts, 3rd Ed., 447.
2. Red. on Railways, vol. 2, p. 276. They cannot free themselves from liability from delays caused by other Companies. *Bealle* v. *G. W. R.*, 18 Sol. J., 972.
3. *Denton* v. *Gt. Northern Rw.*, 5 Ell. & Bl., 868; *In re Oxlade*, 1 C.B., N.S., 454; *Heirn* v. *McCaughan*, 32 Miss., 17.

ing the connection at B; but I remembered that once upon a time a tailor going down into the country to measure his customers, in consequence of the train not having reached a junction at the time advertised, missed his connection and had to spend the night at the junction and pay extra fare the next morning; he sued the company and recovered the amount of his hotel expenses and the extra fare, but not for damages sustained by not reaching his customers at the appointed time [but this rule seems to be almost equivalent to a denial of all beneficial redress in such cases[1]]. The Chief Baron in giving judgment, stated that as a rule, generally, in actions upon contracts "the plaintiff is entitled to recover whatever damage naturally results from the breach of the contract, but not damages for the disappointment of mind occasioned by the breach of contract."[2] It must clearly appear that the damages were sustained without any fault on the part of traveller, and in spite of his utmost efforts to avoid them.[3]

The mere production of a ticket, however, is not sufficient evidence of a contract to carry a passenger to a certain place within a given time, as one Hurst discovered when he sued for various expenses and losses sustained through missing a certain train in consequence of delay in starting; the time-table must be produced to prove the contract.[4] And as I knew that to prove that the table was issued by authority I would have to shew either that it was bought at one of the company's stations, or at one of their recognised receiving offices, or that it was posted up in some office or place where the advertisements of the company were usually placed,[5] I started off on a tour of investigation to see if I

---

1. Red. on Railways, vol. 2, p. 277, n.
2. *Hamlin* v. *Gt. Northern Rw.*, 1 H. & N., 408, and as to damages for remote and collateral consequences, see *Story* v. *N. Y. & Haarlem Rw.*, 2 Selden, 97; *Davis* v. *Talcot*, 14 Barbour, 611; *Horner* v. *Wood*, 16 Barbour, 386.
3. *Benson* v. *New Jersey Rw. Co.*, 9 Bosw., 412.
4. *Hurst* v. *Gt. Western Rw.*, 34 L.J., C.P., 265; *Robinson* v. *The same*, 35 L.J., C.P., 123.
5. Addison on Torts, p. 487.

could pick up the desired article, or evidence that would answer my purpose, keeping in mind how ill fared my friend, Mr. Welfare. He once innocently inquired of a railway porter when the train would be in, and being referred by the official to a timetable hanging upon the wall, he went to consult it; while doing so, down tumbled, through a hole in the roof, a heavy plank and a roll of zinc, and smote Mr. Welfare on the neck, doing him grievous bodily harm; glancing upwards, the poor stricken one beheld the legs of a man upon the roof. Yet for the damages done the company was held not liable, as for aught that my friend showed at the trial the man might have been the servant of a contractor employed to mend the roof, or the misfortune might have been the result of a pure accident.[1] So the sufferings of my friend served but to point a moral—Beware!—and to adorn a volume of reports.

But to return from this digression anent my friend, to the topic on which I was musing. Strictly speaking, a company is not liable for mere delay, special damages must be proved; but whenever, in consequence of the delay, expenses are incurred, there is every ground for making the company liable.[2] Draper, C. J., in one case, held that a time-table could not be treated as a part of the contract, but amounted to a representation only; and that to recover damages one would have to show that he bought his ticket before the time specified for the train leaving, and not merely before the arrival of the train, for if that were after the time specified the would-be passenger would know as well as the company that the time-table had been departed from.[3]

While I was thus deeply ruminating, an old friend appeared— a Q. C., of high standing, at the bar of a neighbouring city; and we went outside to enjoy a chat and weed while waiting for the train. Seeing an elderly female turn up her nose as a whiff of

1. *Welfare* v. *London & Brighton Rw. Co.*, L.R., 4 Q.B., 693.
2. See case cited in 1 U.C., L.J., N.S., p. 336.
3. *Briggs* v. *Grand Trunk Rw. Co.*, 24 U.C., Q.B., 516.

smoke tickled her nostrils, as if it were in very deed a blast from the lower regions, as King James said it was, my friend remarked:

"Did you see that decision of Dillon, C. J., where he held that a woman who found the waiting-room unfit for her occupation—tobacco and other impurities being offensive to her delicate nerves—and so attempted to enter the cars which had not as yet come up to the platform, and was injured by the giving way of the platform steps, was entitled to recover?"[1]

"No," I replied.

"He ruled that it is the duty of railway passenger carriers to provide comfortable rooms for the accommodation of passengers while waiting at the stations, and to enforce such regulations in regard to smoking therein as to enable persons to occupy them in reasonable comfort."

"A very good decision for the ladies, and those who have to wait hour after hour in a dirty room for a train ages behind its time."

"Still I think it is pushing the doctrine of the liability of companies rather far."

"Yes," I returned, "and rather in the teeth of the dictum of Mr. Justice Hannan, in *Liner v. Great Western*,[2] where he said he thought that juries took an exaggerated view of the duties of railway companies: that the companies have done so much for the comfort and convenience of travellers that it is now made the subject of complaint if the highest degree of luxurious care is not attained in all their arrangements."

"His is a much more sensible view of the case;" said Smith who held some railway shares, "and one more likely to produce dividends for unfortunate stock-holders. If people avail themselves of the benefits of railway travellers they should make some allowances. Ah! look at our fair friend!"

---

1. *McDonald et ux.* v. *Chicago & N. W. R. Co.*, 26 Iowa, 124.
2. L. R., 3 Exch., 150.

She was at the far end of the platform, and an engine attached to a freight train seemed to be rushing straight at her; she turned and fled, with a scream, to avoid the charge of the iron horse, and in her hurry tripped over a barrow and fell prostrate. The career of the locomotive was stopped; it appeared that its antics had been caused by the negligent displacement of a switch. We raised the lady and found that although slightly damaged she was more frightened than hurt. We consoled her with the assurance that if she chose to sue the company she could make them pay for the elephantine gambols of the fiery steed which had so disturbed her equanimity.[1]

Seeing a man a short way off to whom I desired to speak, I was on the point of jumping down off the platform, when my Q. C. exclaimed.

"Hold! be not rash! If you jump, instead of going down by the steps, and are hurt you can never make the company pay for the plasters and the salves:[2] besides here's the train."

And so indeed it was at last: up it thundered to the station amid screeching and bell-ringing: out rushed the passengers eager to reach the refreshment room; the crowd pushed my chum against a portable weighing-machine, and, catching his foot in it, he fell and injured himself. Seeing that he was not very seriously damaged I could not help crying out:

"Hold! be not rash! I knew a case on all fours with yours, where the foot of a machine projected above the level of the platform six inches and was unfenced; there it had stood for years without doing any damage, and it was held that there was no evidence to go to a jury of any negligence, the machine being where it might have been seen, and the accident not being one which could have been reasonably anticipated.[3] An exactly similar case. Ho! ho! ho!"

1. *Caswell* v. *Boston & Worcester Rw.*, 98 Mass.
2. *Forsyth* v. *Boston &c.*, 103 Mass., 510.
3. *Cornman* v. *Eastern Counties Rw.*, 4 H. & N., 781; see also *Blackman* v. *London B. & S. C. Rw.*, 17 W.R., 769.

"I wish the whole platform had given way with the weight of that mob, and then there would without doubt have been evidence of negligence. Besides I might have had the pleasure of seeing you break your leg;" testily replied the Q. C.

"Ah! my dear sir, one must be careful and walk circumspectly about a station. You know where a man fell, seriously hurting himself, on a staircase down which some forty thousand people had passed every month without an accident, the court held that there was no evidence of negligence on the part of the company to go to a jury, although the brass covering on the step had been worn smooth, and said that " the mere fact of a man having fallen and hurt himself is not sufficient to charge the company with negligence in the construction of their station; and the Court is in an especial manner bound to see that the evidence submitted to the jury in order to establish negligence, is sufficient and proper to go to them."[1]

---

1. *Crafter* v. *Metropolitan Rw. Co.*, L.R., 1 C.P., 300. Where on the platform there were two doors in close proximity to each other, the one for necessary purposes, had painted over it the words "For gentlemen,' the other had over it "lamp room." The plaintiff having occasion to go to the former, enquired its whereabouts and was directed to it; by mistake he opened the door of the lamp room, fell down some stairs and was injured: Held that in the absence of evidence that the place was more than ordinarily dangerous, a nonsuit was right. *Toomey* v. *London B. & S. C.*, 3 C.B., N.S., 146.

CHAPTER IV.

TICKETS.

Man and wife double as to baggage—Money in Trunk—Authority of American decisions — Annual tickets — Badge of officers — Legislature outwitted — "Tickets, sir"—"Good for this day only"—"Good for this trip"—Stepping off—Lose a ticket, and pay again—The Acts.

JUST as we were starting I overheard an altercation between the baggage-man and a woman of a rather masculine appearance, " with angular outlines and plain surface, hair like the fibrous covering of a cocoa-nut in gloss and suppleness as well as colour, and a voice at once thin and strenuous—acidulous enough to produce effervesence with alkalies, and stridulous enough to sing duets with the katydids." He was asserting that she had too much baggage and that she must pay freight; the woman demurred to this, and protested that as she and her husband were travelling together they were entitled to a double quantity of luggage. In this she was clearly right, as, though the law considers that a man and a woman joined together in the bonds of wedlock are one, still as respects baggage they are two,[1] or half-a-dozen if one may judge from Saratoga trunks. The disputants moved off and I did not hear the functionary's decision.

As my companion opened his pocket book to put in his checks I noticed that he had nothing therein except a few cents, so I remarked jokingly:

" You don't appear to have much of the needful about you."

He replied. "Pshaw! I am not such a goose as to carry money in my pocket to afford the light-fingered gentry an opportunity of enriching themselves at my expense."

1. *Great Northern Rw.* v. *Shepherd*, L.R., 8 Ex., 30.

" But how do you manage to travel without money ? I should like to learn the secret." I said.

" So should I. I carry my cash in my trunk."

" In your trunk! suppose you lose it ? "

" Well the company's liable ;" he replied.

" Shouldn't think so," I said.

" But I am sure of it. It has been held that common carriers of passengers are responsible for money *bona fide* included in the baggage of a passenger for travelling purposes and personal use, to an amount not exceeding what a prudent man—like myself for instance—would deem proper and necessary for the purpose.[1] But they are not responsible for money beyond such an amount, or intended for other purposes, unless, of course, the loss is occasioned by the gross negligence of the carriers or their servants."[2]

" Well, I don't think you are a prudent man ; besides I fancy that's only an American authority." I remarked.

" Only an American authority! suppose it is, it is not to be despised. Bramwell, B., once said that although the American authorities are not indeed binding upon us, still they are entitled to respect as the opinions of professors of English law, and entitled to respect according to the position of those professors and the reasons they give for their opinions,[3] and Spragge, C., in a late case, uses a similar expression.[4]

" Of course I bow to the dictum of the learned baron and chancellor. But doubtless there are American cases the other way."

" Perhaps. In fact I know there are.[5] But the great American authority, Judge Redfield, thinks they are incorrect.[6] I can

1. *Jordan* v. *Fall River Rw.*, 5 Cush., 69 ; see Chapter IV, Book III.
2. *Orange County Bank* v. *Brown*, 9 Wend., 85 ; *Weed* v. *Saratoga & Sch. Rw.*, 19 Wend., 534 ; *Duffy* v. *Thompson*, 4 Smith, 178.
3. *Osborn* v. *Gillett*, L.R., 8 Ex., 92.
4. *Deedes* v. *Graham*, 20 Grant, 270.
5. *Grant* v. *Newton*, 1 E. D. Smith, 95 ; *Chicago & Aurora Rw.* v. *Thompson*, 19 Ill., 578.
6. Red. on Railways, vol. 2, p. 56-58.

give you a Pennsylvanian case sustaining the Massachusetts one I quoted: and that is where the company in their advertisements stated that passengers were prohibited from taking anything as baggage but wearing apparel, which would be at the risk of the owner, and the trunk of a passenger contained specie—the extra weight beyond the usual allowance was paid for and the company's agent took charge of it. The trunk wandered from the right way, went astray and was lost; and it was held that it was not incumbent upon the passenger to inform the carrier of the contents of the trunk unless he was asked, and that it was immaterial whether it was to be considered baggage or freight, and that the company was liable for its loss through the negligence or fraud of their agents."[1]

"Well, such may be the law on the other side of the line, but in this hyperborean Dominion of ours I must say that I think it is somewhat different. I think that if the conduct of the traveller has in any way contributed to the loss, he has no ground at common law for demanding compensation from the carrier.[2] Why there is that old case in Burrows where a prudent man like yourself hid £100 stg. in an old nail-bag with some hay, and gave it to a common carrier to be taken to a banker; the money was lost, but the carrier was held not responsible, as the consignor had neglected to tell him the exceeding value of the bag and so prevented him taking due care of it.[3] Then there was the case of the guineas tied up with a bit of string in a brown-paper parcel;[4] the case of the sovereigns in the tea,[5] and the banknotes and gold in the school-boy's box,[6] in all of which the

---

1. *Camden & Amboy Rw.* v. *Baldauf* 16 Penn. (4 Harris), 67; see also *Walker* v. *Jackson*, 10 M. & W., 16, as to not inquiring contents, and *Crouch* v. *L. & N. W. Rw.* 14 C.B., 255, as to right to inquire.
2. *Butterworth* v. *Brownlow*, 34 L.J., C.P., 267.
3. *Gibbon* v. *Paynton*, 4 Burr., 2298.
4. *Clay* v. *Willan*, 1 H. B., 298.
5. *Bradley* v. *Waterhouse*, 3 C. & P., 318.
6.

carriers were held relieved from liability. Then in England there is the Carrier's Act (11 Geo. 4. and 1 Wm. 4. c 68), applying to all goods above £10."[1]

Here I was interrupted by the sudden cry of "Tickets! Tickets!" which rang through the car. The conductor entered, and stopped in front of a gentleman who said:

"I have not got my ticket here. I hold a season one."

"That won't do, sir;" said the man. "Holders of annual tickets travelling on the line are bound to produce their tickets as much as ordinary passengers.[2] So take your choice, show your ticket, pay your fare, or out you go."[3]

"Well," replied the gentleman, "sooner than be turned out with my baggage, wherever you in your wisdom should deem best, I will pay my fare."

"Don't do it, sir," I almost without intending it called out, so eager was I in my crusade against the company. "The conductor has no right to demand the tickets, nor receive any fare, nor in fact can he exercise any of the powers of his office, or meddle or interfere with any passenger or his baggage unless he has upon his hat or cap a badge indicating his office;[4] and a company before they can enforce any law as to the production of tickets must bring themselves strictly within the terms of the law."

"Sold again," cried the wretched official as he lugged out from his coat pocket a small cap ornamented with the word "*Conductor,*" and showing it to me he added, "You pretend to know a great deal about the law, so perhaps you recollect that the statute

---

1. By it no carrier is liable for loss or injury to any articles of great value in small compass, or for money, bills, notes, jewellery, &c., above £10, unless the value and nature of the property has been declared, and an increased charge paid for it. As to carriers by water, see 37 Vict. (Ont.), ch. 25, s. 1, Imp. St., 17 & 18 Vic., ch. 104, s. 503, and Act of Congress, March 3, 1857, referred to infra Chapter IV, Book III.
2. *Woodard* v. *Eastern Counties Rw.*, 7 Jur., N.S., 971, 4 L.T., N.S., 336; *Downs* v. *N. Y. & N. H. Rw.*, 36 Conn., 287.
3. Railway Act, 1868, sec. 20, ss. 12.
4. The Railway Act, 1868, sec. 20.
5. *Jennings* v. *Gt. N. Rw.*, L.R., 1 Q.B., 7.

does not say that the cap or hat, with the badge, is to be worn on the head. The law in its wisdom assumed that officers of the company would or must have caps or hats, and that they would or must wear them, and wear them upon the head, but it did not enact that they should do so.[1] It never entered the wise noddles of the legislators at Ottawa that a man might own two caps, a jolly fur one for use, and another little chap for show."

"I acknowledge that I spoke with undue haste," I meekly replied, feeling very crestfallen as I heard audible smiles from several of the passengers.

But the remorseless railway man continued: "It is plain by the law of Canada that a passenger is not obliged to purchase a ticket before he enters the company's car, he may pay the conductor, if he pleases, the fare. But if the passenger pays and receives a ticket, then he accepts the ticket upon the condition that he will produce it and deliver it up when required by some duly authorized person, and in such case it is part of the contract:[2] so my dear sir," he said soothingly to the gentleman, though to me his words were very swords, "please produce your ticket, or pay a second time."

When the conductor at length came up for my ticket I quietly shewed it, and telling him of the circumstances connected with the refusal of the baggage-man to check my trunk, asked him to refund the fare; this, as I expected, he refused to do, adding that my friend would do as a witness to prove that I had made the demand in case I chose to sue the company.

After this obnoxious individual had departed, the Q. C. entered into a lengthy disquisition concerning railway tickets; he remarked that the words usually printed on them, "'Good for this day only, A to B,' created a contract on the part of the company to convey the holder in one continuous journey from A to B, to

---

1. *Farewell* v. *G.T.R.*, 15 U.C., C.P., 427.
2. *Duke* v. *Great Western Rw.*, 14 U.C., Q.B., 377.

be commenced on the day of issuing the ticket," and that if a passenger alighted at an intermediate station he would forfeit all his rights under the ticket, and could not claim to be carried on to his journey's end in a subsequent train without paying a new fare.[1] And the same rule holds good when the ticket is marked "Good for this trip only;"[2] and when marked "Good for one passage on this day only," it can only be used on the day of its date.[3] And where a ticket with the words, "Good for this trip only," marked upon it, and unmutilated, but a few days old, was presented, it was held that it was *prima facie* evidence that the holder had paid the regular fare, was entitled to be carried between the places named, and that the ticket had never been used; and also, that such words referred to no particular trip, or time, but only to a continuous trip which might be made on the date or any subsequent day.[4] Some companies give their conductors power to allow passengers to stop by the way by endorsing permission on the ticket.[5]

Companies have no intention of allowing a man after he has travelled on a ticket for a time by one train to leave it, and afterwards at his august pleasure to resume his seat in another train at some intervening part of the road;[6] such proceedings would lead to endless confusion, trouble and annoyance. But it appears that when one has tickets, in the coupon form, over distinct lines, if they contain no restrictions one may delay as long as he likes at the different changing places.[7]

One Craig bought a ticket in Buffalo marked "Good only for

---

1. *Briggs* v. *G. T. Rw.*, 24 U.C., Q.B., 510; *Dietrich* v. *Penn. A. Rw.*, 8 C. L.J., N. S., 202; *McLure* v. *Phil. Will. & Balt. Rw.*, 34 Md., 632; *Boice* v. *Hudson R. Rw.*, 61 Barb., 611.
2. *Cheney* v. *Boston & Maine Rw.* 11 Met. 121.
3. *State* v. *Campbell*, 3 Vroom, 309.
4. *Pier* v. *Friel*, 24 Barb., 514.
5. *McLure* v. *Phil. Will. & Balt. Rw.*, 34 Md., 532.
6. *State* v. *Overton*, 4 Zabriskie, 438; *Cincinnati, Columbus & C. Rw.* v. *Bartram*, 11 Ohio, U.S., 457.
7. *Brooke* v. *Grand Trunk Railway*, 15 Mich. 332.

twenty days from date," from Buffalo to Detroit; after viewing the glories and magnificence of thundering Niagara he took his seat in the afternoon accommodation train of the Great Western at the Suspension Bridge. This train ran on to London, but Craig for his own pleasure got out at St Catharines and went up to see the town. As the night express was going through that fashionable watering place he applied to be allowed to travel by it on the ticket he held, and on being refused sued the company. The court, however, considered that the ticket bound the company to carry the plaintiff on one continuous journey from the Suspension Bridge to Detroit, giving him the option of taking any passenger train from the point of commencement, and if that train did not go the whole distance, to convey him the residue of the journey in some other train—the whole journey to be completed in twenty days; but that it did not give the holder the right to stop at every or any intermediate station as Mr. Craig contended.[1] If one has left the train in which he started on his journey, the fact that he has subsequently entered another train and travelled over a part of the remaining distance without being required to pay fare by the conductor in charge, does not prejudice the company or renew the contract.[2] But, said my friend, "I believe that in this last case Agnew, J., guarded his meaning by saying that there might be exceptions to the general rule, where from misfortune or accident, without his fault, the transit of the passenger is interrupted, and he afterwards resumes his journey."

While I was listening intently to the words of knowledge that were flowing like some mighty river from the lips of the learned counsel, and wondering how and why he was so deeply read on the topic, he suddenly stopped in his discourse, pointed his finger

---

1. *Craig* v. *Great Western Rw. Co.*, 24 U.C., Q.B., 504; *Boston & Lowell Rw.* v. *Proctor*, 1 Allen, 267; *Shedd* v. *Troy & Boston Rw.*, 40 Vt., 88. A bill was introduced into the Ontario Legislature last session, enacting that notices, &c., on tickets to the effect that holders shall only be entitled to a continuous journey or on particular days shall be void. But the bill came to naught.

2. *Dietrich* v. *Penn. A. R. R. Co.*, supra.

at a little child who had got possession of his mother's ticket and was quietly by a process of suction reducing it to an unsightly and undistinguishable pulp; then raising his voice, Smith, Q. C. exclaimed:

"Excuse me, madam, you ought to be more careful of your ticket, for if you lose or destroy it, the conductor (unless he knows for a fact that you actually did pay your fare and obtain a ticket,) will be justified in demanding repayment from you, and, if you refuse it, may put you off the cars. Just listen to what the late lamented Chief Justice Robinson says on this very point, and where a married woman, and for aught I know a mother like yourself, was turned off the train, or had to pay her fare a second time, I forget which."

And before the lady had recovered from her astonishment he dived into his red bag, produced an extensive brief, and read, as follows:

"It may seem hard to a man who has lost his ticket, or perhaps had it stolen from him, that he should have to pay his fare a second time; but it is better and more reasonable that a passenger should now and then have to suffer the consequences of his own want of care, than that a system (the system of issuing tickets as now in vogue) should be rendered impracticable, which seems necessary to the transaction of this important branch of business. It is not for the sole advantage, or for the pleasure and caprice of the railway company that these things are done in such a hurry. The public, whether wisely or not, desire to travel at the rate of four or five hundred miles a-day, and that rapidity of movement cannot be accomplished without peculiar arrangements to suit the exigency which must be found sometimes to produce inconvenience. If the passenger in this case, who I have no doubt lost her ticket, could claim as a matter of right to have it believed on her word that she had paid her passage, everybody else in a similar case must have the same right to tell the same story and to be carried through without paying the conductor, and without showing to him a proof that he had paid any one."[1]

"But," said the lady, who during the delivery of the judgment had time to recover her senses and her ticket; "but my friend here could vouch for me that I spoke the truth."

"Ah, my dear madam, do not deceive yourself: reflect that in *Curtis* v. *G. T. R. Co.*[2] that ornament of the bench, Draper, C. J., remarked that he supposed that a man who produced no ticket, but asserted that he had paid his fare and had lost his ticket and therefore declined to pay again, would—though a bystander corroborated the assertion—be deemed refusing to pay, within the meaning of the Acts."

"I do not see what the Acts have to do with it. I never saw anything about such things in the Acts," said the lady, getting rather puzzled over the matter.

"What, madam, do you read such things? I should have imagined that a fair creature like yourself would have found them too dry to read."

"No sir: I am a member of the association of the Church of the New Jerusalem, and I read the Acts of the Apostles as well as every other part of the Bible," eagerly responded the lady.

Amid broad smiles, giggling he-hes, hearty ha-has, guffawing ho-hos, the Q. C. hastened to explain.

"Oh, my dear madam, I meant no allusion to Holy Writ; I meant 31 Vic. c 68—commonly called the Railway Act of 1868, which says at sec. 20 : "Any passenger refusing to pay the fare, may by the conductor of the train and the servants of the company be put off the cars, with his luggage, at any usual stopping place, or near any dwelling house, as the conductor elects, the conductor first stopping the train and using no unnecessary force."

1. *Duke* v. *Great Western Rw. Co.*, 14 U.C., Q.B., 377.
2. 12 U.C., C.P., 90.

CHAPTER V.

PRODUCING TICKETS, OR EVICTION.

Carried past — Jumping off — Junctions — Cave canem — Conductors refusing change — Fighting in the cars — Turned out in the dark — No seats — Coloured persons — Tickets lost and found too late — Conductor's conduct — Damages for wrongful ejectment — Go quietly — Companies heavily mulcted — By law as to producing Tickets — A lover, his mark — Getting off for a moment.

FORTUNATELY for my friend the attention of our fellow travellers was drawn away from him by the language, more forcible than elegant, of a man who had been carried past a small way station at which he desired to alight, and for which he had a ticket. He vowed vengeance against the company because the train was not stopped and a reasonable opportunity given him to alight, and threatened loudly to sue the company for the damage which, he said, he would inevitably sustain through his non-delivery at his destination. And no doubt he would be successful, judging from American authorities, in recovering compensation for the inconvenience, loss of time, and the labour of travelling back to the haven where he would be, because these are the direct consequences of the wrong done him.[1] The ticket must always be taken to be the contract between the passenger and the company for the special purpose, and upon the terms which are contained in it.[2]

Somebody — not a Solomon — asked the man why he had not jumped off: he, sensibly — considering he was in a passion — replied :

---

1. *Damont* v. *New Orleans & Carolton Rw.*, 9 Louis. Am., 441 ; *Ill. Cen. Rw. Co.* v. *Abell*, cited in 8 Can. L.J., N.S., 172 ; Red. on Railways, vol. 2, 276 ; Hodges on Railways, 619
2. *Farewell* v. *Grand Trunk Rw.*, 15 U.C., C.P., 427.

"If I had been so foolhardy as to jump off while the train was in motion, without doubt, any court in the land would hold that I did it at my own risk, and, if hurt, could coolly tell me that for my gross imprudence I had nobody but myself to blame;[1] if, however, they had stopped but for a moment, I would have run the risk of being injured by their starting before I was quite off, for then they would have been liable."

"But," said my legal luminary to me sotto-voce—for he was afraid to draw attention to himself again—"if a passenger is induced to leap from a car under the influence of a well-grounded fear of a collision that would be fatal to limb or life, it seems to be regarded as well settled that he may recover against the carriers, even though he would not have been hurt in the slightest degree, had he philosophically remained quiet."

By this time we had reached the Junction, and friend Smith and myself and several other persons got out to take the cars of the one or the other of the two other companies whose lines here cross. The stations of the three companies are all open to each other, and the passengers of each pass directly from the one to the other, "no pent up Utica contracts their powers" of pedestrianism, the whole area being used as common ground by the travellers on all three roads. While here, a porter of the B. and E. Co., who was trundling a truck laden high with luggage, let a portmanteau fall off and injure the toes of one of our fellow travellers who was on the part of the platform owned by the B. and E. R. W. Co. on his way to the terminus of the other line. (I afterwards heard that the court held that the negligence being an act of misfeasance by the servant of the company in the course of his employment, the maxim *respondeat superior* applied, and that the

---

1. *Damont* v. *New Orleans & C. Rw.*, supra; *Lucas* v. *Taunton & New Bedford Rw. Co.*, 6 Gray, 64.
2. *Penn. Rw.* v. *Kilgore*, 32 Penn. St., 292.
3. *Ingalls* v. *Bills*, 9 Met., 1; *Eldridge* v. *Long Is. Rw.*, 1 Sandf., 89; *Rw. Co.* v. *Aspell*, 23 Penn. St., 147-150; *Stokes* v. *Saltonstall*, 13 Peters (U.S.), 181.

company were liable; but the judges doubted whether the railway would have been responsible supposing the man had been injured from the state and condition of the platform, as he had no business on it.)[1]

As I was trudging along an ugly dog of the cur tribe with a *noli me tangere* expression of countenance dashed past me and rushed up to an innocent-looking individual, seizing him violently by the posterior part of the most indispensable portion of a man's attire, and judging from the row the fellow kicked up, by something more sensitive than pantaloons as well: shaking vigorously, the dog detached a piece of cloth and drew a little blood. The victim had a heavy stick in his hand, and the little doggy's lively career was stopped then and there. I remarked to the man, "My friend, if you find out that that unfortunate puppy belonged to the company or to any of their servants, sue them for damages—if not, don't trouble yourself to do so unless you can show that they were able to dispose of the fractious animal and did not do it."

Shortly after we were again under way a little excitement was occasioned by an altercation between the conductor and a man who had not fully made up his mind (whether owing to the magnitude or insignificance thereof, we cannot say) how far he intended to ride, and so did not wish to settle for the present. The strife of tongues waxed warm and the sound of the conflict rose high above the rattle and the din of the train.

The conductor said that if he did not at once pay the fare to some place or other he would have the pleasure of walking there. The man still hesitated, so the official pulled the check-rope, and on the stoppage of the train proceeded to eject the traveller, who at the last moment tendered a $20 gold piece, and told the con-

---

1. *Tebbutt* v. *Bristol & Ex. R. Co.*, L.R., 6 Q. B., 73; *Stokes* v. *Cardiff Steam Nav. Co.*, 33 L.J. (N.S.), Q.B., 310.
2. *Smith* v. *Gt. East. Rw.*, L.R., 2 C.P., 4; *Barrett* v. *Malden & Melrose Rw.*, 3 Allen, 101.

ductor to take the fare to the next station (some $1.35): the latter declined now to receive the money and put the man off, leaving him alone in his glory, breathing curses loud and deep.[1] Doubtless the official was justified in so doing, as in a somewhat similar case the court said that even an officer at a ticket office might reasonably object to an offer of a $20 gold piece to pay a fare of $1.35, on account of the trouble and risk involved: and that a person rushing into the cars without a ticket has no reason to expect that he will find the conductor prepared to change a $20 gold piece, for he relies upon receiving tickets from the passengers, or, if money be paid to him instead, he expects that it will be paid with reasonable regard to what is convenient under the circumstances.[2]

I may as well inform the general public here that it is considered a reasonable condition for railway companies to require passengers to procure tickets before entering the train.[3]

My friend was just beginning to dilate upon the subject of ejecting passengers, when his voice was drowned by a crash, a scream, and a general uprising of our fellow-travellers. I verily thought within myself that there was a collision—that we were off the track—that—that—that, I don't know what I did not think in the few moments that elapsed before I saw that it was only a fight between some men who had been indulging deeply in that cup which inebriates and brutalises as well as cheers. The conductor soon arrived and quelled the disturbance. In this case fortunately it was not necessary—as it may sometimes be—for him to stop the train, call to his aid the engineer, the firemen, brakesmen and bellicose passengers, and leading the way himself —like some valiant knight of the middle ages—expel the disturbers of the peace, or else show by an earnest experiment that

1. *People* v. *Tillson*, 3 Parker, C., 234.
2. *Fulton* v. *Grand Trunk Rw.*, 17 U.C., Q.B., 433.
3. *Hurst* v. *G. W. R.*, 19 C.B., N.S., 310.

to do so was impossible.¹ If this latter contingency were to happen, the conductor must either discontinue the trip, or give the other passengers an opportunity of leaving the cars; otherwise the company will be responsible for the acts of the rioters.² A conductor is not bound to wait until some act of violence, profaneness, or other misconduct has been committed before exercising the power reposed in him of excluding or expelling offenders.³ Of course he is never bound to receive passengers who will not conform to reasonable regulations, or who from their behaviour, state of health or person, are offensive to the other travellers.⁴

Where the company issue excursion tickets, stipulating to run trains in a particular manner, they cannot excuse themselves, by showing that the carriages are all filled.⁵ In England, in ordinary cases, the ticket is issued subject to the condition that there is room in the train; otherwise those who are booked for the greatest distance have the preference.⁶ A considerable discussion has taken place in some of the states of the Republic as to how far railway companies can require coloured persons to sit in a particular place or car; the right to do so was maintained by the Supreme Court of Pennsylvania,⁷ but other tribunals have denied it. In Illinois it was decided that a company could not from caprice, wantonness or prejudice, exclude a black woman from the ladies' car on account of her negro blood; although it might not be an unreasonable rule to require coloured persons to occupy seats in a separate car, furnished as comfortably as the others.⁸

1. *Pittsburgh, Fort Wayne, &c. Rw.*, v. *Hinds*, 7 Am. Reg., 14.
2. Redfield on Railways, Vol. 2., p. 234.
3. *Venton* v. *Middlesex Rw.*, 11 Allen, 306.
4. Hodges on Railways, 553.
5. Patteson, J., *Hawcroft* v. *G. N. R.*, 16 Jur., 196.
6. Hodges on Railways, 553.
7. *Westchester Rw.* v. *Miles*, 55 Penn. St., 209.
8. *Chicago & N. W.* v. *Williams*, 55 Ill., 185.

It is said to have been held by some court, in a case of *Toland* against *The Hudson River Railway*, that a passenger who is not provided with a seat is not obliged to pay any fare, and if expelled from the cars for refusing such payment may sustain an action against the company. But this doctrine must be taken *cum grano salis*. If a passenger is not accommodated as he should be he may decline any compromise, and sue the company for refusing to carry him, as their contract by the ticket or their duty required; and he doubtless will succeed unless the company prove some just excuse. But if one chooses to accept a passage without a seat, the general understanding undoubtedly is that he must pay. If, however, he goes upon the cars expecting proper accommodation, and is put off because he declines going without, he may still sue.[1] So much by way of parenthesis and digression.

"Well, what have you got to say about ejectment?" I asked my chum.

"Oh, that it is deuced hard that every dunderhead of a conductor may put a poor wayfaring-man off, even at the noon of night, near any dwelling-house he may choose. In one case the night was dark and cloudy; from where the ejected man was placed, the lights of the last station were visible, although no house was nigh, yet the court held that the servants of the company had not exceeded their authority."[2]

"How would it be, old boy, if the poor wretch was short-sighted?" I inquired.

"That defect in one's optics would impose no additional obligation on the company; at least so it would appear from the authorities."[3]

"What would be the consequences if a fellow was to mislay his ticket, and find it again after he had been ignominiously expelled: could he recover against the company?"

---

1. Redfield on Railways, vol. 2, p. 281.
2. *Fulton* v. *G. T. R.*, supra.
3. *Bridges* v. *N. London Rw.*, L. R., 6 Q. B., 377.

"I remember where one Curtis was travelling between St. Mary's and London, and had put his ticket away so safely—lest he should lose it—that he could not find it. The conductor called upon him to produce it; in vain Curtis ransacked pocket after pocket in coat, waistcoat and trousers, pulling out papers, letters, newspapers, wool and all that precious olio to be found in a man's pockets. The other travellers were greatly edified and delighted at the exhibition of this *omnium gatherum*, and their laughs and jests added not a little to the confusion of the poor wretch searching for his little talismanic piece of paste-board. At length the conductor stopped the train and turned C. off, though while being put off he offered to pay his fare. He sued the company, and got $300 out of them, the court holding the company liable for the acts of their officers duly authorised and styled (under the Act) conductors, when not committed in excess of authority which in this case had not been overstepped. The company applied for a new trial, but the court declined to disturb the verdict (it being the second one recovered by Curtis) although it considered the damages excessive."[1]

"I suppose the courts assume that the conductors are the agents of the company and authorised to do all legal acts for the properly collecting tickets, keeping order, running the train, and removing persons who misbehave or will not pay, and such?" I queried.

"Yes," replied my friend who was suffering from an acute attack of *cacoethes loquendi*, "and if in assuming to carry out what he is legally empowered to do, he forcibly removes from the cars (without any excuse) a passenger who has paid his fare he will be liable for the assault; but if while being removed the man should slip, fall, and be injured, the company will not be responsible for his scratches and bruises, or his sprains and strains, such things being the remote, and not the proximate, consequences of the ejectment."[2]

1. *Curtis* v. *G. T. R.*, 12 C.P., 90.
2. *Williamson* v. *G. T. R.*, 17 U.C., C.P., 615.

"Suppose a man suffered serious detriment to his business by being wrongfully turned out of the cars, could he recover for such losses?" I asked.

"It has been so considered in the great Republic, if he declares specially in regard to them.[1] But it has been held—and I think rightly—that one cannot get vindictive or punitive damages against a company, unless they expressly or impliedly participate in the wrongful action by authorising it beforehand or approving of it afterwards;[2] or the case be one of gross negligence or wilful misconduct."[3]

"What is it, then, exactly, that a man can get for being with indignity and insolence hustled out of a train, amid the laughs and jeers of the vulgar and the sneers of the polite?"

"Damages for actual injury, loss of time, pain of body, money paid to the doctor, or for injuries to the wounded feelings of the evicted one, may be allowed."[4]

"Suppose one was killed, and sent off unprepared to the happy hunting grounds of his fathers?" I queried.

"Then the company would be liable under Lord Campbell's Act:"[5] answered my Nestor.

"I presume," I continued, still indulging my unquenchable thirst for knowledge, "that when a conductor gets into his cranium the idea that it is the proper thing to put one off, the best plan is quietly to submit to the inscrutable and go?"

"Undoubtedly—spoken like a veritable Solon. In such an evil case it will be wise and prudent to gather together one's surroundings and belongings, and peaceably succumb to the powers that be, for if you leave any articles behind you, you cannot recover their value—unless you can show that the company got

---

1. *Holmes* v. *Doane*, 3 Gray, 328.
2. *Hogan* v. *Providence & W. Rw.*, 3 Rhode Is., 88.
3. *Barrow* v. *Baltimore & O. R.R.*, 24 Md., 188; *Baltimore & O. R.R.* v. *State*, Ib., 271.
4. *Hogan* v. *Prov. & W. Rw.*, supra.
5. *Penn. Rw. Co.* v. *Vandiver*, 42 Penn. St., 365.

them, or that the violence or suddenness of your ejection rendered it impossible for you to take them with you and so they were lost. This point Mr. Glover had the pleasure of settling: he was trying to do the London and South-Western by giving half his ticket to a friend to save expenses, and when put out of the cars left a pair of glasses behind him, and the court told him that he had only himself to blame for the loss.[1] The courts never like the idea of mulcting railway companies in heavy damages for the sins of commission of their servants and conductors; and so where a verdict of £50 was given against the G. W. R. because the conductor put the plaintiff off the train, though the inconvenience to him was a mere bagatelle, and the conductor had acted *bona fide* under an impression that the fare had not been paid, and had used no harshness or violence, a new trial was granted on the ground of excessive damages, and the Chief Justice stigmatised the verdict as 'outrageous:' but there the jurors of our Lady the Queen and my lord differed; and so on the second trial the yeomen of the county gave the man only £5 less, and the company submitted.[2] And in another case the same Canadian court spoke regretfully of the exorbitant amount of damages (£50) where the company were not otherwise concerned than through the act of their conductor, who thought that he had only been doing his duty, as England expects every man to do.[3] And where an American jury gave $1000, no special damage being shown, a new trial was granted."[4]

"To return to the question of tickets." I said, "I saw an English decision the other day, which shows how one may save a little in going to an intermediate place, where opposition lines are running to some place beyond."

"How is that?" was asked.

1. *Glover* v. *London & S. W. Rw.*, 3 Q.B., 25.
2. *Huntsman* v. *G. W. R.*, 20 U.C., Q.B., 24.
3. *Davis* v. *G. W. R.*, 20 U.C., Q.B., 27 and Life of Lord Nelson.
4. *Crocker* v. *New London, Will. & Pat.*, 24 Conn., 249.

"Why often if two lines run to B. or there is an excursion thither, the fare is cheaper than to A., which, perhaps, is not half the distance, and one can buy a ticket to B, and get off at A if he so wishes."

" Would that be a safe dodge ? "

" It appears to have been decided in England that one may pay his fare to one place, and yet leave the cars at some intermediate place where the train stops, although the fare to the latter place may be greater than it is to the former."[1]

" I saw another rather funny decision. By a by-law, passengers not delivering up their tickets when required were made liable to a penalty; a man took a return ticket, yet after returning to the place whence he started, did not get off, but went on to a further station, without, however, any intention to defraud; it was held that he could not be convicted under the by-law, for it only applied to the case of a person wilfully refusing to show his ticket *when he had one*, while here the man had none! It was held, also, that the by-law only applied to people travelling minus a ticket with intent to defraud.[2] Where a gentleman took tickets for himself and three servants, keeping the tickets in his own custody, and telling the guard that he had them, and the servants were permitted to enter the car without having or showing each his ticket, the court held that the company were estopped from raising the objection that the by-law, as to the production and delivery up of tickets, had been infringed."[3]

" I believe," I remarked, when a pause enabled me to squeeze in a remark, " a company if it chooses may allow a discount off tickets bought before entering the cars; but that those who enter without their magic scraps of card-board cannot claim such indulgence[4] even though they have been prevented purchasing them from the fact of the office being closed."[5]

---

1. *The Queen* v. *Frere*, 4 E. & B., 598; *Moore* v. *Metropolitan Rw.*, 8 Q.B., 36.
2. *Dearden* v. *Townsend*, 12 Jur., N.S., 120, 13 L.J., N.S., 323.
3. *Jennings* v. *G. N. R.*, 1 L.R., Q.B., 7.
4. *The State* v. *Gould*, 53 Maine, 279; *Chicago and Alton Rw.* v. *Roberts*, 40 Ill., 503.
5. *Crocker* v. *New London, Will. & Pat. Rw.*, 24 Conn., 249.

"I see that in England some companies have a by-law that if a passenger loses his ticket he shall be liable to pay the full fare from the most distant place on the line."

"That's rather hard lines."

"Don't pun—fortunately they cannot enforce their by-law by detaining the traveller himself."[1]

The legal disquisitions on railway companies were suffered to subside for a time, while the train rattled on. I gazed about on my companions. In the seat in front of me sat a young couple, and, judging from the orange blossoms in the bonnet of the one, and the clean shave and kid gloves of the other, not many hours had elapsed since they had stood side by side at Hymen's altar. The male had a little piece of sticking-plaster on his lower lip. As I was staring at the youthful couple, the train dashed into a tunnel and all was darkness: I heard a prolonged sucking sound as of a cow drawing her hind foot out of a mud-hole—to quote a western poet of renown—and when again we emerged into the daylight, ho! presto! the plaster was reposing securely on the ruby lip of the orange-bonneted one—all else was serene and tranquil, and the two looked childlike and bland. How was this? here was a mystery as interesting as any involved in railway law; I meditated deeply on the point until I recollected what in our ante-nuptial days my Elizabeth and myself were wont to do, then all became clear and plain.

We stopped at a small wayside station for a few minutes while the engine took a draught of water; a gentleman got out to take a breath of air or something of the sort, and while he was wandering up and down the platform, off started our train without a solitary premonitory screech, leaving the individual wildly waving his arms and frantically shouting after the hindermost car. In thus quietly slipping off, the company were wrong, for a traveller who alights temporarily, but without notice, invitation or objec-

---

1. *Chilton* v. *London & Croy Rw.*, 16 M. & W., 212.

tion, while the train is stopping at an intermediate station, does no unlawful act, and although for a time he surrenders his place and rights as a passenger, he may resume them again before the train starts, and the officers of the railway are bound to give him reasonable notice of starting,[1] and must not steal off silently like a thief in the night.

1. *State* v. *Grand Trunk Rw.*, 4 Am. Rep., 258; 58 Me., 176.

CHAPTER VI.

PLATFORMS AND ALIGHTING.

Right to safe ingress, egress and regress—Defective platforms—The Englishman and the C'rum cat'or—Getting out of cars—Train not at platform—Calling out name; is it invitation to alight—Ladies jumping—Must have safe place to alight—Leaving train in motion.

"WELL here we are at last at H." said my friend who was learned in the law.

"Yes, now we have a chance of getting some grub (carefully collated from the plates of those who were here before us), and taking the epidermal covering off the interior of our mouths with a scalding decoction dignified by the name of tea," I replied.

"Ding-dong-all gone—come along—one-all," sounded forth the bell of the refreshment room, as the train drew up to the platform, and all the weary travellers sprang up eager to stretch their limbs and to replenish the inner man. Out they rushed. Night had thrown her sable mantle (she has no other except for moonlight wear) over nature's tired bosom, so some of our fellow travellers, in the gloom, were precipitated into a hole in the platform, which the company carelessly suffered to be there—yawning open-mouthed—unmindful of the fact that passengers have the same rights to safe ingress, egress, regress and progress over the stations and platforms at the intermediate places where the trains stop for refreshment, as they have at the termini of the line;[1] although it would appear that where a stoppage is made only for the purposes of the railway and people are not expected to get in or out, the rights of the travelling public and the liability of the company are both greatly curtailed.[2] As soon as one

---

1. *McDonald* v. *Chicago, &c.*, 26 Iowa, 124.
2. *Frost* v. *Grand Trunk Rw.*, 10 Allen, 387.

procures a ticket he is to be regarded as a passenger, and is entitled to a safe passage to his seat.

Though the unfortunates kissed mother earth, they were not seriously damaged; one indeed—as a medical witness afterwards put it—suffered "from a severe contusion of the integuments under the left orbit, with a great extravasation of blood and ecchymosis in the surrounding cellubas, having also a considerable abrasion of the cuticle," or, as the judge in common place Anglo-Saxon expressed it, " had a black eye." Soon comestibles of all sorts, kinds and descriptions were vanishing rapidly by means of down grades into sub-waistcoat and sub-bodice regions.

When we had finished our repast the train still seemed quiescent —appeared as motionless as a painted ship upon a painted ocean —so it was suggested that a little of something slightly stronger than tea might not be unpalatable: but, alas! spirits were tabooed on the line, so there was nothing for it but to make a foray into the adjoining neighbourhood for additional stimulants. A porter kindly showed the way to a public house on the opposite side of the highroad passing the station: we were soon all practising with great success at the bar, but while enjoying ourselves to the full, the engine-bell rang out sharp and clear on the frosty air. Off we all rushed helter-skelter, and to save time, instead of returning by the way we came, we took what we thought was a bee-line for the station lights (but which turned out to be the engine's) across some unfenced ground. Before we well knew where we were we were all tumbling pell-mell, one over the other, into a wide ditch some three feet deep. However, we gained the cars in time, and then one of our chance acquaintances—who, having been leading in the race, went down first and was trampled upon by the rest—found that his arm was badly hurt; so the Q. C. and myself tried to console him with the assurance that he was safe to recover a verdict against the company if he only en-

---

1. *Warren* v. *Fitchburg Rw.*, 8 Allen, 227.

trusted his case into the hands of either of us, for a railway company is bound so to fence its station that the public will not be misled, by seeing a place unfenced, into injuring themselves by passing that way, it being the shortest road to the platform.[1] (Though by the way, a Canadian court has considered that companies are not responsible if parties come to grief through taking short cuts, if the proper way of ingress and egress to the station is safe, convenient and well-lighted.)[2]

Thinking that the man was an American citizen, I told him that Mr. C. J. Dillon, of the State of Iowa, had said on a comparatively recent occasion that "railway companies are bound to keep in a safe condition all portions of their platforms and approaches thereto to which the public do and would naturally resort, and all portions of their station-grounds reasonably near to the platforms, where passengers, or those who have purchased tickets with a view to take passage in their cars, would naturally or ordinarily be likely to go."[3]

"And, my dear sir," said the Q. C. who, more observant than myself, had noticed a pile of Hs accumulating in front of the man, "there is a much stronger English case, where one Martin arrived at a station less than two minutes before the time for the train to leave, and while running along the line—in a place where he should not have gone—in order to reach the train which was a little ahead, he stumbled over a switch handle, fell on his elbow, and was considerably hurt. The jury considered that the company had been guilty of negligence and want of proper care, and gave Martin £20, and the court would not interfere."[4]

"Vell, hi think the Hinglish case is the one for my money," quoth our new found friend. "Hand hi'll rub my harm with a

---

1. *Burgess* v. *G. W. R.*, 32 L. J., 76.
2. *Walker* v. *G. W. R.*, 8 U.C., C.P., 161.
3. *McDonald* v. *Chicago, &c.*, 26 Iowa, 124.
4. *Martin* v. *G. Northern Rw.*, 16 C.B., 179; and see the case of stumbling over the hampers, *Nicholson* v. *Lancashire & York Rw.*, 3 Hurl & C., 534.

little hof this to prevent any 'arm," he added, producing a pocket comforter that Job never knew of.

"Don't waste good stuff that way," said Mr. Smith. "Apply it internally, and rub your arm with the bottle."

"Ho-ho-ho!" laughed John Bull at the wretched joke, which doubtless was first perpetrated "when the Memnonium was in all its glory." He took the advice, however, and the brandy with a vengeance.

Some little while after I saw him steadying himself as he stood up on the seat and poking with his stick at the top of the car : supposing he was striving to open the ventilator, I paid little attention to him. In a few minutes the train suddenly stopped—in a few seconds more the conductor came rushing into the car, excitedly asking if any one had pulled the rope or communicator.

"C'mum 'cat'or?" asked J. Bull, "I wang the bell for some bwandy 'n-vater. And dooced 'ard work hi 'ad to reach hit. Where's the 'andle?"[1] Speedily the train was again under weigh.

At length after several hours more of journeying we arrived at our destination, thankful that as yet all bones were safe and sound. Alas, I was hallooing before I was out of the wood, for as I emerged, the light being very dim I fancied I was stepping on to the platform, but as I landed violently on the ground I found that the car was some feet beyond the platform. Of course railways should bring their trains to a halt at places convenient for passengers to alight. Bringing a car to a solemn stand-still at a spot at which it is unsafe to get out, under circumstances which warrant one in believing that it is intended he shall alight and that he may do so in safety, (without giving him warning of his danger,) amounts to negligence on the part of the company, for which an action may be maintained if the passenger has not in any way contributed towards the accident.[2] This highly sensible rule

---

1. See Punch for Feb'y, 1874.
2. *Cockle* v. *London & S. E. Rw. Co.*, L.R., 7 C.P., 721. (Ex. Ch.)

was adopted in the case of one Praeger, where—as I afterwards found—Lord Chief Justice Cockburn, of Geneva award renown, said : "I adopt most readily the formula which has been suggested as applicable to these cases, viz., that the company are bound to use reasonable care in providing accommodation for passengers, and that the passengers are also bound to use reasonable care in availing themselves of the accommodation provided for them."[1] Of course if it had been daylight and I could have used my eyesight to any practical purpose, and had noticed that the car was not in the ordinary position with regard to the platform, I would certainly have exercised a little more caution in getting out and not have been such a ninny-hammer as to step down in the way I did, for, I can assure the general public, that it is anything but agreeable to step upon thin air and be thrown violently upon one's nasal organ—which always seems tremendously projecting on such occasions—abrasing one's elbows and knees.

As I had my homeward journey to perform by rail, and there seemed a chance of my being reduced to an atomic condition before I once again saw the wife of my bosom, I then for the benefit of my numerous readers (for, of course, I meant to publish a book as every one does now-a-days) dotted down a few decisions which I thought might be useful for them to bear in mind in case they ever came to grief in alighting from a railway train; and here they are *pro bono publico*.

(N.B.—Those frivolous persons who only read to pass the time had better turn at once to the next chapter.)

Where the train overshot the platform so that the car in which one Whitaker was sitting stood opposite to the parapet of a bridge, the top of which in the dusk looked like the platform; the porters having called out the name of the place, W. getting out on the parapet in the *bona fide* belief that he was stepping on the platform, fell over and was injured, but recovered from the company.

---

1. *Praeger v. Bristol & Exeter Rw.*, 24 L.J., N.S., 105.

Bovill, C. J., held that on this occasion there was a clear invitation to alight at a dangerous place, and that W. was misled by the appearance of the parapet, and so distinguished the case from the Bridges one, to which I will refer in a moment or two.[1] Where in the dark, a passenger on alighting fell into a culvert, over which the car had stopped, the company were held liable.[2]

Owing to the length of the train in which a Mr. and Mrs. Foy were journeying, there was not room for all the cars to be drawn up at the platform, and some of the passengers were desired to get out upon the line beyond it. The distance from the carriage to the ground was only three feet; Mrs. F., (instead of sensibly availing herself of the two steps of the carriage,) with the aid of Mr. Foy jumped from the first step to the ground, and—not being a practised athlete or gymnast but a sweet little thing—came down upon the ground like a barrel of sugar with such a thud that the vertebræ of her back were jarred and the spine injured. The jury found that the company were guilty of negligence in not providing reasonable means of alighting, and that the lady had not contributed to the accident, and they gave her £500 to pay her doctor's bills; and the court considered the verdict warranted and declined to interfere with the damages.[3] Bovill, Q. C., urged that if the lady, instead of jumping as she did, had turned herself round and availed herself of the assistance of both steps and of the handles of the carriage, the accident would not have happened; but Williams, J., said severely that "in the present fashion of female attire, the mode of descent suggested by the learned counsel would be scarcely decent!" This judgment was given in 1865, and as fashions change two or three times a year, one can hardly decide what a lady might or should do in this present year of grace, especially as the virtuous judge did not

---

1. *Whitaker* v. *Manchester & S. Rw. Co.*, L.R., 5 C.P., 464.
2. *Col. & Ind. C. Rw. Co.* v. *Farrell*, 31 Md., 408.
3. *Foy & wife* v. *London B. & S. C. Rw. Co.*, 18 C.B., N.S., 225.

insinuate wherein such a descent would lie the lack of woman's crowning glory, modesty.

Old Siner and his wife arrived in daylight at Rhyl station and the carriage in which they were, overshot the platform; the passengers were neither told to keep their seats nor to get out, nor did the train move until it started on its onward journey. After exhausting his stock of patience, S. following the example of his fellow travellers alighted, without asking the company's servants to back the train to the platform or holding any communication with them whatever. The wife then, standing on the iron steps of the carriage, grasped both her husband's hands and jumped down, straining her knee in the act. She did not use the footboard. There was no evidence of any carelessness or awkwardness except what might be inferred from these facts. In an action brought against the company for this injury, the court held (Kelly, C. B., *diss.*) that there was no evidence of negligence in the defendants, and that the accident was entirely the result of the woman's own act in awkwardly and carelessly jumping.[1] The *Foy* case was distinguished, as there an express invitation to alight was given.

Where a gentleman, the corners of whose eyes were far more convex than those of the generality of the genus *homo*, who well knew the station, got out of the train while the carriage in which he had been sitting was still in a tunnel, and in making his way to the platform stumbled over some rubbish and fell, breaking his leg and otherwise injuring himself so that he shortly died from the effects; it was held by the House of Lords (reversing the decision of the court below) that the train having come to a standstill, the calling out the name of the place was an invitation to alight, and that the company's servants calling out afterwards "Keep your seats," showed that it had been improvidently uttered, and therefore furnished evidence of negligence, and that the per-

---

1. *Siner v. Great Western Rw. Co.*, L.R., 3 Ex., 150.

sonal representative of Mr. Bridges was entitled to recover against the company.[1] The shortsightedness of the deceased imposed no additional duties on the company. In another case the court thought that the conduct of a traveller, who fell down between the car and the platform, which curved gracefully back from the line, amounted to contributory negligence, and so made absolute a rule to enter a nonsuit.[2]

In Bridges' case it was unanimously held by the whole court, that the calling out the name of a station is not in itself an intimation to the passengers to alight; whether it is so or not must depend on the circumstances of each particular case. Willes, J., said, "nobody who travels by rail who has a head on his shoulders would ever say that calling out the name was an invitation;" but many a man with a head on his shoulders, and with something in that head too, acts as if he did,—indeed C. J. Redfield says that Bridges only did what the great majority of men would have done under similar circumstances. (In fact Redfield considers that in the late cases the English courts have overstrained things in favour of the companies.)[3] Baron Cleasby thought that in reality the stopping of the train at the station is the invitation to alight. Bovill, C. J., said that whether calling out was a request to get out or not was a question for a jury.[4] In a late case Mr. Justice Blackburn gave it as his decided opinion, that calling out the name is merely an intimation to all on the train that the place at which the cars are about to stop is that particular station named; and he adds, (most truthfully) that every person must have heard porters at stations call out something which, if the traveller happens to know the name of the place, is recognisable, but if the name is not known no reliable information is gained from the

---

1. *Bridges* v. *North London Rw. Co.*, L.R., 6 Q.B., 377. In appeal, Weekly Notes, 27 June, 1874.
2. *Praeger* v. *Bristol & Exeter Rw.*, L.R., 5 C.P., 460, n. 1; also *Plant* v. *Midland Rw. Co.*, 21 L.T., N.S., 836; and *Harold* v. *Great Western Rw.*, 14 L.T., N.S., 440.
3. Redfield on Railways, vol. 2., p. 264.
4. *Whitaker* v. *Manchester & S. Rw.*, L.R., 5 C.P., 464.

porter's cry.¹ In a still later case it was said that the train having overshot the platform and the name of the place having been called out, the omission of the company's servants to caution passengers not to alight until the train had been brought up at the proper place, was evidence of negligence, or according to Honeyman, J., negligence itself.²

Companies are bound to provide platforms, or safe places of deposit, for passengers to alight at their stations and to deliver them there. If there is any difficulty in the passengers getting out the officers should assist them to do so.³ If the place where one is required to alight is in fact dangerous, it is his duty to request the train to be put in its proper place; and this is a request which no station master would venture to refuse, knowing the risk he would incur if an accident happened through his refusal. If the defendants will not place the train properly, the plaintiff should stay in the carriage. So, at least, said the Judges in *Siner v. Great Western Railway* (supra);⁴ but we can well imagine the surprised look—tinged strongly with scorn—of a conductor upon any one of our Cis-atlantic railways, were he asked to move his train forwards or backwards merely for the convenience of his living freight.

If a man persists in getting off a train while it is in motion especially if he has been warned by the conductor not to do so, he has no claim against the company for any damage he may receive in the act;⁵ and so when one attempted to get on a train while moving and was killed in the attempt, it was held, as a matter of law, that no recovery could be had.⁶ But otherwise where one lost his life in jumping off by the direction of the con-

---

1. *Lewis & wife* v. *London C. & D. Rw.*, L.R., 9 Q.B., 66; *Cockles* v. *London & S. E. Rw.*, (supra) distinguished.
2. *Weller* v. *London, Brighton & S. C. Rw.*, L.R., 9 U.P., 126.
3. *Memphis & Charleston Rw.* v. *Whitfield*, 44 Miss., 466.
4. See also *Memphis & C. Rw.* v. *Whitfield*, supra.
5. *Ohio & Miss. Rw.* v. *Schiebe*, 44 Ill., 460.
6. *Knight* v. *Ponchartrain Rw.*, 23 La. Am., 462.

ductor.[1] The courts of Mississippi has laid it down clearly that it is the duty of railway companies to announce audibly in each car the name of the station reached, and then allow sufficient time for the passengers safely to leave the carriages; and that on the other hand it is the duty of the passengers to use reasonable care, and to conform to the customs and usages of the company so far as they know and understand them.[2]

Ah me! I fear that this long dilating will cause my Diary to be sent

> To bind a book, to line a box,
> Or serve to curl a maiden's locks.

1. *Lambeth* v. *North Carolina Rw.*, 66 N.C., 494.
2. *Southern Rw.* v. *Kendrick*, 40 Miss., 374.

CHAPTER VII.

BAGGAGE.

Gone.—Company liable for lost baggage.—Carelessness of owner.—Checking. What is baggage?—Papers.—Spring-horse.—Household goods going west.—Luggage left in cloak-room.—Limitation of liability.—Taking change.—Railroad police.—Beauties of checks.—Fall of a window.—Legs and arms outside.—Officials squeezing fingers.—Stern Boreas.

MISFORTUNES never come singly, for birds of a feather flock together. Scarcely had I got to the hotel and begun ruefully examining the discolorations on my nether limbs, and putting a piece of sticking plaster on the top of my proboscis, when a thought struck me, and really hurt me, so that I involuntarily exclaimed, "Why, where's my bag?" Of one thing I was soon satisfied, namely that it was not there. I ran my fingers through my hair to let the cooling air as near as possible to my heated brain, and after mature reflection came to the conclusion that I had seen nothing of it since I had left it in the car while I went out after those refreshments already referred to, for on my return, finding in my seat a lovely girl, with long dark eyelashes, soft tender dark-blue eyes, a bewitching smile and dimples which rippled round her ruby lips as she talked and laughed with a young fellow of a vinegar aspect who sat beside her, I had located myself elsewhere: both these individuals had got out at the next station, but I had never again noticed, or even thought of, my bag.

When I met the Q. C. in the dining-hall I told him of my loss.

"What had you in your bag?" he enquired with the air of a man who thought that he knew a thing or two about lost luggage.

"Nothing but my brushes and razors, pen and ink; some shirt-fronts *alias* dickeys, and other clothing."

"Ah well! you are all right! you can easily recover the value of the waifs and strays from the company; for all those things have been held to be such personal baggage as a traveller has a right to carry with him.[1] Have you got your check?" He added.

"No. It was not checked. I carried it into the car with me, and left it to keep my place when we got out for refreshments and it was gone before I got back into my seat—at least I have not beheld it since."

"*N'importe!* as the frog-eaters say. You are entitled to recover, for your ticket gives you a right to be carried with your luggage;[2] and a by-law to the effect that a company will not be responsible for baggage unless booked, has been held bad in England.[3] Of course, if you had kept exclusive control over your bag, the company would not ordinarily be liable.[4] And when a man has his traps taken into the car with him for his own convenience he impliedly undertakes to use reasonable care; and if one were to leave his portmanteau in one car while he went and travelled in another, and the portmanteau was rifled, he could not recover for his loss;[5] nor, if he stupidly forgot to take his overcoat with him, when he left the train."[6]

"I had an idea," I said, "that a Canadian judge had expressed an opinion to the effect that the system of checking in vogue in this enlightened country was notice to passengers that all articles must be checked or handed to the company's servants, except what they desire or prefer to keep under their own personal care and at their own risk. Did you ever meet with such a dictum or decision?"

1. *Hawkins* v. *Hoffman*, 6 Hill, (N.Y.) 559; *Duffy* v. *Thompson*, 4 E. D. Smith. 178.
2. *Gamble* v. *G. W. Rw.*, 24 U.C., Q.B., 407; *Le Couteur* v. *London & S. W. Rw.*, L.R., 1 Q.B., 54.
3. *Williams* v. *G. W. Rw.*, 10 Ex., 15; see also *G. W. R.* v. *Goodman*, 12 C.B., 313.
4. *Tower* v. *Utica & Sch. Rw.*, 7 Hill, (N.Y.) 47; and Wilde, J., in *Richards* v. *London B. & S. C. Rw.*, 7 C.B., 839.
5. *Talley* v. *G. W. R.*, L.R., 6 C.P., 44.
6. *Tower* v. *Utica & Sch. Rw.*, supra.

"Oh yes, I noticed the case only the other day. Morrison, J., did speak to that effect, but he was over-ruled, and Draper, C. J., said that he considered checking only as additional precautions taken by the company, beyond what is customary in England, in order to prevent the luggage from being given up to the wrong person; that the company would be liable for a loss in case no such means of checking was in use, and if, notwithstanding, a loss occurs, the liability is unchanged, in the absence of express notice on their part that they will be responsible only for articles checked.[1] By the way, were there any papers in your bag?"

"No: they were all in my pocket. I have not many with me, and I remember seeing it decided that title deeds, which an attorney was carrying with him to produce on a trial, were not baggage for the loss of which a carrier would be responsible."[2]

"Prudent man!" replied my friend, as he turned on his heel and departed.

What I did at the place where I now was concerns nobody except those who had the pleasure of paying my travelling expenses to and fro and my hotel bill while there. To dilate with any particularity on the subject might lead one into a breach of that well-established rule concerning privileged communications between attorneys and their clients.

At length my labours were at an end and I was at perfect liberty to return to my *Lares et Penates* at my earliest convenience. My readers must not suppose, from the fact that my bag and baggage had been lost, that I was acting the Nazarite all this time: no indeed; I had bought all the necessary articles of a gentleman's toilet and some changes of raiment, and with these in a bran new valise I was ready to start *en route* for the place whence I had come forth.

I was rather amused, while awaiting the arrival of my train at the station, by a controversy between what was evidently a "fond

---

1. *Gamble* v. *Great Western Rw.*, 24 U.C., Q.B., 407.
2. *Phelps* v. *London & N. W. Rw.*, 19 C.B., N.S., 321.

parient" of rural origin and the baggage master. The father had invested in a spring-horse for his youthful son and heir to exercise upon; the creature was 44 inches long and weighed 78 pounds. The man wished it passed as luggage.

"No, you will have to pay freight for this," said he of the chalk and checks.

"But I have nothing else, and I am certainly entitled to carry something," urged the man.

"Yes," returned the other, "you are entitled to take your personal baggage with you; but if you have none, that does not give you the right to take other things instead,[1] and a horse of this color is personal luggage by no manner of means."[2]

Just then a friend came up to me and asked what was included in the personal baggage which a man was entitled to take with him, free of charge. I said:

"My dear sir, that is a question which has often pressed itself seriously upon the consideration of a contemplative traveller and philosophic jurist like myself, when on entering a crowded train I have found one half of the seats occupied by a 'stern realities' or bipedal extremities, and the other half by bundles and bandboxes, nursery paraphernalia, and the oleaginous and saccharine products of the kitchen and the cook-shop; and also when I have considered how gravely the question has agitated Courts of Justice. One of our own learned judges has forcibly remarked that 'the authorities and references show it is much easier to say what is not personal or ordinary luggage, than it is to decide what it is which a carrier is bound, or which it is usual for him to carry along with his passengers."

"You have made a long oration, but have not answered my question; just like you lawyers, always darkening counsel by words."

"State your question more definitely," I remarked.

---

1. *Pardee* v. *Drew*, 25 Wend., 459.
2. *Hudston* v. *Midland Rw.*, L.R., 4 Q.B., 366.

"Well then, there is a poor man here, moving west with his family. He has a bed, pillows, bolsters and bedquilts in a trunk, or a box, with his clothes; he is carrying them for his own use. Should he be compelled to pay freight on them? He says that he has no money; and I don't want to see the poor beggar put upon."

"Yours is a question which I cannot definitely answer. In England, it was decided that such things were not personal baggage[1]. In Vermont it was held a matter for a jury to pronounce upon, after considering the peculiar circumstances, the value, the quantity and the intended use of the articles."[2]

> "He would not, with a peremptory tone
> Assert the nose upon his face, his own;
> With hesitation, admirably slow
> He humbly hopes, presumes it may be so;"

said my friend mockingly, and then added pepperishly, "you unsatisfactory lawyers will never give a sensible reply to the simplest question."

"Granted. But yours was not the simplest question. Were an ordinary layman like yourself, to read but a tithe of what has been written on the moot point of personal luggage or not, you would be a sadder, if not a wiser man than you now are; so voluminous are the decisions that a Saratoga trunk would fail to contain all."

"Well you are not luminous anyway.

> "Lawyers each dark question shun
> And hold their farthing candle to the sun.

I'm off to get my traps in the cloak-room."

"I'll go with you," I replied.

When we got to the room we found the door locked, and that the man in charge was off for an hour or so.

---

1. *Macrow* v. *Gt. Western Rw. Co.*, L.R., 6 Q.B., 612.
2. *Ouimet* v. *Henshaw*, 35 Vt., 605.

"Well that is a pretty how-do-ye-do, my train will be going in a few minutes, so what am I to do?"

"Have you got a ticket for your baggage?" I enquired.

"Yes, and paid tuppence for it. Here it is." On the back of it were some printed conditions, but nothing was said as to the hours the cloak-room was kept open, or at what time the box was to be re-delivered.

"It is clear," I remarked, "that the company is bound to give you your box on your reasonable request, and at any reasonable time."[1]

"But what good does that do me, if they are not here to give me my things now? I must go on whether I get them or not."

"You can sue them," I remarked.

"All very fine, but I have a case of patterns which I need with me; and suppose it is lost?"

"Well, of course, you can't recover damages beyond the actual value of the goods: no warehouseman is responsible beyond the actual value of the article lost or damaged, unless there was a special contract.[2] What was the value?"

"Thirty or forty pounds."

"What!"

"Can't you hear? I say thirty or forty pounds."

"Well, I am very sorry for you. Did not you see the notice on the ticket that 'the company will not be responsible for any package exceeding the value of £10.'"

"Oh, but I did not read that."

"The legal inference, however, is that you did read it, and did assent to it; and so I am afraid that the company, in case of a loss, will not be liable as your goods exceed the prescribed limit.[3] For the same reason they may also be excused for delay in re-delivering them, at least if such tardiness is not caused by any

---

1. *Stallard* v. *Gt. W. R.*, 2 B. & S., 419; 8 Jur., N.S., 1076.
2. *Anderson* v. *North Eastern Rw.*, 4 L.J., N.S., 216.
3. *Van Toll* v. *South Eastern Rw. Co.*, 12 C.B., N.S., 75; 6 L.T., N.S., 244.

wilful act or default of their own, and is without their privity or knowledge.[1] Samples and patterns are not considered personal baggage."[2]

"Many thanks for all your information. I think I can see my box through this crack, and here comes the man with the key; so I am all right."

"Well, good-bye! there's my train, anyway, so I am off. Don't forget you owe me a fee for this."

As I was passing into the car, I saw a crowd gathered round the ticket-office, and an unfortunate man—quite respectably habilitated—struggling in the clutches of a policeman. I made inquiries as to the cause of the arrest and was told that the prisoner had been buying a ticket at the office, and in giving change the clerk handed him two sous, a French piece, the man, whose name was Allen, objected and demanded a British penny in its place, and as the clerk would not take back the sous, Allen determined to help himself: the bowl of the till containing copper coins appearing to be within easy reach, he put in his hand to get the money. Upon this the agent raised the hue and cry, summoned the conservator of the peace on duty, and gave A. into custody on the charge of attempting to rob the till. It seemed rather a hard case as the poor fellow was only trying to help himself to his change. (Being dubious as to what would be the upshot of the affair, I bore the matter in mind, and after the usual time required for issuing a writ, bringing a case to trial, moving in term, and giving judgment, I discovered that in the action brought by A. against the company for false imprisonment it was held, that as the arrest, after the attempt had ceased, could not be necessary for the protection of the company's property, but was merely to vindicate justice, the clerk had no implied authority to arrest the man; his authority only extended to the doing of such acts as were necessary for the fulfilment of the duties entrusted to him, and

---

1. *Pepper* v. *South Eastern Rw. Co.*, 17 L.J., N.S., 469.
2. *Bayley* v. *Lancaster Rw. Co.*, 18 Sol. J., 301.

that the company was, therefore, not liable for the act of the clerk, nor for that of the policeman who took A. into custody. Blackburn, J., was inclined to think that if a man in charge of a till were to find that a person was attempting to rob it, and he could only prevent his stealing by taking him into custody, he might have an implied authority to arrest the offender; or, if the clerk had reason to believe that the money had been actually stolen and he could get it back by taking the thief into custody, and he took him up for that purpose, it might be that that also would be within the authority of the clerk.[1]

A man standing by me asked how it was that the policeman had not on the same style of garments as those of his fellows who perambulate in blissful ease and quiet serenity the city streets. I told him that railway companies had power to appoint constables to act on their lines for the preservation of peace, and securing persons and property against felonies and other unlawful acts on such railways and their works, and in all places not more than a quarter of a mile distant therefrom, and to take before a justice of the peace any person guilty of an offence punishable by summary convictions under any act or by-law.[2]

This time I had my *impedimenta* checked, and thus was relieved of the trouble of carrying them in and out of the car. All the world knows that the possession of a check is evidence against the company of the receipt of the baggage: the piece of metal has been compared to a bill of lading, in fact said to be identical therewith.[3] It is always the source of great wonderment to me that the British public do not insist upon the British railways introducing the system on their lines; the continental plan of registering, though far in advance of the English, is still much more troublesome than the simple process of checking, and very expensive. How convenient is our enlightened plan, when

---

1. *Allen* v. *London & S. W. Rw.*, L.R., 6 Q.B., 65.
2. Railway Act, 1868, s. 49.
3. *Dill* v. *R. W. Co.*, 7 Rich, 158.

one has to change cars *en route:* no trouble looking after baggage; one simply has to walk out of one train into the other, ticket for the whole journey and checks in your pocket; and if your traps are lost you can sue either or any of the companies.[1]

The car being rather crowded the atmosphere soon became rather close and stifling. A gentleman, after a considerable amount of coaxing, pushing, shoving and pulling, persuaded one of the windows to allow itself to be lifted up to admit the sharp, clear, exhilarating winter's air. The person who opened the window got out and another got in and took his seat beside it, and carelessly allowed his left hand to rest on the ledge: as the train approached a station, the breaks were suddenly put on, and the vibration caused the window to fall athwart the man's fingers, inflicting a serious injury thereon. Aroused and attracted by the grunting and groaning, adjurations and exclamations of the injured one, some officious people came round him, advising and urging the poor fellow to sue the company, for that they were bound to provide windows with good fastenings for the comfort and protection of passengers. I merely said, that without positive proof of the defective construction of the window, the mere falling would not make a *prima facie* case of negligence against the company, as a Mr. Murray found when he sued a London railway company for exactly a similar injury.[2]

Some people seem to be possessed of limbs which do not appear to belong to them of right, and with which they never seem to know exactly what to do, and such uncomfortably constituted mortals are very apt to stretch their heads, or legs, or arms, out of the windows of railway carriages, having no other improper place to put them when travelling by rail; to such eccentric genii I would remark, that if they are injured while in this position they will not be able to recover damages against the company, for the negligence is their own, and the company is not bound to put bars

---

1. *Hart* v. *Rensallaer & Saratoga Rw.*, 4 Seld, 37.
2. *Murray* v. *Metropolitan District Rw.*, 27 L.T., N.S., 762.

across its carriage windows as careful matrons do over their nursery panes.[1] It was once held that a company, in order to save the upper extremities of their passengers, was bound to provide wire gauzes, bars, slats, or other barricades for the windows,[2] but this fatherly decision has been overruled.[3] Mrs. Holbrook found this to her cost when she had her arm broken (it was projecting from the window) by something coming against it as they were passing other cars on another track.[4] In the State where the principles of Brotherly Love prevail, or are supposed to, it was held that when passengers are liable to have their arms, if lying outside the windows, caught in passing bridges, the conductors should give them notice to put them effectually upon their guard, or the company will be liable for injuries, and printed notices are not sufficient.[5]

Talking about squeezing fingers—a decidedly unpleasant thing to the squeezee, when not done by the human hand divine—railway officials are not allowed, as a rule, to apply extempore thumbscrews and pinch a man's digits in the door: this has been solemnly decided by the Court of Common Pleas, at Westminster Hall. One Fordham, was in the act of getting into a railway carriage, of the usual English make, with doors at the sides opening outwards; having a parcel in his right hand, he very naturally placed his left on the open door to aid him on entering. The guard, without giving any previous warning, flung too the door with a slam: F. having just at that moment his fingers where the door should meet the door-plate, and they possessing that quality of matter, compressibility, had them badly crushed. The Court of Common Pleas and the Exchequer Chamber thought that the guard had been guilty of carelessness and that Fordham had done nothing to contribute

---

1. *Indianapolis & Cincinnati Rw.* v. *Rutherford*, 7 Am. Law Reg. (N.S.), 476.
2. *N. J. R.* v. *Kennard*, 21 Penn. St., 203.
3. *P. & C. Rw.* v. *McClurg*, 7 Am. Law Reg. (N.S.), 277.
4. *Holbrook* v. *Utica & Sch. Rw.*, 12 N.Y., 534.
5. *Laing* v. *Calder*, 8 Penn. St., 483.

thereto, and so gave the latter damages against the railway company.[1] In another case, however, where a porter after he had called out, "Take your seats—take your seats," squeezed a man's thumb in shutting too the door, the same Court considered that the official had closed the door in the ordinary and proper exercise of his duty, and that Mr. Richardson had only to thank himself for his want of caution in leaving his member where it might be so easily crushed.[2]

To return from this digression which my readers will probably have found as dull and heavy as most wanderings of that nature. Before many hours had passed, thick heavy clouds began to scud across the sky; the wind sighed and moaned mournfully around the car; Boreas came raging from the icy regions of the north, and the snow-flakes whirled wildly in ever thickening clouds—as a Longfellow would have said had he been on board that express train:

> "Ever thicker, thicker, thicker,
> Froze the ice on lake and river:
> Ever deeper, deeper, deeper,
> Fell the snow o'er all the landscape,
> Fell the covering snow and drifted
> Through the forest, round the carriage."

Slowly and more slowly did the laboring engine, laden with its long line of cars, make its way against the obstructing showers of feathery ice-morsels, and fears arose in the hearts of the passengers that our progress would soon be entirely stopped, and we would be left to spend the long cold night imbedded in the rapidly rising banks of snow.

A lady, shivering as she gazed out into the now pitchy darkness, asked me in quivering tones, what would be done if we came to a complete standstill and the engine was unable to move at all. I replied,

---

1. *Fordham* v. *London B. & S. C. Rw.*, L.R., 3 C.P., 368, and 4 C.P., 619, Ex. Ch.; also *Coleman* v. *S. E. Rw.*, 4 H. & C., 699.
2. *Richardson* v. *Metropolitan Rw.*, L.R., 3 C.P., 374, n.

"If a line becomes blocked up and impeded by snow, the company is bound to use all reasonable exertions to forward the passengers, although that may put the company to extra expense, which of course they have no way of recovering from the travellers;[1] so I presume ere long extra engines and snow ploughs will come to our rescue."

"It is to be hoped that the fuel will last," said the lady. "How I pity those poor cattle that we heard lowing so plaintively as we passed them at the last siding:" she added tenderly.

"Yes; no great efforts will be made for their convenience; if a snow storm comes, the company is not bound to forward them by extraordinary means and at additional expense."[2]

"Poor things," said my fair companion, who seemed

> "A very woman ; full of tears,
> Hopes, blushes, tenderness, fears,
> Griefs, laughter, kindness, joys and sighs,
> Loves, likings, friendships, sympathies ;
> A heart to feel for every woe,
> And pity, if not dole, bestow."

"Poor things, unless in the hereafter there is a place where the spirits of animals be at rest, they have to bear a very heavy share of the primeval curse, and pay dearly for Adam's transgression and fall."

1. Addison on Torts, 3rd Ed., 448.
2. *Briddon* v. *Gt. Northern Rw.*, 28 L.J., Ex. 51.

CHAPTER VIII.

DUE CARE.

Snowed up – Pacific Railway—Passenger carriers not insurers—Company must use due care—Defective machinery—Broken axle—Company must account for accident—Difference between goods and men—What is due care—Latent defects in cars—English rule—Rule in New York—Moralising.

AS the train came to a solemn pause in a deep cutting, a number of us gathered together in the warm and cosy Pullman, the *ne plus ultra* of railway cars, far surpassing in comfort and luxury an English or Continental first-class carriage, though not adorned as are the Italian cars, with those abominations of the sterner sex—tidies for the head to rest against. And here, each in turn related railroad adventures and accidents; tales which excited laughter and joyous merriment, of engagements, love scenes, marriage ceremonies, undress exhibitions in sleeping cars; tales of sorrow and grief, collisions, explosions, helpless people crushed, boiled, roasted to death; dozens plunged into eternity in a moment by the simple derangement of a switch, the starting of a rail, a flaw in a wheel, a sleepy pointsman or a weary telegraph clerk.

One told that, in India, railroad traffic is seriously affected by the stagnation of the matrimonial market, a wedding there being an occasion of great pomp and the gathering together of friends; that the railways are breaking down the castes, as the conductors tumble into the same car proud, lofty, blue-blooded Brahmins, poor despised Pariahs, blood-thirsty Thugs, sun-worshiping Parsees, and learned Musselmans: and go together these must, notwithstanding the dogmas of Shasters, Vedas and Korans, or else jump out and die. Another told of having found nuggets of gold, th e remains of melted jewellery, among the charred and blackened remains of unfortunates consumed at the Komoka (Ont.) accident. While a third in graphic terms described the efforts made to break through a snow blockade on the Central Pacific ; the snow was a solid mass twenty feet high in front of the plough; ten engines were at work ; they backed up about a mile, then reversing made a spring forward, locomotives shrieking and screeching, men yelling and gesticulating, volumes of smoke pouring forth from every funnel and hanging like a pall over the scene : the loud rumbling of the huge iron-beaked monster flying over the track, the hissing roaring din and the chorus of shrieking demons behind made up a scene that would blanch the boldest cheek ; with the force of a thousand giants the plough rushed upon the snow and hurled it in enormous masses, like mighty billows, down the mountain sides, crushing through the lofty pines, and glistening and gleaming like frosted silver as it fell upon the frozen cataract below ; but the charge was well nigh in vain.

Thus with the flow of reason and the feast of soul passed some weary hours. At last, one gentleman turning to me, said :

"I believe that a carrier of goods is liable for his freight in every event : is a carrier of passengers responsible to the same extent ?"

"No," I responded, "all jurists are agreed that railway companies are only liable for negligence, either proximate or remote, and not for injuries happening to passengers from unforeseen accident or misfortune, where there has been no negligence or default on the part of the carrier;[1] still it is the bounden duty of a company to use due and proper care and skill in conveying travellers ; and this duty laid upon them does not arise from any contract made between the company and the persons conveyed by them, but is one which the law imposes. If railways are bound to carry, they are also bound to carry safely : it is not sufficient for them to bring merely the dead body of their passenger to the end of the journey, and there deliver up the remains,

---

1. *Aston* v. *Heaven*, 2 Esp., 533 ; *Frink* v. *Potter*, 17 Ill., 496.

parboiled or cut into sausage meat, to his executors and administrators[1]. The fact that injury is suffered by any one while upon the company's train, as a passenger, through any failure of the means of safe transportation, is regarded as *prima facie* evidence of their liability;[2] and such evidence, if not rebutted by the company, will justify a verdict against them which a court will not set aside."[3] And having delivered myself of this harangue, I looked around with a self-satisfied air " and rubbed my hands with invisible soap, in imperceptible water," *à la* Tom Hood.

"Yes," said an engineer, "a company is bound to use the best precautions in known practical use to secure the safety of their passengers, but not every possible preventive which the highest scientific skill might have suggested,[4] nor every device which ingenuity might imagine.[5] But it appears hard that a company should be held liable—as they have been—for injuries arising from a crack in the axle of a car indiscoverable by any practical mode of examination,[6] and be bound to provide roadworthy carriages, absolutely and irrespectively of negligence."

"Yes, that is the rule in New York State: but it has been somewhat questioned in later cases, and in fact it was laid down that a company is not responsible for injuries caused by *vis major*, as the breaking of a rail through extreme cold."[7]

"Wal, strangers," quoth a regular long, lean, lanky down-Easter, "look ye har, down in my State, a carrier is bound to use the highest degree of care that a reasonable man would use."[8]

"That is substantially the same as the rule in the English

---

1. *Collett* v. *London & N. W. Rw.*, 16 Ad. & Ell., N.S., 984.
2. Denman, C.J., in *Carpue* v. *London & B. Rw.*, 5 Q.B., 747; *Laing* v. *Colder*, 8 Penn. St., 479—483.
3. *Dawson* v. *Manchester S. & L. Rw.*, 5 L.T., N.S., 682; but see *Hammond* v. *White*, 11 C.B., N.S., 587.
4. *Ford* v. *London & S. W. R.*, 2 F. & F., 730, per Erle, C.J.
5. *Baltimore & Ohio Rw.* v. *State*, 29 Md., 252.
6. *Alden* v. *N. Y. Central Rw.*, 26 N.Y., 102.
7. *McPadden* v. *N. Y. C. Rw.*, 44 N. Y., 478; 47 Barb., 247.
5. 13 Conn. 326.

cases," I said, "and has, I believe, been followed in most of the States, and in the United States Supreme Court."[1]

"I presume," said the machinist; "companies are liable for defects in their cars whether they manufacture them or purchase them?"

"Oh yes," I rejoined, "the companies are alike bound to see that in the construction no care or skill has been omitted for the purpose of making their engines and cars as safe as care and skill can make them."[2]

"I remember," spake the man of science, "hearing of one case where the engine ran off the track, and it was found that a fore-axle was broken, but no evidence was given as to whether the accident caused, or was caused by, the breakage; yet a traveller who had his shoulder contused, and his hat crushed, and was rendered insensible for a time and sick for a longer period by the accident, recovered a large sum against the company.[3] And in another English case[4] an accident happened from the breaking of the tire of a driving-wheel; the defect could not have been discovered by the original testing, but *might have* been if it had been repeated when the tire was returned, after being considerably worn. The company was held liable."

"Yes," said one who had not yet spoken; "I was on a jury in a case against the Great Western of Canada: the axle of the tender had broken, and the tender and a car went off the track, and a man who was in the car had his arm broken. At the trial the company proved by the engineer in charge of the train, that he had examined the axle shortly before the accident and that all appeared in good order. The judge charged in favour of the defendants, but we found a verdict for the plaintiff, which the

---

1. Redfield on Railways, vol. 2., 222 n.
2. *Hageman* v. *Western Rw.*, 16 Barb.. 353, affirmed by Court of Appeals, 13 N.Y., 9.
3. *Dawson* v. *Manchester L. & L. Rw.*, 5 L.T., N.S., 682; see also *Skinner* v. *London B. & S. C. Rw.*, 5 Ex., 787; *Carpue* v. *Same*, 5 Ad. & E., N.S., 747; *Reid* v. *Gt. Northern Rw.*, 28 L.J., Ex., 3.
4. *Mauser* v. *Eastern Counties Rw.*, 3 L.T., N.S., 585, Exch.

court refused afterwards to interfere with, as we were the proper judges as to whether or not there had been negligence on the part of the company."¹

"I think that it was in that case that Chief Justice Macaulay remarked, that the accident having happened unaccountably, and without any proximate or active cause to account for it, constituting as the cases say some evidence of negligence, it rested with the company to explain and reconcile it with perfect innocence on their part. It has been held, too, in England, that the plaintiff is not bound to show specifically in what the negligence of the company consisted; but that if some inevitable fatality caused the accident, it is for the company to prove it:² in New York, too, the same view is taken."³

"Wal, stranger, what is yer law about this yer in the old country? Not that I care three shakes of a dead possum's tail about the old country, and all yer lawyers and judges with their horse tail wigs, but still I calkerlate I kind o' like to know what they do say on this here point; as it appears to me that the great Amerikin eagle has got rather mixed up." And to add emphasis to his query, our friend of the land of wooden-nutmegs, fired from between his teeth a perfect *feu de joie* of extract of nicotine.

Thus appealed to, I cleared my throat, pulled up my shirt-collar, crossed my legs, assumed as authoritative expression of countenance as Dame Nature ever permits me to do, and thus began:

"So long ago as the days of Sir James Mansfield it was held⁴ that there is a decided difference between a contract to carry goods and one to carry passengers. In the former case the carrier is liable for his freight in any event, but he does not warrant the safety of his passengers. His undertaking as to them extends no further than this, that as far as human care and foresight can go,

---

1. *Thatch* v. *Gt. W. R.*, 4 U.C., C.P., 563.
2. *Skinner* v. *London B. & S.C.*, 5 Ad. & E., N.S., 747.
3. *McPadden* v. *N. Y. C.*, 44 N.Y., 478.
4. *Christie* v. *Griggs*, 2 Camp., 79.

he will provide for their safe conveyance. So, if the breaking of a coach is purely accidental, the injured traveller will have no remedy for the misfortune he has encountered. The contract made by a general carrier of passengers is to take due care to carry his living freight safely; and it does not amount to a warranty that the carriage or car shall be in all respects perfect for its purpose, *i.e.*, free from all defects likely to cause a catastrophe, although those defects were such that no skill, care, or foresight could have detected their existence.[1] The obligation to use all due and proper care is founded on reasons obvious to any one with a semi-optic; but to impose on the carrier the burden of a warranty that everything he necessarily uses is absolutely without spot or blemish and free from defects likely to cause peril—when from the nature of things defects must exist which no skill can detect, and the effects of which no care or foresight can avert—would be to compel a man by implication of law and not by his own will, to promise the performance of an impossible thing, and would be directly opposed to the maxims of law, 'Lex non cogit ad impossibilia,' 'Nemo tenetur ad impossibilia.' (Here the audience coughed.) 'Due care,' however, undoubtedly means (having reference to the nature of the contract to carry) a high degree of care, and casts on carriers the duty of exercising all vigilance to see that whatever is required for the safe conveyance of their passengers is in fit and proper order. But the duty to take due and proper care, however widely construed, however vigorously enforced, will not, as that man Readhead sought to do, subject a railway company to the plain injustice of being compelled by law to make reparation for a disaster arising from a latent defect in the machinery which they are obliged to use, which no human skill or care could have prevented or detected, or eye descried unless of 'the patent double

---

1. *Readhead* v. *Midland Rw.*, L.R., 4 Q.B., 379, Ex. Ch.; also L.R., 2 Q.B., 412, and the cases therein cited.

million magnifyin' gas microscopes of hextra power kind' to which Mr. Weller, Jr., refers. In that case, the accident was caused by the breaking of the tire of one of the wheels of the carriage, owing to a latent defect in it, which was not attributable to any fault on the part of the manufacturers, nor was it discoverable previously to the breakage. The rule laid down in that case (Readhead's) seems to be that although the carrier of passengers may be responsible for deficiencies caused by want of skill or care in the manufacture of the carriages used, he is not to be so held when the defect could not have been avoided in the making, or detected on examination. It is so extremely improbable that such a case should happen, that the practical difference between this and the New York rule of absolute responsibility[1] is not of much importance, although the theoretical difference is. But the rule in New York does not seem to be fully approved of even on this side of the Atlantic.[2] The truth seems to be that carriers of persons must be held to the utmost degree of care, vigilance and precaution, but not to such a degree of vigilance as would be wholly inconsistent with the mode of conveyance adopted, and render it impracticable. Nor is the utmost degree of care which the human mind is capable of imagining required. Such a rule would require such an expenditure of money and employment of hands so as to render everything safe, as would prevent all persons of ordinary prudence from engaging in that kind of business. But the rule does necessitate that the highest degree of practicable care and diligence that is consistent with the mode of transportation adopted, should be used."[3]

I stopped; one universal sigh of relief uprose from those of my listeners who were not nodding approvingly from the borders of Dreamland. The Yankee said:

1. *Alden* v. *New York Central Rw.*, 26 N.Y., 102.
2. *McPadden* v. *N. Y. C.*, 44 N.Y., 473, *Meir* v. *Penn. Rw.*, 27 Phil. Rep., 229 and *Ingalls* v. *Bills*, 9 Met., 1, where the Court said, "if the injury arise from some nvisible defect which no ordinary test will disclose, the carrier is not liable."
3. *Fuller* v. *Talbot*, 23 Ill., 357.

"Wal, stranger, that was a yarn. I guess I'll go and have a smoke, and see if I can calkerlate what in blazes you did mean by all that long pow-wow." And he departed.

"I think," said the juror, "that the law ought to be the most stringent possible in order to put a stop to such barbarous and inhuman sacrifice of multitudes, such horrible mangling of bodies and limbs, such frightful cases of burning alive and scalding to death that have occurred so frequently of late."

"Yes, I hope that the day is not very far distant when all our courts will hold, that all who undertake the transportation of passengers by the dangerous element of steam, and with the great speed of railway trains, are responsible for the use of every precaution which any known skill or experience has yet been able to devise, and that passengers need not judge for themselves how many of these precautions it is safe to forego."[1]

"But," urged another, "people now-a-days wish cheap and rapid travelling in all directions and everywhere."

"Suppose they do; we do not allow monomaniacs or brigands to commit suicide or murder without interference, because it is their pleasure or their interest to do so; and I see no good reason why railway passengers or railway managers should be allowed to roast a hecatomb in human sacrifice, because it seems desirable or convenient to the one or the other class concerned in the immolation, or because the one class demands and the other consents, to use a mode of transportation which inevitably produces these results."[2]

"Ah," said a lady, "I fear these dreadful accidents will continue until every train is compelled to carry a director of the company, or a general manager, upon the cow-catcher; experience will then soon induce them to be a little more careful of the bodies and lives of others."

1. Redfield on Railways, vol. 2, p. 237.
2. Redfield on Railways, vol. 2, p. 238.

CHAPTER IX.

ACCIDENTS TO TRAVELLERS.

Standing on platforms of cars—Room and seats to be furnished—Riding in express cars—in caboose car—Rule in Illinois—Walking through the train—Innocent blood—Damages to infants and juveniles—Child's fare unpaid—$1,800 for a baby's leg and hand—Negligence of a nurse—Travelling on free pass—Conditional liability—Company exempt—Pat and Sambo—Home again from a foreign shore.

OUR Connecticut friend went out of the car and stood on the platform, in defiance of the notice posted up on the door forbidding people to stand there; and, gazing out into the storm and the night, he tried, like sister Ann, to distinguish whether there were any signs of relief coming to us in our benighted condition. As he balanced himself on his long slender legs and stretched forward his lean and lank corpus to look ahead, the engine gave a sudden puff and plunge, Conn. lost his balance and fell to the ground: the snow prevented much damage happening to his fragile body, but unfortunately his foot rested partly on the rail and the wheel of the car badly crushed his big-toe. The violent ear-piercing howls that issued from his tobacco-seasoned throat brought assistance very soon, and he was speedily helped back into the car; his damaged pedal member was dressed by a young member of the Æsculapian fraternity who chanced to be on board, and seemed eager to show his surgical skill.

The injured man soon became violent in his denunciations of the carelessness of the company, in his threats of vengeance in the form of suits for damages. He was, however, suddenly checked in the outpouring of the vials of his wrath by one of the passengers remarking

"Perhaps you do not know that in these hyperborean regions people can claim no compensation for injuries received while on the platform of a car (or on any baggage, wood or freight car), in violation of the printed regulations posted up conspicuously, and where there is proper and ample accommodation for the passengers inside the car."[1]

"And there is a similar statute in New York State," added another.[2]

"Yes," I said, "no one can recover for an injury of which his own negligence was in the whole, or in part, the proximate cause."[3]

"Wal, but the old conductor saw me thar and didn't say nothink agin' it," quoth the wounded man.

"That makes no difference.[4] If there had been no notice up you might get something out of them."[5]

"I think," I said, "that it has been held, in one case at least, to be a question for the jury, whether the passenger had notice not to stand outside, and whether the fact of his disregarding it contributed to the injury; and they having failed to find these facts, the Court of Appeals let the plaintiff keep the $10,000, awarded him."[6]

"Oh, Jee-ru-sa-lem and Jee-ri-cho, I go in for that slick and quick," cried the victim, at the sound of the almighty dollars.

"Ha-ha; but the company, if you sue them, will only have to show that there was room and an unoccupied seat inside the cars for you. Of course, one is not obliged to displace either the persons or property of other passengers, or urge them to give up half a seat, or even a whole one, needlessly occupied by them;[7] that is the duty of the conductor."

1. Railway Act, 1868, s. 20 sub-sec. 13 (Canada).
2. Redfield on Railways, vol. 2., p. 252.
3. *Robinson* v. *Cone*, 22 Vt., 213; *Butterfield* v. *Forrester*, 11 East., 60.
4. *Higgins* v. *N. Y. & Harlem Rw.*, 2 Bosw., 132.
5. *Colegrove* v. *N. Y. & N. H. Rw.*, 6 Duer, 382.
6. *Zemp* v. *W. & M. Rw.*, 9 Rich, 84.
7. *Robinson* v. *Fitzburg & Worcester Rw.*, 7 Gray, 92; *Willis* v. *Long Island Rw.*, N.Y., 670.

"But," asked a lady, "should a passenger go through all the train searching for a place wherein to bestow her weary frame?"

"No; it is no compliance with the duty of the company to provide proper accommodation, that there is sufficient room in a carriage remote from the place where the passenger was allowed to enter."[1]

"How would it be where a passenger is in the baggage car with the knowledge of the conductor, and is there injured?" asked one.

"It was decided in Canada, in such a case, that the traveller could recover damages. There a man went into the express company's compartment (which was not intended for passengers, but whither they oft times resorted to smoke the pipe of peace): a notice was usually put upon the inside of the doors of the passenger cars and on the outside of the door of the baggage car, forbidding travellers to ride in the latter, but it was not shewn that it was there on that particular day; the conductor passed through the car twice while the man was in there and made no objection. By a collision, this Watson had an arm broken, while none of those in the passenger car were much hurt, and the Court held that even if W. was aware of the notices, yet the Company were not thereby excused, under the circumstances.[2] But where a man rode free of charge on an engine, after the engineer had told him that it was against the rules for him to do so, it was held that he was a wrongdoer, and could not recover for injuries sustained while he bestrode the iron horse, as the consent of the engineer conferred no legal right.[3] If, however, passengers are carried, and charged fare, in the caboose car (whatever that may be) of freight trains, they have the same right to be conveyed safely as if luxuriating in a gorgeous Pullman palace car,[4] and so where one rides on a

---

1. *Willis* v. *Long Island Rw.*, supra.
2. *Watson* v. *Northern Rw. Co.*, 24 U.C., Q.B., 98; see also *Carroll* v. *N.Y. & N.H. Rw.*, 1 Duer., 571. where a man took a seat in the Post Office department of baggage car with the assent of the conductor.
3. *Robertson* v. *N. Y. & E. Rw.*, 22 Barb., 91.
4. *Edgerton* v. *N. Y. & H. Rw.*, 39 N.Y. St., 227.

gravel train.[1] And where the conductor, though against the rules, allowed a passenger to travel in a freight car, charging him a first-class fare, the company were held to have incurred the same liability for his safety as if he had been in a regular passenger train.[2] Ditto where the conductor of a coal train invited a man to take a ride and charged him naught."[3]

"That may be true enough down east, but out west if a passenger takes a freight train he takes it with the increased risk and diminution of comfort incident thereto, and if it is managed with the care requisite for such trains, it is all he has a right to expect or demand;"[4] remarked one who hailed from the city of Widow O'Leary's celebrated cow.

"By the way," said a gentleman, who had been listening attentively to all the conversation; "can any of you gentlemen, who seem to have the whole law appertaining to railways at your finger's ends or the tips of your tongues" (whichever expression be the more correct or implies the greater knowledge), tell me whether it is safe for one to promenade from one end of the train to the other for the sake of exercise or to see who is on board? Down in New York State the jury must decide whether it is right so to do, in order to find a seat."[5]

"Out west," said the Chicagoian, "it has been decided that passengers have no right to pass from car to car, unless for some reasonable purpose;[6] and heaven only knows what twelve enlightened men from the body of the country would, in their wisdom, deem to be reasonable."

"Humph, you don't seem to have a very high opinion of juries," said the representative of that class, who had already joined in the conversation.

1. *Lawrenceburgh & Upper Miss. Rw.* v. *Montgomery*, 7 Porter (Ind.), 474.
2. *Dunn* v. *G. T. Rw.*, 18 Am. Law Reg., N.S., 615.
3. *Eaton* v. *Del., Lack. & W. Rw.*, 1 Am. Law Record, 121, Sup. Ct., N.Y.
4. *Chicago B. & Q. Rw.* v. *Hazzard*, 26 Ill., 373.
5. *McIntyre* v. *N. Y. Central Rw.*, 37 N. Y., 287.
6. *Galena & Chicago Rw.* v. *Yarwood*, 15 Ill., 468.

"I rather think not; who could, when they elaborate such queer decisions from their brains and shew such ignorance. I know one case where an intelligent jury brought in a verdict of 'guilty' against the plaintiff in a libel suit; of another, where, at the close of a lengthy trial, the foreman coolly asked the judge to explain 'two terms of law, namely plaintiff and defendant.' Many of them would be decidedly improved were occasional punishment inflicted as in the good old days of yore, when sometimes a juryman was fined and had his nose split; and the usual fate of a disagreeing jury was to be put into a cart and shot into the nearest ditch."

Our train had been released from bondage and under weigh for some time, and just at this juncture the conversation was stopped by a collision taking place. Fortunately the drivers of the approaching engines had discovered the danger some time previously; they were, therefore, enabled by putting on the breaks so to deaden the speed that the trains barely touched each other—gently kissed, as it were—and although some of the passengers were jerked forward in an uncomfortable manner as if they had been suddenly punched in a sensitive part, still no persons were seriously hurt except two. One of these unfortunates was the newsboy who in passing from one car to another was thrown to the ground and had a leg badly crushed; the other was a beautiful little child of some three or four summers who had been playing with a lady and was knocked violently down, and in falling hit his head against the side of a seat. From his pure white forehead a purple stream was slowly trickling, dying his golden ringlets, as he lay unconscious upon his weeping mother's knee. While some tried to restore the child, and others to console the parent, I took a business-like view of the transaction, and "with all the homage due to a sex of which I am enthused dreadful," as Col. Morley of the Parisians would say, I approached and said,

"Madam each drop of that child's blood is worth money: you may lay the foundation of his future fortune now in the days of his youth by recovering damages against the company for the injury they have done to him;" she heeded not, but I continued. "Why in one case a child two years old was wandering on a track and being run over by a train lost a leg and a hand, and the jury gave it $1800:[1] why that sum put out at compound interest would——"

"Oh, you horrid man," exclaimed the mother, "to talk that way. But I did not buy a ticket for him, and I should have, as he is over three years old." And the mother's grief broke out afresh, as she thought she had lost this golden opportunity.

"Don't trouble yourself, madam, that makes no difference: the contract made with you when you bought your ticket was that both you and your child should be carried safely, and if there was any misrepresentation on your part as to the little sufferer's age, although it might render you liable for the fare that should have been paid, or for a penalty, still it does not alter the position of the company, and they were and are bound to carry you and the little dear safely."[2]

"Ah!" sighed the mother, "if that nasty woman had only held him up, and not have let him fall:—perhaps the jury will say she ought to have done so?"

I was glad to see that the thought of the almighty dollar was applying a golden salve to the mother's wounded heart, if not to the boy's forehead, for I hate tears, crocodile or otherwise, and was therefore willing to enlighten her ladyship as much as possible, especially as I make it a constant practice to give advice gratuitously (when I think it won't be paid for), and putting down the usual charge for it to the account of my charitable disbursements; so I said:

"The misconduct of one assuming to take charge of a child, but

---

1. Redfield on Railways, vol. 2, p. 243, n.; *Ranch* v. *Lloyd*, 31 Penn. St., 358.
2. *Austin* v. *Gt. Western Rw.*, L.R., 2 Q.B., 442.

to whom it has not been entrusted, will not preclude a recovery on its part for the negligence of the company."[1]

Alas, for the poor mother's peace of mind, there was a Job's comforter on board, and he opened his mouth, and although he did not bray as he should have done, being what he was, he spake thus:

"The law in the State of Massachusetts is that, the negligence of those who have the charge of children, or invalids, unable to take care of themselves, will injuriously affect their right of action."[2]

"Thank goodness we are not near the Hub of the universe now," I exclaimed, sharply.

"Well then," the wretch continued to drawl on, "in England where a child five years old was in the charge of his grandmother and was injured by a train while crossing the track, it was held that he was so identified with his old granny that on account of her carelessness an action in his name could not be maintained against the company.[3] And where a passing train cut off the leg of a three and a half year old child, the court considered that the company were not responsible, unless it was shown that he had strayed upon the track through their negligence or default."[4]

"Never mind his croaking, madam, these cases do not apply to you: and besides, on this side of the water a parent may suffer a four year old to cross a track by itself to school,[5] or wander about a station,[6] without freeing the company from liability. Parents need only be ordinarily careful in not allowing their small fry to get into danger.[7] But I must go and see the newsboy."

1. *N. Penn. Rw.* v. *Mahoney*, 57 Penn. St., 187.
2. *Holly* v. *Boston Gas Light Co.*, 8 Grey, 123; *Wright* v. *Malden & M. Rw.*, 4 Allen, 283.
3. *White* v. *North Eastern Rw.*, El., Bl. & El., 719.
4. *Singleton* v. *Eastern Counties Rw.*, 7 C.B., N.S., 287.
5. *Lynch* v. *Smith*, 104 Mass., 52.
6. *Stout* v. *S. C. & P. Rw.*, 11 Am. Law. Reg., N.S., 226.
7. *Pittsb. A. & M. Rw.* v. *Pearson*, 29 Law Intell., 372.

Off I started instanter—

> "For a virtuous action should never be delayed,
> The impulse comes from heaven, and he who strives
> A moment to repress it, disobeys
> The god within his mind."

I found the youth in the baggage car with his leg tightly bandaged. The pallor spread over his countenance, the beads of perspiration on his brow, and his closely pressed lips, told that his sufferings were great; but with Spartan courage he repressed every voluntary sign of pain. A group of rough, yet tender men were gathered round him, and they told me that it was feared he would have to lose his leg; that he was the only son of his mother, and she was a widow with no stay nor support save the earnings of her boy.

"I say, mister," said one of the party to me, "I kind of calculate you are a lawyer from what I heard you say before we left the station, and I want to know whether a man who has not got a ticket can sue the railway for damages."

I replied, "Every person is a passenger and entitled to be carried safely (so far as due care will provide for his safety), who is lawfully on the train;[1] and the *onus* is on the company to prove affirmatively that he is a trespasser.[2] Any one permitted to ride in a train as a passenger is entitled to demand and expect the same immunity from peril whether he pay for his seat or no: the confidence induced is a sufficient legal consideration to create a duty in the performance of the service undertaken;[3] so, if one is injured by the culpable negligence or want of skill of the company's servants he is entitled to recover although he is a deadhead.[4] Thus, a newspaper reporter travelling on a free ticket

---

[1] *Gt. Western of Canada* v. *Brand*, 1 Moore P.C., N.S., 101.
[2] *Penn. Rw. Co.* v. *Books*, 7 Am. Law Reg., N.S., 524.
[3] *Coggs* v. *Bernard*, Holt, 13
[4] *Ohio & Miss. Rw.* v. *Muhling*, 30 Ill., 9.

—even if granted to another brother of the press;[1] the president of one company riding by request of the president of another;[2] a mail-clerk travelling in charge of the mail bags,[3] and a child for whom no fare has been paid;[4] were all held entitled to damages when injured. Nor—though this is rather beside the matter—does the fact that the train has been hired for an excursion excuse the negligence, or remove the liability of the company."[5]

"All right," said the man to the boy; "cheer up, sonny; you will get a pot of money for this that will keep you like a fighting-cock till you get round again."

"I did not say that," I remarked, gloomily shaking my head.

"Why, what do you mean?" was anxiously queried by several.

"Railway companies may stipulate for exemption from all responsibility for losses accruing to passengers from the negligence of their servants, unless, indeed, it arise from their fraudulent, reckless or wilful misconduct;[6] and where it has been agreed that, in consideration of a free pass, the passenger should travel at his own risk, or where he takes a free ticket having an express condition printed thereon 'whereby the holder assumes all risk of accidents and expressly agrees that the company shall not be liable under any circumstances, whether of negligence by their agents or otherwise, for an injury to the person, or for any loss of or injury to the property' such agreement or condition is good, and will exclude all liability on the part of the company for any negligence (save gross or wilful)[7] for which they would other-

1. *Gt. Northern Rw.* v. *Harrison*, 12 C.B., 576; *Gillenwater* v. *Madison & Indian Rw.*, 5 Ind., 340.
2. *Phil. & Read. Rw.* v. *Derby*, 14 How. (U.S.), 483.
3. *Collett* v. *London & N. W. R.*, 16 Ad. & El., N.S., 984; *Nolton* v. *Western Rw.*, 10 How. Pr. R., 97.
4. *Austin* v. *Gt. Western Rw.*, supra.
5. *Skinner* v. *London, B. & S. C. Rw.*, 5 Ex., 787; *Cleveland* v. *Terry*, 6 Ohio, N.S. 570; but see *Peoria Br. Ass.* v. *Loomis*, 20 Ill., 235.
6. *Welles* v. *N. Y. C.*, 26 Barb., 641; *Indiana Central Rw.* v. *Mundy*, 21 Ind., 48.
7. *Ind. Cent. Rw.* v. *Mundy*, supra; *Welles* v. *N. Y. C. Rw.*, 26 Barb., 641; *Bissell* v. *N. Y. C.*, 29 Barb., 602; *Ill. C. R.* v. *Read*, 37 Ill., 484.

wise have been liable. That has been held in Canada;[1] in New York State,[2] in other States and in England the company is not even liable for wilful or gross negligence.[3] But of course such an agreement does not extend to an independent wrong, as an assault or false imprisonment, or any rights as to criminal proceedings,[4] nor where the traveller is carried under an agreement between the company and some third party which says nothing about the traveller taking the risk himself."[5]

"What's the use in such a long palaver," rudely interrupted my questioner, "the boy had no ticket at all."

"Well, where a newsboy of the name of Billy Alexander, while on the platform of a station, was struck by a piece of wood projecting from a passing car and so hurt that he died, it was held to be a good defence that he was a newsboy in the employ of Chisholm, selling papers on the company's trains under an agreement between Chisholm and the company, that the latter should not be liable for any injury to the newsboys or their goods, whether occasioned by the company's negligence or otherwise."[6]

"Do you mean to tell me," cried a listener, indignantly, "that in this free land of ours the life of a child can thus be sold by his employer?"

"Ah," I returned, "that is a question which Richards, C. J., did not decide: the case, however, has gone to the Court of Appeal. But if you want to know anything more on the subject call on me at my office, and I shall be most happy to attend to you," I added, as I left the car.

I now retired to my berth in the Pullman. I was scarcely settled there ere I heard loud and angry voices proceeding from

1. *Sutherland* v. *Gt. W. Rw.*, 7 C.P., 409; *Woodruff* v. *G. W. R.*, 18 Q.B., 420.
2. *Welles* v. *N. Y. C.*, 26 Barb., 641.
3. *McCawley* v. *Furness Rw.*, L.R., 8 Q.B., 57.
4. *Ibid.*
5. *Woodruff* v. *G. W. R.*, 18 U.C., Q.B., 420.
6. *Alexander* v. *Toronto & N. Rw.*, 32 U.C., Q.B., 474.

the front end of the car, and recognised our Hamitic conductor's tones in the words—

"I tell you, sah, this is a sleeping car, and you can't come in without a ticket."

"Shure and I had a ticket, and its after slaping I want to be;" was the response in Milesian accents, broad and sweet.

"Whar is it?"

"Shure and I have lost the plaguy thing."

"If you have lost your ticket, sah, can you remember your berth?" asked the African.

A solemn pause, during which Paddy ruminated deeply, then he exclaimed,

"Och, by jabers, it is a hard thing to remember that, though I know I was there at the time; and my old mother, rest her bones, tould me that I was born on Patrick's day in the morning, the year afore the famine, and more by token our old sow had a fine litter of pigs that self same day."

When the burst of laughter that greeted this reply had died away, I quickly subsided into the "arms of Murphy," and knew nothing more of railroads, railroad-law, or railroad travelling, until I was called by the descendant of Noah's naughty son, and informed that we were just at the station which I had left some days previously, and where my journeyings were for a time to end, and from which in a few minutes I would be transported to the bosom of my beloved spouse. Right glad was I when once again I stood—*mens sana in corpore sano*—on the platform of the depot of my native city, and saw the cabby coming from the baggage car with my traps on his brawny shoulder. I will draw the veil of modesty over the reception that awaited me at home.

CHAPTER X.

INJURIES TO PASSENGERS AND EMPLOYEES.

Inefficient line—Passengers hurt—Employees killed—Lord Campbell's Act—Compensation for death—Solatium for wounded feelings—Scotch law—American law—Hen-pecked husband's will—The rule in Massachusetts—in Pennsylvania—in Maryland—in Canada—Hard to decide—Annuity tables—Bad or diseased—Insured—Children injured.—Parents compensated—Amounts obtained.—A leg at $24,700—For what compensated—Chances of matrimony—Servants injured—Fellow servants—Different companies—Which one to sue—Strangers' acts—Greedy ruminant.

I HAD fondly hoped that no new points, quirks, or quiddities on railway law would arise in the course of my not very extensive practice for some time to come, so that I might have leisure to paddle my own little canoes, and issue little billets doux in the Queen's name to the company on my own account. But alas! I had scarcely settled down in my office on the day of my arrival at home when my young friend, Tom Jones (to whom I referred in the early pages of this interesting and instructive diary of mine), came rushing in.

After a considerable amount of small talk, chit-chat and mutual enquiries after mutual friends and affairs, and things mutually interesting, Tom exclaimed, "I say, old fellow, I have a couple of matters that are bothering me, and I want your advice thereon."

By the way, nearly all Tom Jones' matters bothered him, and when they bothered him he bothered me, for he was not one of those who

"Make law their study and delight,
Read it by day and meditate by night."

"All right," I said, extending my left digits towards him for an *honorarium*.

"Oh, I am not going to pay you," he remarked coolly, "so you need not expect it."

"Ah, well," I returned, quietly and with the air of an ill-used man, "I shall do like old Thurlow did, he could never come to a decision without a fee, and so when he had to decide upon some matter for himself he would take a guinea out of one pocket and put it into another. Now what are your questions?" I always preferred answering his queries to lending him books, for although he was a miserable hand at accounts, he was a most excellent book-keeper.

"I suppose you know," began T. J., "that a short time ago owing to a heavy storm, part of the line of the Blank Railway gave way ——"

"That is *primâ facie* evidence of the insufficiency of its construction; and a company is bound to build its works in such a manner as that they will be capable of resisting all extremes of weather, which in the climate through which the line runs might be expected, though rarely, to occur. So say that august assembly, the Judicial Committee of the Privy Council."[1]

"Can't you wait a bit—that's not the point at all;" said Jones.

"Go on then."

"Several men were killed, and, as is usual, they all had large families of small children. Three of the wives have come to me to see if I can get damages against the company for them."

"Were they passengers or employees, for that makes a great difference," I said.

"One was employed on the line, the others were not," replied Tom.

"Well, let us settle about the others first."

"Well, what do you do first to get your damages? I mean under what Act do you proceed?"

---

1. *Gt. Western Rw.* v. *Fawcett—Same* v. *Brand*, 1 Moore, P.C.C., N.S., 101—9 Jur., N.S., 339.

"Under what in England is called Lord Campbell's Act (9 & 10 Vic. ch. 93), the Canadian Act[1] is a transcript of that; and a similar statute has been introduced into most of the States of the Union, to obviate that most heathenish of maxims *actio personalis moritur cum personam*. Our Act provides that when death shall be caused by the wrongful act, neglect or default, of any person, such as would (if death had not ensued) have entitled the party to an action, in every such case an action may be maintained by the executor or administrator of the party injured, and the jury may give such damages as shall be proportioned to the injury resulting from the death of such party, to be divided among the members of his family as the jury shall direct. But, of course, if any negligence of the party himself, or those in charge of him, contribute directly to the injury, there can be no remedy.[2] Have twelve months elapsed since the death?"

"No," was the response.

"All right."

"What damages shall I claim?"

"Only such as will compensate for the pecuniary loss sustained,"[3] I returned.

"But one of my wives—the richest one, too,—went into most awful fits over the death of her husband, and has not been quite *compos mentis* since; and I want something to solace her for her mental sufferings."

"You cannot get it in this country, nor could you in England either. If the jury were to enquire into the degree of mental anguish which each member of a family suffers from a bereavement, then not only the child without filial piety, but a lunatic child and one of very tender years, and a posthumous child, on the death of the father, although getting something for pecuniary loss, would

---

1. Con. Stat. Can., ch. 78.
2. *Willets* v. *N. Y. & Erie Rw.*, 14 Barb., 385, where a lunatic was left by himself and in consequence was killed.
3. *Blake* v. *Midland Rw.*, 18 Q.B., 93.

not come *in pari passu* with other children, and would be cut off from the solatium. If a jury were to proceed to estimate the respective degrees of mental anguish of a widow and twelve children from the death of the pater-familias, a serious danger might arise of damages being given to the ruin of the defendants: especially would the damages be disastrous if all the relatives mentioned in the fifth section of the Imperial Act (the sixth of the Canadian), the father and the mother, grandfather and grandmother, stepfather and stepmother, grandson and granddaughter, stepson and stepdaughter, not only got compensation for their pecuniary losses, but solatiums for their shattered affections, blighted expectations and broken hearts."[1]

"That is too bad," said Jones, "for I am sure the Scotch law gives a solatium for wounded feelings, even where the death of the man, instead of being a loss, is a gain to the family, owing to his bankruptcy or dissipated habits."[2]

"Yes," I replied, "but the Scotch are always more liberal than other people; they grant a solatium to a man injured in his happiness and circumstances by the death of his wife and child whereas in England a widower will not get anything unless the death of his spouse causes him some pecuniary loss;[3] it being a pure question of pecuniary compensation, and nothing more, which is contemplated by the Act.[4] Nor, I believe, can a husband recover in New York State for the death of his wife.[5] But where the damages are for the next of kin, the services of the deceased mother in the nurture and instruction of her children, had she survived, may be properly considered.[6] I wonder what is the rule as to the solatium in the Republic—let us see."

---

1. *Blake* v. *Midland Rw.*, 18 Ad. & Ell., N.S., 93; *Pym* v. *Great Northern Rw.*, 4 B. & S. (Ex. Ch.), 396.
2. Ersk. Inst., 592, note 13.
3. In argument *Gillivard* v. *Lancaster & Yorkshire Rw. Co.*, 12 L.T., 356.
4. *Armsworth* v. *South Eastern Rw. Co.*, 11 Jurist, 758.
5. *Lucas* v. *N. Y. C*,, 21 Barb., 245; *Worley* v. *Cincinnati H. & D. Rw.*, 1 Handy. 481.
6. *Tilley* v. *Hudson River Rw.*, 29 N.Y., 252.

So saying, I reached down a most useful book on Railways, by Chief Justice Redfield, of Vermont, and concerning "the great learning, research, and power of reasoning displayed" in which, Lord Chief Justice Cockburn speaks with expressions of admiration.

"Here it is: 'There seems no doubt, according to the best considered cases in this country, that the mental anguish, which is the natural result of the injury, may be taken into account, in estimating damages to the party injured in such cases, although not of itself the foundation of an action.'"[1]

"It seems," remarked my friend, "somewhat strange that in Canada a person's feelings should make no difference, for one of my widows feels her loss deeply, whereas the other is evidently one of them 'vidders' against whom Samivel Veller, Senior, would have warned his hopeful boy."

"Both are entitled to the same compensation, although one was as closely joined in sympathy and spirit to her lost spouse as was Chang to Eng, in the flesh; and the other was the Elizabeth referred to in the will of that unfortunate wretch who died in London, in 1791. I must read you that will, though it is rather beside the subject, for it is a perfect model for hen-pecked husbands to follow; here it is. 'Seeing that I have had the misfortune to be married to the aforesaid Elizabeth, who, ever since our union, has tormented me in every possible way; that heaven seems to have sent her into the world solely to drive me out of it; that the strength of Samson, the genius of Homer, the prudence of Augustus, the skill of Pyrrhus, the patience of Job, the philosophy of Socrates, the vigilance of Hermogenes, would not suffice to subdue the perversity of her character; that no power on earth can change her; seeing we have lived apart during the last eight years, and that the only result has been the ruin of my son, whom she

---

1. *Canning* v. *Williamstown*, 1 Cush., 451; *Moore* v. *Auburn & Syracuse Rw.*, 10 Barb., 623; so in California, *Fairchild* v. *California Stage Co.*, 13 Cal., 599.

has corrupted and estranged from me : weighing, maturely and seriously, all these considerations, I have bequeathed and I do bequeath, to my said wife Elizabeth, the sum of one shilling, to be paid to her within six months of my death.' But to return ; as to damages, I see that in Massachusetts by statute[1] the passenger carrier is subject to a fine, not exceeding $5,000, to be recovered by indictment, to the use of the executor or administrator of the deceased for the benefit of his widow and heirs. Under this Act, if the death is instantaneous and simultaneous with the injury, as no right of action accrues to the person injured, there is none to which the Act can apply ;[2] but it is sufficient if one does not die for fifteen minutes, although insensible from the first.[3] In Pennsylvania, the jury were told to estimate damages 'by the probable accumulations of a man of such age, habits, health and pursuits as the deceased, during what would probably have been his lifetime.'[4] In Maryland the jury was directed to give such damages as would yield the family of the deceased the same support as they would have obtained from the labour of the father during the time he would probably have lived and worked, and that they might consider the age, health and occupation of the man killed, and the comfort and support he was to his family at the time of his death."[5]

"I see," said Tom, who seemed unwilling that I should do all the talking, " that our own Chief Justice Robinson, on one occasion, confessed himself utterly at a loss to make a satisfactory computation of the amount of damages to be awarded, or of the pecuniary loss sustained by a widow and her children through the death of the head of the house : he said he had no means of determining whether they would have been better off if the father's life had

1, 1842, c. 89.
2. *Hollenbeck* v. *Berkshire Rw.*, 9 Cush., 481.
3. *Bancroft* v. *Boston & Worcester Rw.*, 11 Allen, 34.
4. *Penn. Rw. Co.* v. *McClosky*, 23 Penn. St., 526, 528.
5. *Baltimore & Ohio Rw.* v. *State*, 24 Md., 271.

run its natural course, or not; it was mere conjecture. The father might have become extravagant or intemperate, and squandered his property; or from too great eagerness to grow rich, might have lost it by grasping at too much, or might have died from natural causes within a year or a month, leaving his family no better off than he did leave them when carried away by the sad accident.[1] And I think that I would be equally puzzled were I on a jury; I don't see how in the world a jury, except by drawing lots, can calculate the damages arising from the loss of the income, and of the care, protection and assistance of the father."

" Yes, it must be rather a nice calculation."

"Suppose," continued Jones, " there was an accident to a train containing an archbishop, a lord chancellor, a bank director, a lunatic, a wealthy but immoral man, and one virtuous but bankrupt, and all these respectable persons came to final grief: how could any ordinary jury estimate the pecuniary value of the conjugal and paternal care, protection and assistance of each of these."

" You need not put such an unlikely case," I said, " merely suppose that there were together one who—

> 'Scorned life's mathematics,
> Could not reckon up a score,
>   Pay his debts, or be persuaded
> Two and two are always four.
>   That another was exact as Euclid,
> Prompt and punctual, no one more.'

" Still," I added, " these difficult calculations have to be made."

" But how ? "

" In England, it has been decided that the damages are not to be estimated according to the life of the man, calculated by annuity tables, but the jury should give what they consider a reasonable compensation;[2] although, in the United States, it was thought proper for the judge in charging the jury to allude to the expecta-

---

1. *Secord* v. *Great Western Rw.*, 15 U.C., Q.B., 631.
2. *Armsworth* v. *South Eastern Rw.*, 11 Jur., 759.

tion of life according to the tables deduced from the bills of mortality;[1] and even in England, in such cases, the average and probable duration of the life is a material point, which cannot be better shewn than by the tables of insurance companies, who learn it by experience.[2] And the probable benefits of the continuance of the life of the father, as to the children, is to be estimated with reference to their majority, and as to the widow, with reference to the expectation of life as determined by the tables.[3] Of course, the jury are not to attempt to give damages to the full amount of a perfect compensation for the pecuniary injury, but must take a reasonable view of the case, and give what they consider, under all the circumstances, a fair compensation."[4]

"Would it make any difference were the man of a bad character, or diseased?"

"If the man had a fatal disease which would be sure to kill him in a short time, the amount of damages given should be less. And as to character, the loss is supposed to be of a man as he ought to be. It has been held not to be necessary that the widow, or next of kin, should have any legal claim upon the deceased for support."[5]

"How would it be if he was insured, and by his death the family rather made than lost?"

"Well, I presume that if the insurance goes to a man's family, it would be a good reason for reducing the amount of damages. There appears to be only one English case on this point, and that was at *Nisi Prius* and is not reported at length; in it Lord Campbell told the jury to deduct from the amount of damages the amount of an insurance against accidents, and any reasonable sum

---

1. *Smith* v. *N. Y. & Harlem Rw.*, 6 Duer, 225; *City of Chicago* v. *Major*, 18 Ill., 349.
2. *Rowley* v. *London & N. W. Rw.*, 29 Law Times Rep., N.S., 180.
3. *Balt. & Ohio Rw.* v. *State*, 33 Md., 542; *Macon & Western Rw.* v. *Johnson*, 38 Ga., 439.
4. *Rowley* v. *London & N. W. Rw.*, supra.
5. *Birkett* v. *Whitehaven Junction Rw.*, 4 H. & N., 732.
6. *Railway Co.* v. *Barron*, 5 Wallace, 90.

they should think fit in respect of life insurance.[1] In a Canadian case, McLean J., said that if the interest on the insurance would exceed the annual value of the testator's income while living and exercising his ordinary avocations, it would surely be competent for the company to shew that the widow had sustained no pecuniary damages, and that only nominal damages should be given, if indeed any.[2] But, I should say that if the insurance went to some of the family only, the others would still have their right to substantial damages."

"I believe," continued the irrepressible Jones, "that if an injured man settles with the company for a sum of money, that puts an end to the whole matter, and if he afterwards shuffles off this mortal coil nothing more is to be had."

"Yes: once and forever, is the rule, even if the unfortunate makes a mistake and takes too little."[4]

"Can you make money out of the slaughter of children?"

"Oh, certainly: though in England doubts have been suggested as to whether damages were obtainable to compensate for the loss of the services of a child so young as to be unable to earn anything;[5] but in New York a mother recovered $1,300 for the death of a daughter seven years old."[6]

"That was a pretty good figure for a female youngster."

"Yes, as the pecuniary loss is not supposed to be extended beyond the minority of the child.[7] In England, however, a father recovered for the loss of a son twenty-seven years old, but unmarried, who had been accustomed to make occasional presents to his

---

1. *Hicks* v. *Newport A. & H. Rw.*, mentioned in 4 B. & S., 403.
2. *Ferrie* v. *Great Western Rw.*, 15 Q.B., U.C., 517.
3. *Pym* v. *Great Northern Rw.*, 4 B. & S., 397, Ex. Ch.
4. *Read* v. *Great Eastern Rw.*, L.R., 3 Q.B., 555; but see remark of Erle, C.J., in *Pym* v. *Gt. N. Rw.*, 4 B. & S., 406; and Coleridge, J., in *Blake* v. *Midland Rw.*, 18 Ad. & Ell., N.S., 93.
5. *Bramhill* v. *Lee*, 29 Law Times, 111.
6. Court of Appeals, 14 N.Y., 310.
7. *State* v. *Baltimore & Ohio Rw.*, 24 Md., 84; but see *Penn. Rw.* v. *Adams*, 55 Penn. St., 499.

parents.¹ There the old man rather tried to stick it on: he had a swell funeral and bought crape for the family and wanted the company to pay for them: the jury said 'Yea,' but the court said 'Nay.' In one case, however, a mourning husband recovered the funeral expenses of his wife.² As a rule, damages of a pecuniary nature must be shown; so, where a son was in the habit of assisting his father by carrying round coals for him, it was held that £75 was too much to give the old man for compensation for his death.³ In an Irish case, where a boy of fourteen, earning no wages and whose business capabilities were valued at *six-pence* per day, was killed, it was considered that the probability of his assisting his mother was good evidence to go to the jury.⁴

"What sums have been given and allowed by the Court?"

"Well, it was considered that $12,000 was not too much for the widow and three children of an industrious well-to-do farmer;⁵ in an English case £1,000 was given to the widow, and £1,500 to each of eight young children, $65,000 in all;⁶ then $1,300 for that baby girl.⁷ But when $20,000 was given as damages for the death of a blacksmith—the inventor of a patent plough—who was killed at the celebrated Desjardins Canal accident, a new trial was granted, as the Court thought the sum enormously excessive.⁸ On the other hand, in one case, twelve miserable jurymen, who doubtless would have eagerly skinned a mosquito for the sake of its hide and tallow, gave £1 to a poor widow, and ten shillings each to her two fatherless children.⁹ So you see the sum goes by the rule of thumb."

1. *Dalton* v. *S. E. Rw.*, 4 C. B., N.S., 296.
2. Redfield on Railways, Vol. 2., p. 275.
3. *Franklin* v. *S. E. Rw.*, 3 H. & N., 211; *Duckworth* v. *Johnson*, 4 H. & N., 653.
4. *Camden* v. *Great Southern & Western Rw.*, 16 Ir. C.L.R., 415.
5. *Secord* v. *Great Western Rw.*, 15 U.C., Q.B., 631.
6. *Pym* v. *Great Northern Rw.*, 4 B. & S., 397 Ex. Ch.
7. Court of Appeals, 14 N.Y., 310.
8. *Morley* v. *Great Western Rw.*, 16 U.C., Q.B., 504.
9. *Springett* v. *Balls*, 6 B. & S., 477.

"So it appears," answered my young friend, who sucked in knowledge as a sponge does water—only to lose it again. "But some of those are not bad figures."

"Certainly not; yet they are by no means as good as some people have got and had the pleasure of spending themselves. In one case, a man received $6,000 for a broken leg, which got well in about eight months;[1] another got $24,700 (Canada money) for the loss of his leg."[2]

"What a leg that must have been—a match for Miss Kilmansegg's precious limb, which

> Was made in a comely mould,
> Of gold, fine virgin glittering gold,
>   As solid as man could make it—
> Solid in foot, and calf and shank,
> A prodigious sum of money it sank;
> In fact 'twas a branch of the family Bank,
>   And no easy matter to break it.
>
> All sterling metal—not half-and-half,
> The Goldsmith's mark was stamped on the calf—
>   'Twas pure as from Mexican barter.
>
> 'Twas a splendid, brilliant, beautiful leg,
> Fit for the Court of Scander-Beg,
> That precious leg of Miss Kilmansegg!"

Exclaimed Tom Jones glowing with poetic fire, his eye in a fine frenzy rolling at the thought of the bawbees.

"Cease exhibiting your Hood," I said severely. "In another case $10,000 was obtained for something or other, when if the man had been killed outright his friends would only have got $5,000.[3] But in these three cases, new trials were granted, as will always be the way where the damages are so excessive as to strike every one as beyond all measure unreasonable and corrupt, and as showing the jury to have been actuated by passion, corrup-

---

1. *Clapp* v. *Hudson R.R.*, 19 Barb., 461.
2. *Batchelor* v. *Buffalo & Brantford R.R.*, 5 U.C., C.P., 127.
3. *Collins* v. *Albany & Sch. Rw.*, 12 Barb., 492.

tion or prejudice.[1] Where, however, a woman had lost one arm and the use of the other, and was so bruised, battered, blackened and injured that she was in constant pain, and her health and memory were impaired, and in three successive trials recovered $10,000, $18,000, and $22,250 respectively, the first two verdicts were set aside, but she was allowed to keep the third.[2] And where one was disabled for two years, $4,500 was held not exorbitant compensation;[3] and in Connecticut, $1,800 to a two year old baby for the loss of a leg and hand were given and retained.[4] As these things rest a good deal in the discretion of the jury, they must of necessity be more or less uncertain."

" Can you sue more than once ? "

" No, you must go for all your damages, present and prospective in one action."[5]

" What do you actually get paid for ? "

" The effect of the accident—both at the present time and in the future—upon one's health, use of limbs, ability to attend to business and pursue the course of life that one otherwise would have done, the bodily pain and suffering endured, and in fact all injuries that are the legal, direct and necessary results of the accident.[6] In some cases the plaintiff has been allowed to add to his actual damages of loss of time, expense of cure, pain and suffering, and prospective disability, if any—counsel fees not recoverable as taxable costs;[7] but this rule is not now followed.[8] A husband may recover for the expense of the cure of ¡his wife, and for the loss of her services.[9] Expenses incurred by sick-

---

1. *Coleman* v. *Southwick*, 9 Johns., 45 ; *Gilbert* v. *Berstenshaw*, Cowp., 230 ; *Hewlett* v. *Cruch*, 5 Taunt., 287.
2. *Shaw* v. *Boston & Worcester Rw.*, 8 Gray, 45.
3. *Curtis* v. *Rochester & S. Rw.*, 20 Barb., 282.
4. Redfield on Railways, vol. 2, p. 243.
5. *Hodsoll* v. *Stallebras*, 11 Ad. & El., 301 ; *Whitney* v. *Clarendon*, 18 Vt., 252.
6. *Curtis* v. *Rochester & S. Rw.*, 20 Barb., 282.
7. *Baranrd* v. *Poor*, 21 Pick., 381 ; *Sanback* v. *Thomas*, 1 Stark, 306.
8. *Grace* v. *Morgan*, 2 Bing., N.S., 534 ; *Jenkins* v. *Biddulph*, 4 Bing., 160.
9. *Hopkins* v. *Atlantic & St. Lawrence Rw.*, 36 N.H., 9 ; *Pack* v. *Mayor of New York*, 3 Comst., 489 ; *Campbell* v. *G. W. R.*, 20 U.C., C.P., 345.

ness of a wife caused by the death of her child;[1] and damages for premature labour, and birth of a still-born child caused by collision, are recoverable.[2] One young lady, who was seriously injured by the upsetting of a passenger car, sought to get additional damages because the prospects of her forming a matrimonial alliance were lessened by her injuries, but the poor thing failed in her attempt for lack of evidence on the point, and because her attorney had neglected to insert the special claim in the declaration."[3]

"Oh that was too bad," said Jones, " for the desire of marriage —her chances of which had been lessened—arises naturally from the principle of reproduction which stands next in importance to its elder born correlative, self-preservation, and is equally a fundamental law of existence : it is the blessing which tempered with mercy the justice of the expulsion from Paradise ; it was impressed upon the human creation by a benevolent Providence, to multiply the images of Himself, and so promote His own glory and the happiness of His creatures. Not man alone but the whole animal and vegetable kingdoms are under an imperious necessity to obey its mandates. From the lord of the forest to the monster of the deep ; from the subtlety of the serpent to the innocence of the dove; from the celastic embrace of the mountain Kalima to the descending fructification of the lily of the plain, all nature bows submissively to this primeval law. Even the flowers which perfume the air with their fragrance and decorate the forests and the fields with their hues, are but curtains to the nuptial bed. The principles of morality, the policy of nations, the doctrines of the common law, the law of nature and the law of God, unite in condemning any act which hinders people entering into the holy estate of wedlock."

1. *Ford* v. *Monroe*, 20 Wendell, 210.
2. *Fitzpatrick* v. *Great Western Rw.*, 12 U.C., Q.B., 465.
3. *Hanover Rw.* v. *Coyle*, 55 Penn., 396.

"My conscience, Tom Jones, how did you become master of such mighty and glowing strains of high toned eloquence," I asked, as I 'astonied stood and blank.'

"Oh, I have an action of breach of promise coming on to-morrow, and I thought I would see if I knew the peroration of my address to the jury."

"Did you compose it?" I asked.

"Not quite. Mr. Justice Lewis, of Pennsylvania, originally uttered the words in giving judgment in a will case. Now then," said Jones, after a pause, "what about the employee that was killed."

"Ah! more of them are killed every year than the number of soldiers who died during the Ashantee war; 1300 appears to be the annual number. But it is clearly settled both in England and America, that a servant who is injured through the negligence or misconduct of a fellow servant, can maintain no action against the master,[1] if the latter has taken due care not to expose him to unnecessary danger,[2] and has made a proper selection of servants—competent and trustworthy—and has a sufficient number of them,[3] and has himself not been guilty of negligence,[4] and takes care to furnish and maintain suitable and safe machinery and structures;"[5] and if a servant continues his work knowing that his fellows are incompetent, or the machinery defective, he is guilty of contributory negligence.[6]

"It seems," remarked my friend, "strange that if my coachman runs over a stranger and kills him, I have to make repara-

---

1. *Priestly* v. *Fowler*, 3 M. & W., 1; *Farewell* v. *Boston & W. Rw.*, 4 Met., 49; *Brown* v. *Maxwell* 6 Hill, N.Y., 592.

2. *Hutchinson* v. *York &c. Rw.*, 5 Ex., 353; *Wigget* v. *Fox*, 11 Ex., 837; *Ketgan* v. *Western Rw.*, 4 Selden, 175.

3. *Tarrant* v. *Webb*, 18 C.B., 805; *Frazer* v. *Penn. Rw.*, 38 Penn. St., 104; *Wright* v. *New York Central*, 28 Barb., 80; *Hurd* v. *Vermont & Canada Rw.*, 32 Vt., 473.

4. *Ormond* v. *Holland*, 1 El., Bl. & El., 102.

5. *Bartonshill Coal Co.* v. *Reid*, 3 Macq. H. L. Cas., 266; *Tarrunt* v. *Webb*, 18 C.B., 797; *Weems* v. *Mathieson*, 4 Macq., 215.

6. *Holmes* v. *Clark*, 6 H. & N., 349; 7 *ib.*, 937.

tion, but if he runs over the footman and disposes finally of that man of buttons, it is a matter of no importance. And in this case it will prove very hard on the poor family."

"Ah, well! judges and juries must not be drawn out of the path of duty even by their feelings for the widow and the orphan. The reason of the law is, that when a servant engages to serve a master he undertakes to run all the ordinary risks of the service, which includes, of course, the negligence of fellow servants acting in the discharge of their duty towards their common master.[1] If the rule was otherwise it might become very hard on the master; as Lord Abinger suggests, the footman who sits behind the carriage would have an action against his master if he came to grief through the negligence of the coachmaker or harness maker, or through the drunkenness, neglect or want of skill of the coachee; in fact the poor master would be liable to his servant for the negligence of the chambermaid, in putting him into a bed with damp sheets, whereby he took the rheumatism; for that of the upholsterer in sending him a crazy bedstead, whereby he fell down while asleep and injured himself; or for the negligence of the cook in not properly cleaning the copper vessels used in the kitchen, of the butcher in supplying the family with meat injurious to health, of the builder, for a defect in the foundation of the house whereby it fell, and injured both the master and the servants in its ruins."[2]

"But what is a fellow servant?"

"In England all the servants of the same person, or company, engaged in carrying forward the common enterprise—although in different departments, widely separated or strictly subordinated to others—are fellow servants and are bound to run the hazard of any negligence or wrong doing which may be committed by any of their number,[3] and it makes no difference that the negli-

---

1. *Morgan* v. *Vale of Neath Rw.*, L. R. 1 Q. B., 149.
2. *Priestly* v. *Fowler*, 3 M. & W., 1.
3. *Tunney* v. *Midland Rw.*, L.R., 1 C.P., 291; see also *Plant* v. *G. T. R.*, 27 U.C., Q. B., 78.

gence is imputed to a servant of superior authority, whose directions the other was bound to obey. But in some of the American cases, it has been held that employees, who are so far removed from each other as that the one is bound to obey the other, are not fellow servants within the rule;[2] other judges, however, have denied this qualification;[3] and now it seems settled that it is sufficient to bring the case within the general rule, if the servants are employed in the same general service,[4] or under the same general control."[5]

"All this may be very true, but then you see, my dear Eldon, my man was killed in consequence of the state of the track;" said Jones.

"Why in the name of all that is sacred and profane did you not remind me of that before. In one case a company was held responsible for an injury to one of its servants through the track being out of repair,[6] but in others it was considered that if the line was properly built and inspected it was all that could be required.[7] So you can draw your own conclusions, for I am getting tired of you."

"Well, I'm off, and am much obliged. But, oh, one point more before I leave you. One of the men was coming from Chicago and had a coupon ticket which he purchased at the station there, does that make any difference?"

"Through tickets do not import a contract with the purchaser on the part of the company selling to carry him beyond the limits of their own line: the coupons are to be considered as so

---

1. *Feltham* v. *England*, L.R., 2 Q.B., 33.
2. *Coon* v. *Syracuse & Utica Rw.*, 1 Selden, 492; *Louisville & N. Rw.* v. *Collins* 5 Am. Law Reg., U.S., 265·
3. *Farewell* v. *Boston & W. Rw.*, 4 Met., 49, 60; *Gillshannon* v. *Stoney Brook Rw.*, 10 Cush., 228; *Chicago & N. W. Rw.* v. *Jackson*, 55 Ill., 492.
4. *Wright* v. *N. Y. C.*, 25 N.Y., 552; and see *Baird* v. *Pettit*, 29 Phil. Rep., 397.
5. *Abraham* v. *Reynolds*, 5 H. & N., 142; *Hurd* v. *Vermont, &c.*, 32 Vt.. 475.
6. *Snow* v. *Housatonic Rw.*, 8 Allen, 441.
7. *Faulkner* v. *Erie Rw.*, 49 Barb., 324; *Warner* v. *Same*, 8 Am. Law Reg., N.S., 209.

many distinct tickets for each road, sold by the first company as agent for the others;[1] and each successive company is responsible for all injuries to through passengers while upon its own line and in passing to the next company's line.[2] The companies cannot be considered partners so as to render each liable for injuries or losses occurring upon the whole route."[3]

"Is not that different from the rule as to carrying goods and baggage, and the rule in England?"

"As to carriers of goods or baggage taking pay and giving checks or tickets through, the first company is ordinarily liable for the entire route;[4] and in England it has been decided[5] that where a railway company contracts to carry a passenger from one terminus to another, and on the journey the train has to pass over the line of another railway company, the company issuing the ticket incurs the same responsibility as that other company, over whose line the train runs and by whose default the accident happens, would incur if the contract to carry had been entered into by them. The company issuing the ticket is liable for the negligence of the servants of any other company over whose line the passenger has to pass to reach his journey's end; the contract with the passenger being the same whether the journey be entirely over the line of the first company, or partly over that of another company, and whether the passage over the other line be under an agreement to share profits or simply under running powers; and that contract is, not only that they will not be themselves guilty of any negligence, but that due care will be used in carrying the passengers from one end of the journey to the other, so far as is within the compass of railway management.[6] In fact the

---

1. *Sprague* v. *Smith*, 29 Vt., 421 ; *Hood* v. *N. Y. & N. H. Rw.*, 22 Conn., 1.
2. *Knight* v. *P. S. & P. R. Rw.*, 56 Me., 234 ; 2 Redf. Am. Rw. cases, 458.
3. *Ellsworth* v. *Tartt*, 26 Ala., 733.
4. *McCormick* v. *Hudson*, 4 E. D. Smith, 181.
5. *Great Western Rw.*, v. *Blake*, 7 H. & N., 987, Ex. Ch.
6. *Thomas* v. *Rhymney Rw. Co.*, L. R., 6 Q.B., 266, Ex. Ch. ; and *John* v. *Bacon*, L. R., 5 C.P., 437.

rule in regard to companies that run over other roads than their own seems now to be pretty well established and it is, that the first company is responsible for the entire route and must take the risk of the employees of the other companies;[1] and where another company has running powers over the first company's line, the first company is not liable for any injury arising through the negligence of such other company; though if it were a case of goods they would be liable, because they are then insurers."[2]

"I suppose in England you can only sue the company granting the ticket."

"Yes. I would just add, so that you may have an exhaustive discourse on the subject, that if mischief arises from the act of a stranger in leaving a log of wood across the railway, or doing any other act which might endanger a railway train passing along the line of another company, an action cannot be maintained against the railway company, because in that case there would not be any direct or undirect breach of duty, or breach of contract, on their part; they would not be liable on their own line, or on any other company's line for that; the same doctrine was held where a stranger had wilfully and maliciously placed a stone upon the track which threw off the train.[4] If, however, a man falls off the cars on to the track, because he has no proper place to sit and his body throws the train off, this will afford no excuse for damages to the man's luggage from such upsetting.[5] So, where the covetous greed of a young bullock induced him to

---

1. Redfield on Railways, vol. 2, 303; *Railway Co.* v. *Barron*, 5 Wall, 90; *Ayles* v. *S. E. Rw.*, L.R., 3 Ex., 146; *Birkett* v. *Whitehaven Junction Rw.*, 4 H. & N., 730; *Sprague* v. *Smith*, 9 Verm., 421, was an exceptional case.

2. *Wright* v. *Midland Rw.*, L.R., 8 Ex., 137.

3. *Mytton* v. *Midland Rw.*, 4 H. & N., 615; *Great Western Rw.* v. *Blake* 7 H. & N., 987, Ex. Ch.; *Weeds* v. *Saratoga Rw.*, 19 Wends., 534.

4. *Latch* v. *Rimmer Rw.*, 27 L·J., Ex., 155; see also *Cunningham* v. *Grand Trunk Rw.*, 31 U.C., Q.B., 350; *Curtis* v. *Rochester & Syracuse Rw.*, 18 N.Y., 534; *Teiriery* v. *Peppinger*, 1 Wallace, 543; *Thayer* v. *St. Louis, &c.*, 22 Ind., 26; *Pitts. Ft. Wayne & Chicago* v. *Maurer*, 21 Ohio, U.S., 421.

5. *Goldey* v. *Penn. Rw.*, 30 Penn. St., 242.

force his way through a hedge to gain some tempting grass that grew luxuriantly on the track, and the collision with him of the train hurt Mr. Buxton who was on board; and it appeared that B. had been a passenger on the defendants' railway to be carried from Y. to T., and to reach T. it was necessary to travel over the line belonging to another company, and while journeying over the latter line the affair of the bullock took place. The court held that the contract having been made with the defendants they were the proper parties to be sued. A new trial was, however, granted because the judge had directed the jury that, it was negligence in the defendants if the fences were insufficient: the court considering that there was no statutory obligation on the company, towards their passengers, to keep up the fences."[1]

"What would it have been if the bullock had jumped over the hedge instead of pushing through?" asked Jones.

"I don't understand." I returned.

"Why a case of cattle-lept-sy to be sure. Au revoir."

1. *Buxton v. North Eastern Rw.*, 3 Q.B., L.R., 549.

CHAPTER XI.

BAGGAGE AGAIN.

Epistolary model—Dog lost—Quitting a moving car—When liability for luggage commences—Goods of third party—Left in the car—Baggage lost—English rule—Limited liability—Personal luggage, what it is—Watch—Rings—Pistol—Railroad porter—Hotel 'bus—Tools and pocket pistols—Fiddles and merchandize—Farewell.

MY DEAR WIFE,

Your letter announcing your safe arrival at M——if indeed, you can be said to have arrived safely considering all that befell you, made me happy this a.m. The tale of your disasters was really quite amusing, and I have passed some of my lonely hours most agreeably considering the law on the various points.

So poor Fox is gone; doubtless the mangled remains of that poor cur lie stark and cold upon the railway line, and crows are gathering in the leaden skies to assist at his funereal obsequies; or, perchance, he may be gracing the board at some restaurant in the familiar form of sausages. You say it appears that he slipped his head through the noose of the string by which he was tied in the baggage car, if this be so the baggage man might have seen that he was not securely fastened; and it was his duty to lock him up, or otherwise keep him safely.[1] Make out your bill, dearest, we'll make the company pay. At what figure do you value him? (I had, however, better add that in a late case where a dog was fastened in the ordinary way, and there was nothing to show that he was likely to escape, the carrier was held

---

1. *Stuart* v. *Crawley*, 2 Stark, 324.

justified in trusting to the owner having properly secured the animal).[1]

Poor Miss Smith ought to have been more careful when she would insist upon going into the car to bid you a last adieu, even though her young man was waiting for her. She most certainly should not have attempted to leave the carriage after it was in motion, and when the conductor warned her not. Even if the conductor was to blame in negligently starting the train without the usual premonitory screech, and the unnecessary jerk assisted in the catastrophe, the company was not responsible; her conduct was the mere outcome of that perverseness which is the characteristic trait of the feminine nature.[2]

You never told me that Eliza Jane had taken her trunk to the station some half dozen hours before the train was to start; it was rather verdant of her so to do. I presume the desire to have a quiet drive with her John was the motive. The loss of her finery will teach her a lesson; however, it will not really matter, as she can recover the value of her "things," for the responsibility of the company as common carriers attaches as soon as their servants receive the baggage of the traveller at the proper place; and the giving of the check does not control the time of the responsibility attaching. The fact that you took and paid for her ticket will not prevent E. J. maintaining an action for her loss;[4] for it makes no difference whether a passenger pays her own fare, or some one else kindly does it for her.[5] In fact, if one is travelling on a free pass by which the company stipulates to be excused from all loss or damage, still they are responsible for the wilful or careless misconduct of their servants.[6]

1. *Richardson* v. *North Eastern Rw.*, L.R., 7 C.P., 75, note.
2. *Lucas* v. *Taunton & New Bedford Rw.*, 6 Gray, 64.
3. *Camden & Amboy Rw.* v *Belknap*, 21 Wendell, 354; *Hickox* v. *Naugatuck Rw.*, 31 Conn., 281.
4. *Marshall* v. *York, N. & B. Rw.*, 11 C.B., 655.
5. *Van Horn* v. *Kerniet*, 4 E. D. Smith, 453.
6. *Mobile & Ohio Rw.* v. *Hopkins*, 41 Ala., 486.

But, unfortunately, I fear that you must quietly submit to the loss of those things of yours which she had in her trunk, for the contract to carry was with her alone; the company thought that the trunk contained her luggage, if they had been told that it was not they might have objected to carry, considering the Saratogas you had, not to speak of bandboxes, bundles and parcels; and even if you had had no luggage yourself it would have been all the same;[1] and as they were not Eliza Jane's I don't suppose she can sue for them either.

And so that pretty dressing-case which I gave you on that memorable day when we twain became one flesh, is gone! you say that you put it under your seat in the car, and that it must have been left there when the porter carried your traps to the cab at your journey's end; well, I cannot say that placing it where you did was a very wise thing, still as another lady who once did the same in England recovered the value of her dressing-case, (although she failed to recover the case itself),[2] so doubtless if money will dry your tears for the loss of that memento of our wedding-day, you will be consoled. Probably the fact of your name and address not being on it will not affect your rights in the matter.[3] A railway company is liable for the loss of a passenger's luggage though carried in the carriage in which he himself is travelling.[4] Very special circumstances, and circumstances leading irresistibly to the conclusion that the traveller takes such personal control and charge of his luggage as to altogether give up all hold upon the company, are required before a court will say that the company as common carriers are not liable in the event of a loss.[1] Even if luggage is never given to a railroad servant but kept by the passenger in his own possession,

---

1. *Beecher* v. *G. E. Rw.*, L.R., 5 Q.B., 241.
2. *Richards* v. *London, B. & S. C. Rw.*, 7 C.B., 839.
3. *Campbell* v. *Caledonian Rw.*, 14 Ct. of Sess. Ca., 2 Ser., 806; 1 S. M. & P., 742.
4. *Le Couteur* v. *London & S. W. Rw.*, L.R., 1 Q.B., 54.
5. *Ibid.*

still in the eye of the law it is considered to be in the custody of the company, so as to render them responsible for the loss. In England, a railway company that receives goods or luggage, and books it for a certain place beyond the terminus of its road, is responsible for any evil that befalls it before its arrival at its journey's end, even though it happens while the goods are passing over the rails of another company;[2] in fact one has no remedy except against the company with whom the contract is made. But the justice and soundness of the English decisions have been seriously questioned by the American courts, who think that the carrier is only liable for the extent of his own route, and for safe storage, and safe delivery to the next carrier.[3] Many cases, however, follow the English ones, and others hold that the responsibility is only *prima facie*, and may be controlled by general usage among carriers, whether such usage be known to the traveller or not.[4] (But this subject is so mixed that I will show you what Judge Redfield says when you get back again).[5] Where different railways—forming a continuous line—run their cars over the whole line and sell tickets for the whole route, checking baggage through, an action lies against any company for the loss of baggage.[6]

Of course if there was any notice on your ticket limiting the liability of the company with regard to your traps, you are bound thereby, even if you never read it;[7] for railway companies, as well as other carriers, may limit their responsibility by special

---

1. *Great Northern Rw.* v. *Shepherd*, 8 Ex., 30; but see *Tower* v. *Utica & Sch. Rw.*, 7 Hill, N.Y., 47.
2. *Muschamp* v. *Lancaster & Preston Junction Rw.*, 8 M. & W., 421; *Watson* v. *Ambergate &c.*, 15 Jur., 448; *Bristol & Ex. Rw.* v. *Collins*, 7 Ho. Lords Ca., 194.
3. *Farmers' & Mechanics' Bank* v. *Champlain Trans. Co.*, 16 Vt., 52; 18 Vt., 131; 23 Vt., 186; *Van Lantvoord* v. *St. John*, 6 Hill, N.Y., 158.
4. *Southern Express Co.* v. *Shea*, 38 Ga., 519; *Cincinnati &c. Rw.* v. *Pontius*, 19 Ohio, U.S., 22.
5. Redfield on Railways, vol. 2., p. 126, *et seq.*
6. *Hart* v. *Rensselaer & Saratoga Rw.*, 4 Seld, 37.
7. *Zung* v. *South Eastern Rw.*, L.R., 4 Q.B., 539.

contract of which notice is given to the passenger or owner, and to which he assents or does not object, subject to such exception, limitation or qualification as reason and justice may require and a judge and jury decide with reference to each particular case.[1]

I don't exactly know what you had in that dressing-case of yours, but the rule is, "that whatever a passenger takes with him for his own personal care and convenience, according to the habits or wants of the particular class to which he belongs, either with reference to the immediate necessities or the ultimate purpose of the journey, must be considered as personal luggage" for the loss of which the carrier is liable;[2] and articles of jewellery such as a lady usually wears are considered personal luggage.[3] So is a watch;[4] though in Tennesee a watch was not deemed a proper part of necessary baggage.[5] Where was yours? So are finger rings. In one case a man was allowed to have two gold chains, two gold rings, a locket and a silver pencil-case;[7] so I will leave you to calculate how many a lady should be allowed to carry about with her. Your swell gold spectacles would also come within the category;[8] and by the way, that linen which you bought for my new shirt fronts would be included,[9] (if you were good enough to take it with you to make them up, and unfortunate enough

---

1. *Carr* v. *Lancashire & York Rw.*, 7 Ex., 707; Redfield on Railways, vol. 2., p. 101. Where the condition on ticket was "that the company does not hold itself responsible for any delay, detention, or other loss arising off its lines," and the baggage was never delivered to any other company, held that meaning of the last words was "out of the custody of the company." *Kent* v. *Midland Rw.*, Weekly Notes, Nov. 7, 1874.
2. Cockburn, C.J., in *Macrow* v. *Great Western Rw.*, L.R., 6 Q.B., 623; *Great Northern Rw.* v. *Shepherd*, 8 Ex., 38.
3. *Brooke* v. *Pickwick*, 4 Bing., 218; *McGill* v. *Roward*, 3 Penn. St., 451.
4. *Jones* v. *Voorhes*, 10 Ohio, 145; *Miss. C. Rw.* v. *Kennedy*, 41 Miss., 471.
5. *Bonner* v. *Maxwell*, 9 Humphrey, 621.
6. *McCormick* v. *Hudson River Rw.*, 4 E. D. Smith, 181.
7. *Bruty* v. *Grand Trunk Rw.*, 32 U.C., Q.B., 66.
8. *Re H. M. Wright*, Newberry Admiralty, 494.
9. *Duffy* v. *Thompson*, 4 E. D. Smith, 178.

to lose it); and that little present you were taking for your sister—perhaps.¹ I don't know what else you had in that case which will now know its place on our dressing table no more forever. Of course, your brushes, razors—*pardonnez moi, madame*, I forgot to whom I was writing—pen and ink &c., are fairly baggage within the meaning of the term.²

Not content with the abandonment of your dressing-case, you say you lost a bandbox by stupidly letting a porter carry it for you to a cab, which you could not afterwards find: well, if it is the custom on that line for the company's porters to assist passengers to obtain cabs, within the station grounds, and place their baggage therein, the company will be liable for this loss also. This my old friend Butcher satisfactorily established: he had a carpet-bag with him containing a large sum of money, and this he wisely kept in his own possession while journeying up to London. On arriving at the station there, however, he unwisely—even Jove sometimes nods—let a porter take it from him for the purpose of securing a cab. The porter put the bag in a fly and then returned to the platform to get my friend's other luggage. Meanwhile cabby disappeared and the bag and all that was therein was lost. The court considered the company liable as there had been a delivery of the bag to them to be carried, and no re-delivery to Butcher.³

Your next misfortune was the loss of that new book I gave you, wherewith to beguile the weariness of the way; you say you left it in the omnibus that took you up to the hotel; well, omnibus drivers who take passengers from the stations about the towns are unquestionably responsible as common carriers. Although in England it has been held that a cab-driver or hackney-coachman was not;⁵ still they are bound to use an

---

1. *Great Western Rw. v. Shepherd*, 8 Ex., 38.
2. *Hawkins v. Hoffman*, C. Hill, N.Y. Rep., 589.
3. *Butcher v. London & S. W. Rw.*, 16 C.B., 13.
4. *Peixotti v. McLaughlin*, 1 Strob., 468.
5. *Brind v. Dale*, 8 C. & P., 207; *Ross v. Hill*, 2 C.B., 887.

ordinary degree of care. If the hotel proprietor undertakes to provide free transit to and from the cars, and you lost your book in his 'bus, he is liable.[1]

Although it deeply pains me to find the slightest fault with my spouse, still I must say that I think that you have been a little careless during this trip; in fact you have shown that the character your mother gave you was not quite a libel, when she said that you would lose your head were it not securely fastened on, and your tongue were it not in incessant use.

While I am writing to you in this strain, I may as well give you a little further information concerning what you may, and what you may not, carry as personal baggage; though doubtless you will soon forget all that I say, or if not—at all events—will not heed it, such is the forgetfulness and perverseness of that sex whose love, as Prince Charles Edward said "is writ on water, whose faith is traced on sand."

Besides what I have already mentioned, if you are a sportsman you may take a gun, if a disciple of the gentle Izaak Walton, the necessary *instrumenta bella* ;[2] if you are a joiner —I don't mean a parson—you may take a reasonable amount of tools with your clothes,[3] although perhaps you can't;[4] you may take new clothing and materials for yourself and family, though not for others ;[5] if you are of a nervous disposition and desire to defend yourself against thieves and robbers you may take a pocket pistol—don't suppose I mean a brandy flask —if you are a bellicose man of honour a couple of duelling pistols will be allowed,[6] although in Maryland, one was not allow-

---

1. *Dickenson* v. *Winchester*, 4 Cush., 115.
2. *Macrow* v. *Great Western Rw.*, L.R., 6 Q.B., 623 ; *Hawkins* v. *Hoffman*, C. Hill, N.Y. Rep., 589.
3. *Porter* v. *Hildebrand*, T. Harris Henn. Rep., 129.
4. *Bruty* v. *Grand Trunk Rw.*, 32 U.C., Q.B., 66.
5. *Dexter* v. *S. B. & N. Y. Rw.*, 42 N.Y., 326.
6. *Woods* v. *Devon*, 13 Ill., 746 ; *Bruty* v. *G. T. Rw.*, 32 U C., Q.B., 66.

ed to take a colt.[1] A theatre goer may take an opera glass;[2] a student on his way to college, manuscripts necessary for the prosecution of his studies;[3] but an artist cannot carry his pencil sketches as luggage in England; although Cockburn, C. J., thought he could.[5] J. Wilson, in a Canadian case, thought that one musically inclined might take a concertina, or a flute, or that instrument in the playing of which a western writer says "the resined hair of the noble horse travels merrily over the intestines of the agile cat;"[6] but fortunately for mankind in general the majority of the court held otherwise.

You cannot carry merchandize, either in England,[7] the United States,[8] or the Dominion of Canada,[9] unless, indeed, it is carried openly, or so packed that the carrier can see what it is and does not object to it; nor samples, if you belong to the confraternity of commercial travellers;[10] nor can a banker take money as such;[11] nor can one carry silver spoons, nor surgical instruments, unless he is a disciple of Galen and Hippocrates.[12]

But really, my dear, I must draw these remarks to a close, as the parsons say in their sermons. You cannot complain that this letter is too short. There are several items of news—of babies born, brides be-wed, bodies buried—and such like trivialities, of which I might have told you; but as you spoke about your

1. *Giles* v. *Fauntleroy*, 13 Md., 126.
2. *Toledo & Wabash Rw.* v. *Hammond*, 33 Ind., 379.
3. *Hopkins* v. *Westcott*, 7 Am. Law Reg., U.S., 533.
4. *Mutton* v. *Midland Rw.*, 4 H. & N., 615.
5. *Macrow* v. *Great Western Rw.*, L.R., 6 Q.B., 623.
6. *Bruty* v. *Grand Trunk Rw.*, 32 U.C., Q.B., 66.
7. *Great Western Rw.* v. *Shepherd*, 8 Ex., 30; *Macrow* v. *Great Western*, supra.
8. *Pardee* v. *Drew*, 25 Wend., 459; *Collins* v. *Boston & Maine Rw.*, 10 Cush., 506.
9. *Shaw* v. *Grand Trunk Rw.*, 7 U.C., C.P., 493.
10. *Cahill* v. *London & N. W. Rw.*, 13 C.B., N.S., 818; *Belfast, B. L. & C. Rw.* v. *Keys*, Ho. Lords, Cas., 556; *Hawkins* v. *Hoffman*, 6 Hill, 586; *Dibble* v. *Brown*, 12 Ga., 217.
11. *Phelps* v. *London & N. W. Rw.*, 19 C.B., N.S., 321.
12. *Giles* v. *Fauntleroy*, 13 Md., 126.

losses I concluded that I would send you an instructive note, and let vain trifles rest quiescent until your return.

Though you may think that this epistle smacks somewhat of business, yet please reflect that you are my sleeping partner and spend the greater portion of the profits of my office, and so 'tis becoming that you should be slightly acquainted with legal matters, especially as you are the daughter of my mother-in-law.

Adu! adu! O reservoir!

Your
SPANISH GRANDEE.

CHAPTER XII.

TELEGRAMS AND FIRE.

Assault—Authority of officials—A dear kiss—Arresting passengers—Telegraphic messages—Interesting examples—Who can sue for mistake—Fire-fiend's pranks—Train arrives—Liability ceases—Trunks in warehouse—Baggage left at station—Dissolving domestic view.

WHEN the day arrived on which my wife was to return to me, I determined to go and meet her at N., so as to be on the spot to keep an eye on her baggage when she reached the station and avoid further loss and accident.

I bought my ticket and got into the proper car, but just as the train was on the point of starting I asked the porter if I was in the right carriage, he replied, I was not, and must get out; I hesitated, as the train was in motion, so he caught hold of me and violently pulled me out. We fell on the platform and I was considerably hurt, and what was as bad, the cars went on and left me behind. I went in search of the general superintendent of the line, as I was determined to seek redress, for a person who puts another in his place to do a class of acts in his absence necessarily leaves him to determine, according to the circumstances which arise, when an act of that class is to be done; consequently he is answerable for the wrong of the person so intrusted, either in the manner of doing such an act, or in doing such an act under circumstances in which it ought not to have been done; provided that what is done is not done from any caprice of the servant, but in the course of the employment.[1] And in a similar case it was held that the act of the porter, in pulling a man out of the carriage, was an act done within the course of his employment as the

---

1. *Bayley* v. *Manchester &c.*, L.R., 7 C.P., 415.

company's servant, and one for which they were therefore responsible.[1]

Railway companies are liable for all the acts of their servants and agents committed in the discharge of their business and their employment, within the range of such employment, whether wilful or negligent.[2] The injured person has to show that his assailant was not only a servant of the company, but that he had authority so to treat him, or that such conduct was subsequently ratified by the company;[3] although the daily press asserts that a jury gave a verdict of $1,000 against the Chicago and North Western Railway because a conductor of theirs wrongfully and without their order or approval kissed and caressed a young lady passenger.

A railway is supposed to have at their stations officers with authority to do all such things as are necessary and expedient for the protection of the company's property and interests, and for the apprehension of wrong doers; and where there are persons present who are acting as if they had express authority, it is *prima facie* evidence that they had such authority;[4] and the company will be answerable if their officers, in the exercise of their discretion, make a mistake and apprehend an innocent person, or commit an assault through an excess of duty, or do any other act that cannot be justified.[5] And it makes no difference with regard to the responsibility of the company that the servant disobeyed the directions of his superiors, if he was acting within the scope of his employment at the time.[6] But when he does an act which he has no authority to do, the company is not

---

1. *Bayley* v. *Manchester, &c.*, L.R., 7 C.P., 415.
2. *Derby* v. *Phil. & Read. Rw.*, 14 Howard, 468; *Noyes* v. *Rutland & Burl. Rw.*, 27 Vt., 110; *Yarborough* v. *Bank of England*, 16 East., 6.
3. *Roe* v. *Birkenhead & Lancaster Rw.*, 7 W. H. & G., 36.
4. *Goff* v. *Northern Rw.*, 3 E. & E., 672.
5. *Giles* v. *Taff Vale Rw.*, 2 E. & B., 822; *Moore* v. *Metropolitan Rw.*, L.R., 8 Q.B., 36.
6. *Phil. & Read. Rw.* v. *Derby* 14 How., U.S., 468.

liable;[1] nor are they when he does an act which the company themselves have no authority to do.[2] And thus a seeming paradox arose in one case where a station master arrested a man for not paying the fare of a horse he had with him, and it was held that (as the company itself could not have done so) the company was not liable, though had the zealous official arrested him for not paying his own fare, damages might have been recovered against the company.[3]

Thus ruminating over my wrongs and chewing the bitter cud of hatred and malice, I found my way into the office of the chief official, but as that important functionary was *non est*, I had to nurse my wrath until some more convenient season.

Just then a friend came up and shewed me a telegram which seemed perfectly enigmatical and worthy of the Sphinx of yore, and we thus got speaking concerning such messages (or as they are often rightly called tell-o-crams). He asked me if I had ever noticed the case where a gentleman telegraphed for *two hand* bouquets, and the operator changed *hand* into *hund* and added *red*, making the order for "Two hundred bouquets." The florist delighted at the extensive order, procured a quantity of expensive flowers, which the other party of course refused to accept, so the poor flower-man had to sue the company for damages, which he recovered,[4] as well on the ground of breach of contract, as of breach of duty, the telegraph company being public servants.

"I believe that where the company gives notice that they will not be responsible except for repeated messages, such a condition will be held good," I said.

"Yes.[5] There have been several cases shewing the damage which the company will have to pay for mistakes in the perfor-

---

1. *Edwards* v. *London & N. W. Rw.*, L.R., 5 C.P., 445.
2. *Poulton* v. *London & S. W. Rw.*, L.R., 2 Q.B., 534.
3. *Ibid.*
4. *N. Y. & Wash. Print. Tel. Co.* v. *Dryburgh*, 35 Penn., 298.
5. *McAndrew* v. *Electric Tel. Co.*, 17 C.B., 3; *Waun* v. *Western &c. Tel. Co.*, 37 Mo. 472.

mance of their duty : in one where a merchant sent the message 'Stop sewing pedal braid till I see you,' and it was delivered 'Keep sewing, &c., &c.,' and in consequence a large quantity of unfashionable braid was manufactured which the merchant received and disposed of in the best manner. He was held entitled to recover the whole loss sustained in consequence of the error;[1] and it was so held where the message was changed from '5,000 sacks of salt,' into 5,000 casks."[2]

"How is the law in England?"

"It has been held there, and in Canada, that the party employing the telegraph company, or sending the message on his own account, is the only party who can maintain an action for any failure to perform their duty in respect of the message.[3] And where a message was sent for *three rifles* and when received it read *the rifles*, and the plaintiff supposing it referred to a former communication sent the sender of the despatch 50 rifles, the number before named; and these were refused; the plaintiff sued the sender for the price, but the Court held that the defendant was not responsible for the mistake in transmitting the message, and that the plaintiff could only recover for three rifles.[4] The American jurists think that the English Courts are guilty of an inconsistency, if not of a blunder, in holding that the only party who can sue the company is not responsible for the mistake. They say that the party who suffers by the mistake should, at all events, be allowed to maintain an action to recover the damage sustained by him; and they say that is the rule throughout the republic."[5]

"It seems to be the law that the regulations of a telegraph company relieving them from liability, unless the message is repeated, are reasonable, and will free them from the effects of many

1. *Lockwood* v. *Ind. Line of Tel. Co.*, N.Y., C.P.. 1865.
2. *Rittenhouse* v. *The same*, 1 Daly, C.P., 474.
3. *Playford* v. *United Kingdom Tel. Co.*, L.R., 4 Q.B., 706 ; *Feaver* v. *Montreal Tel. Co.*, 23 U.C., C.P., 130.
4. *Hankel* v. *Pape*, L.R., 6 Ex., 7.
5. Redfield on Railways, vol. 2, p. 314.

mistakes;[1] but they will not be construed so as to release the company from liability occasioned by their own wilful misconduct or negligence,[2] as where *our* was changed into *your*,[3] or the message was never sent,[4] or delayed in delivery,[5] there must, however, be proof of negligence distinct from the infirmities of telegraphing."[6]

"But suppose one is not aware of these rules and regulations?"

"To prevent one recovering they must be brought home to his knowledge;[7] but he will be presumed to know what is on the blank used, and to make the conditions thereon his own, whether he read them or not."[8]

Thus chatting with my friend about the law and the profits thereof, occasionally indulging in the luxury of that odious weed of the great Sir Walter Raleigh, and frequently practising the bibulistic art, the time passed rapidly and pleasantly enough, and at length the shrill ear-piercing screech of a locomotive announced the arrival of the train, containing, as Horace neatly puts it, *animæ dimidium meæ*, or as ordinary folks say "my better half." After the usual osculatory exercises, I inspected the amount of her bandboxes, bundles, satchels and checks, and concluded that it would be useless to expect a cabby to carry home such a vast amount of baggage, and at well nigh the noon of night it would be equally vain to endeavour to obtain the services of a carter; so, knowing that travellers have a reasonable time to claim and remove their baggage, I determined to leave it at the station for the night.

1. *McAndrew* v. *Electric Tel. Co.*, 17 C.B., 3; but see *Tyler* v. *W. U. Tel. Co.*, 5 Chi. Leg. News, 550.
2. *N. Y. & Wash. Tel. Co.* v. *Dryburgh*, 35 Penn. St., 298 ; *True* v. *International Tel. Co.*, 60 Maine; *Sweetland* v. *Illinois &c. Tel. Co.*, 27 Iowa, 432.
3. *Seilers* v. *W. U. Tel. Co.*, 3 Am. Law Reg., 777.
4. *Birney* v. *N. Y. & Wash. Tel. Co.*, 18 Maryland, 341.
5. *U. S. Tel. Co.* v. *Gildersleeve*, 29 Maryland, 232; *Bryant* v. *Am. Tel. Co.*, 1 Daly, 575.
6. *Ellis* v. *Am. Tel. Co.*, 13 Allen, 226; and *Wann* v. *West. U. Tel. Co.*, 37 Mo., 472.
7. *Camp* v. *West. Union Tel. Co.*, 1 Met., 164.
8. *West. Union Tel. Co.* v. *Carew*, 15 Mich., 525.

With the checks clinking together in my pocket and my wife by my side, and Eliza Jane in front of me, I drove home comfortably, thinking that in the morning the checks would bring forth the trunks; but alas! I leant upon a broken reed, and ere the morrow's light appeared the baggage and my right to recover for its loss had vanished forever and ever, like a morning mist before the rising sun.

A fire broke out at the station and favoured by the winds of heaven it grew into a mighty conflagration, and before the morning watch the devouring element had consumed the station and all that therein was.

After a visit to the charred and smouldering ruins of the once handsome depot—my numerous enquiries having confirmed my worst fears as to the total loss of my wife's apparel—I returned to my office to consult the law on the subject, before I encountered her ladyship with the direful news of the antics of the Fire Fiend. There I quickly found that after a reasonable time and opportunity to take away his baggage has been given to a traveller, the company's responsibility as carriers ends : they are no longer responsible for its absolute security, but degenerate into mere warehousemen bound to exercise only that care which a prudent man ordinarily does in keeping his own goods of a similar kind and value;[1] and that care is exercised by the company placing the goods in a secure warehouse;[2] or, as a Canadian Chief Justice of high repute and great experience says, "the terminus of the transport being reached, the duty of the common carrier is fulfilled by placing the goods in a safe place, alike safe from the weather and from danger of loss or theft."[3] It was perfectly clear that the company was not responsible to me for

---

1. *Shepherd* v. *Bristol & Ex. Rw.*, L.R., 5 Ex., 189 ; *Mote* v. *Chicago & N. W. Rw.*, 1 Am. Rep., 212 ; 27 Iowa, 22 ; *Burwell* v. *N. Y. C.*, 45 N. Y., 187 ; *Rock Island & Pacific Rw.* v. *Fairclough*, 52 Ill., 106.

2. *Bartholemew* v. *St. Louis, Jacksonville, &c.*, 53 Ill., 227.

3. *Inman* v. *Buffalo & L. H. Rw.*, 7 U.C., C.P., 325 ; *O'Neill* v. *Great Western Rw., Ibid.*, 287 ; *Bowie* v. *Buffalo, Brantford & G. Rw., Ibid.*, 191.

the loss of my baggage,[1] through the foul pranks of the fire-fiend. And it would have been just the same if it had been stolen from the warehouse; or if on the arrival of the train I had taken possession of the trunks, and afterwards for my own convenience handed them back to the baggage-master at the station to be kept until sent for, and they had come to grief or been pilfered;[2] unless, indeed, there was some gross negligence on the part of the company. And I found by my books that it is the duty of the company to have the baggage ready for delivery upon the platform, at the usual place, until the owner may with due diligence call for, and receive it; and that it is the owner's duty to call for and remove it within a reasonable time; and that "reasonable time" is directly upon the arrival of the train, making a reasonable allowance for delay caused by the crowded state of the depot at the time; but that the lateness of the hour makes no difference if the baggage be put upon the platform.[4] Or if the traveller does not choose to call and take away his *impedimenta*, (as Julius Cæsar calls it), the company do all they need by putting it into their baggage room and keeping it for him, with the liability of ordinary warehousemen.

Thus conscious that I should wring nothing from the iron grasp of the railway company, and that out of my own professional earnings I should have to replenish my wife's wardrobe, I went home sad, down-cast and dejected to break the direful news to her.

Scarcely had I entered my house, which had been so peaceful and calm during the past few weeks, when my *alter ego* flew at me with a perfect storm of words and questionings as to why her trunks had not yet come up, and assertions that she had literally

---

1. *Roth* v. *Buffalo & State Line Rw.*, 34 N.Y., 548.
2. *Penton* v. *Grand Trunk Rw.*, 28 U.C., Q.B., 367; *Campbell* v. *The same*, Hilary Term, 1873, Ont.
3. *Minor* v. *Chicago & North Western Rw.*, 19 Wis., 40.
4. *Ouimet* v. *Henshaw*, 35 Vt., 60 .

nothing to wear. (Though to the eyes of an ordinary mortal she appeared far from being *in puris naturalibus.)*

When I told of the fate that had befallen her paraphernalia the storm increased into a hurricane, and when it was announced that the company were not liable, a perfect tornado—a cyclone—a typhoon—a simoon—of words, whirled with terrific fury around my head, then a perfect waterspout shot forth; and I, remembering suddenly an appointment down town, vanished from the scenes, resolved that henceforth both myself and my amiable— but hysterical—spouse would eschew the iron horse and his train as much as possible.

BOOK SECOND.—BY STAGE.

CHAPTER I.

EVERYTHING MUST BE SOUND, AND EVERYONE CAREFUL.

The reason why—Literature of stages—Off on wheels—Soundness warranted—Seats taken—Fare paid, either first or last—Damage to trunks—Involuntary aeronautics—Passengers injured—Negligence of passengers, or of drivers—Carrier liable for smallest fault—Not insurers—Genuine accidents—Horses left standing—Driving and upsetting a friend—Pleasures of the weed and rural life.

THE long vacation was rapidly approaching—that season when the heat having lengthened out the days (as it does everything else), the members of the legal profession abandon rejoinders and demurrers, cast briefs and records, with physic, to the dogs, and, satisfied with bills and conveyances, wander off in search of change in cooling streams and pastures green. In my modest household was eagerly discussed the question, " Whither shall we flee ?" The solemn vows that we had taken not to commit our persons or chattels to the step-mother-care of a railway company, shut us off from the usual means of exit from our inland city, and as "*Exeunt omnes*" was the cry, we could not surely stay at home; if we did we would have to lie low in the kitchen and back premises, that we might appear to others to be away. At last I found that there was still a tumble-down old stage-coach making, with the assistance of two skeleton horses, tri-weekly trips to and from the little Village of Ayr, where we could catch a steamboat and thus do in proper style the Lakes and the St. Lawrence, the Ottawa and the far-famed Saguenay.

When this discovery of mine was divulged at home, great was the rejoicing, loud pæans arose, and for days I was deluged with quotations from all the novelists, from old Fielding to poor Dickens anent stages, and coaches, and stage-coaches; I was told of all the heroes of romance, from Tom Brown back to Tom Jones, who had journeyed thereby; I was confidently informed, on the authority of Mr. William Makepeace Thackeray, that in every coach there is sure to be found an asthmatic old gentleman, a fat man, swelling preternaturally with great coats, and snoring indecently, and a lone widow who insists upon all the windows being shut, and fills the vehicle with the fumes of rum which she sucks perpetually from a black bottle. Mr. Thomas Hughes was quoted to prove how much more punctual stages are than railway-trains, for he tells of one that went "ten miles an hour, including stoppages, and so punctual that all the road set their watches by her." The old joke concerning the young man who, on being asked if he had ever been through Euclid, replied, "Yes, I have driven through it on a stage-coach," was given to me once again as if uttered for the first time; and I was informed that an Indian squaw, the first time she saw a coach pass at a spanking trot, and watched the wheels revolving rapidly, clapped her hands in delight, exclaiming, "Run, little one, run! or the big one will catch you!" The subject gradually became monotonous.

At length, however, the day of our departure dawned.

When the coach drove up to the door, at sight of the dusty tumble-down conveyance, my wife—true to her woman's nature—was half-inclined to decline to trust her precious self therein, but as I had paid our fares when booking our places—the driver having asked for the money, as he had a perfect right to do[1]—and as I assured her every stage-coach proprietor warrants that his stage is sufficiently secure to perform the journey proposed, and is bound to examine his vehicles every day, and if he does not is responsi-

1. Chitty on Contracts, 292.

ble for accidents,[1] she consented to start; although I could see from her expression of countenance that the ideal coach which she had been fondly cherishing was very different to the one into which we entered. Our luggage was mounted on top, and soon we were rumbling down the street to pick up other passengers, as we were numbers one and two. A sudden stop to mend some broken harness called forth an exclamation of disgust from the fair being beside me, and a remark from myself to the effect that she need not be anxious, as the owner was responsible that all the equipments of the conveyance, drivers, horses, harness were fit and suitable.[2]

In a few minutes we drew up at the door of a large mansion, from which quickly emerged four old maids; they drew back in horror when they saw my pantaloons, one exclaiming—

"Driver, we engaged the whole inside of the coach, and there's a man in it."

"Yes, mum," said John, "but one of you can sit outside along of me for a bit, the gentleman is not going far."

"You have no right to separate us;[3] or let other persons get inside," replied number one, waxing wrathy.

"No, indeed," chorused the others.

"Ladies," I said, "I will be most happy to give up my place and ride outside; the driver should have told me that the inside had been engaged, and then myself and my wife would have waited until some other day."

"Well," quoth the driver, "the ladies had not paid for the seats, and we were not bound to keep them for them."[4]

With withering sarcasm the eldest maid replied, "Here is your money, sir."

1. *Bremmer* v. *Williams*, 1 C. & P. 414; *Sharp* v. *Gray*, 9 Bing., 457.
2. *Crofts* v. *Waterhouse*, 3 Bing., 321; *Jones* v. *Boyce*, 1 Stark., 493; *Stokes* v. *Saltonhall*, 13 Peters, 181; *Ingalls* v. *Bills*, 9 Metcalf, 1.
3. *Long* v. *Horne*, 1 C. & P., 611.
4. *Ker* v. *Mountain*, 1 Esp., 27.

If a look could have annihilated a coachee never again would that man have mounted a box, or handled the ribbons, after the Medusa glance he then received. I emerged from the inside into which the ladies stowed themselves and several parcels, packages and bandboxes, while several boxes of larger growth, containing their staple goods were hoisted up aloft. After picking up a man we rattled off down the street into the open country.

The last comer had not as yet paid his fare and, at the first stopping place he was asked for it; but he demurred saying, that, as he had not prepaid the fare, it was not due until the whole journey was completed.

"You will have to leave the stage then," said the collector.

"I'll do nothing of the kind," returned the other, "and if you force me off it will be at your peril, for your driver permitting me to commence the journey without prepayment is an acquiescence in my riding to the end before paying up, so you may *howl and swear as much as you like.*"[1]

At this the man of fares subsided, and we resumed our slow jog-trot without any diminution of numbers. The jolting of our vehicle soon caused one of the trunks belonging to one or other of the four sisters to gape and yawn in a manner which exposed the contents thereof in a way which would doubtless have caused the fair owner to blush to the roots of her hair (if it was her own she wore), and it appearing probable that articles of feminine apparel would soon be scattering themselves over the dusty road, and knowing that, the box not having been securely and properly packed and fastened, the carrier would not be liable for any loss or damage happening to it,[2] I persuaded the driver to stop until the mischief could be remedied; for such an injury would vex a saint, much more a shrew of her impatient humour; with much grumbling he consented, and all was soon made taught and right.

---

1. *Howland* v. *Brig Lavinia*, 1 Peters Adm. 126 ; *Detouches* v. *Peck*, 9 Johnson, 210.
2. *Walker* v. *Jackson*, 10 M. & W., 101.

To make up for lost time, we now rushed ahead at a terrific pace, considering the clumsy, cumbrous, jingling, jerking concern in which we were travelling. The ladies within cried one and all:

"Oh, do be careful—don't go so fast." And I, in admonitory tones, told the driver that we would hold him liable for any injuries that might happen to either ourselves or our baggage, in consequence of his racing in such an improper manner.[1]

"All right," said he, "I'm responsible, and I am master too, here; so I'll do just what I like."

Scarce had he uttered these words when we drew near a large spreading tree, standing in the middle of the road: at a glance I saw that the coach must pass under the outstretched branches, and that they were so low that they would assuredly sweep the top of the stage clear of luggage and whatsoever else was thereupon, and unfortunately I myself was thereupon: I had no choice left but to jump off or remain in certain peril; mindful of my early performances in the gymnasium, of the two threatening evils I chose what appeared the least, and as the foremost twigs took off the hat of the driver (who was considerably below where I was perched) I sprang to the ground, and, as if in rage at my escape, the giant forest tree hurled two or three trunks after me—one came with a thud upon my foot and bruised it rather badly.

Of course the ladies screamed loudly as they saw me flying in a graceful parabolic curve through the azure air: the driver as rapidly as possible pulled up his old horses. Some loud conversation took place between myself and the man, interspersed with ejaculations more vigorous than religious, he contending that I had only myself to thank for my injuries, as—if I had bent low enough—I would not have been touched by the tree.

"All very true," I replied, "if I had been the size of the little husband no bigger than a thumb what was put into a quart pot

---

1. *Mayor* v. *Humphries*, 1 C. & P., 251; *Gough* v. *Bryan*, 5 Dowl., 765.

and made to beat a drum; but Mr. Thomas Thumb himself, if he had been on top, could not have escaped from that tree. However, your master is liable to me for the injuries I have received."[1]

"No, he isn't," surlily replied the Jehu, "because I say if you had staid quiet you would not have been hurt."

"Even if that were so, it would make no difference, as I entertained a well founded apprehension of being decapitated by that ugly branch."[2]

I argued not, however, with the man, but limping back to the coach, remounted to my elevated seat, accompanied by the prayers and entreaties of my wife, not to blight her young life by exposing myself to any more such frightful risks outside, but to come within where she was sure there was plenty of room; but I preferred the fresh air and fine view aloft to the close musty smell and narrow field of vision down below.

When again under way, my fellow passenger, who by sitting on the box with the driver, had avoided the collision, began to tell me of his grandmother, one Mistress Elizabeth Dudley, who on one occasion was an outside passenger to the Cross Keys, Chelsea. When in front of the gateway leading to the stable-yard of that inn, the coachman requested the travellers to alight, as the passage into the yard was awkward; as Mrs. Dudley did not wish to soil her pumps in the dirty road, she said she would rather be driven into the yard. Coachee told her to stoop, and then lashed up his horses. The coach was 8 feet 9 in. high, and the archway only 9 feet 9 in., and Betsy not being able to squeeze herself into the interstice of twelve inches, received a severe injury by having her back and shoulders knocked against the archway; she recovered, however, with £100 damages.[3]

I said: "Of course, to excuse the driver from responsibility, it

---

1. *Ingalls* v. *Bills*, 9 Met., 1; *Stokes* v. *Saltonhall*, 13 Pet. (U.S.), 181; *Frink* v. *Potter*, 17 Ill., 406.
2. *Jones* v. *Boyce*, 1 Stark., 493.
3. *Dudley* v. *Smith*, 1 Camp., 167.

must always be shown that the plaintiff was guilty of negligence which contributed directly to the injury.[1] I remember one case where a man was asked by the driver to ride inside a coach, and told that if he remained outside it would be at his own risk; he treated both the request and the advice with silent contempt, and being injured by the overturning of the carriage, sued the owners and got damages, as it appeared that the accident occurred from the negligence of the driver, and that the position of the obstreperous man in no way contributed to it."[2]

"It is clearly settled," returned my new made acquaintance, "that a driver, or his master, although he does not warrant the absolute safety of his passengers is, nevertheless, answerable for the smallest negligence;[3] and that the proprietor is also responsible for all defects in the coach, even though they be out of sight and not discoverable upon an ordinary examination, as a *sharp* fellow once proved."[4]

"An American, however, *in gall* and bitterness was told by a Court, that carriers are not liable for injuries happening through hidden defects which could not from the most careful and thorough examination be discovered."[5]

"Yes," interrupted my friend, "but in the State of Illinois, a *Potter*, who owned a stage-coach, was held liable for an injury to a passenger, which resulted from the breaking of an axletree, through the effect of frost."[6]

"Long ago the Courts in England held that a man established a *prima facie* case by proving his taking passage in a coach, his coming to grief while in it, and the injury he sustained; and then that the proprietor must show, if he could, that his vehicle was as

1. *Colegrove* v. *N. Y. & Harlem &c.*, Rw. 6 Duer., 382.
2. *Keith* v. *Pinkham*, 43 Maine, 501; *Lackawana Rw.* v. *Cheneworth*, 52 Penn. St., 382.
3. *Harris* v. *Costar*, 1 C. & P., 636; *Christie* v. *Griggs*, 2 Camp., 79.
4. *Sharp* v. *Gray*, 9 Bing., 457.
5. *Ingalls* v. *Bills*, 9 Met., 1.
6. *Frink* v. *Potter*, 17 Ill., 406.

good as a vehicle could be, and that the driver was as skilful a handler of the reins as could be found."[1]

"Yes, as Best, C. J., once said, a coachman must have competent skill and must use that skill with discretion; he must be well acquainted with the road he undertakes to drive; he must be provided with steady horses, a coach and harness of sufficient strength and properly made, and also with lights by night. If there be the least failure in any one of these things the duty of the proprietor is not fulfilled, and he is answerable for any injury or damage that happens;[2] he also is so unless the driver exercised a sound discretion at the time of an accident; if he could have exercised a sounder judgment or better discretion than he did, as by driving slower or faster, or by telling his passengers to dismount at a dangerous or difficult place, the owner must make compensation."[3]

"Fortunately, however, for the pockets of carriers they are not considered as actual insurers of the safety of those who intrust their precious bodies to them. Accidents will happen in the best regulated concerns, and it appears to be settled that when they do occur where there is *no* negligence or default, the law will protect carriers from the demands of injured ones."[4]

"Oh, yes, that is a well-established doctrine, and many cases might be quoted to sustain it. Where, for instance, on a dark night the lights were obscured by a fog, or the coachman without any fault of his gets off the road."[5]

"And also," I chimed in, "where extreme cold prevented the driver doing his duty;[6] and where the reflection of the sun upon falling water frightened the horses so that they ran away and

1. *Christie* v. *Griggs*, 2 Camp., 79
2. *Crofts* v. *Waterhouse*, 3 Bing., 319 ; *Farrish* v. *Reigle*, 11 Gratt., 697.
3. *Stanton* v. *Weller*, Hil. Term., 6 Vict., U. C.
4. *Aston* v. *Heaven*, 2. Esp., 533.
5. *Crofts* v. *Waterhouse*, 3 Bing., 321.
6. *Stokes* v *Saltonhall* 13 Peters, 181.

knocked things into pie;[1] and where an axle-tree that was sound and perfect snapped asunder.[2] And where a sleigh or a carriage upsets through mere accident and without culpable neglect on the part of the driver—as where he had been driving along a track in a ditch to take advantage of the small modicum of snow remaining and in turning on to the road again got into a hidden hole and upset—and the horses escape from the hands of the Jehu, and run away and do mischief to the person or property of other people; though undoubtedly the owner would be liable where there was clear negligence on the part of himself or driver which led to the carriage being overturned and the escape of his horses.[3] If a man has carelessly left his horses standing on the highway, while he is drinking or loafing in a tavern, and the horses run away and commit an injury the right to recover damages is clear.[4] But where a pony and chaise were left standing in the street without any person to take care of them, and afterwards the pony was seen running away with the chaise and those who saw the runaway did not know the cause of the starting. The owner of the turnout, however, proved that his wife was holding the nag by the bridle, when a Punch and Judy show coming up frightened the pony, which breaking from the lady ran off, and Lord Denman in charging the jury, said: 'If the facts are true as suggested by the defence I very much think you will be disposed to consider this an inevitable accident, one which the defendants could not prevent.'"[5]

"Of course if one gentleman when out driving offers another a seat in his carriage, he is not liable at all for an accident afterwards occurring; unless, indeed, it were of a gross description; and, as nothing is more usual than for accidents to happen in driving,

1. *Aston* v. *Heaven*, sup.
2. *Parker* v *Flagg*, 26 Maine, 181 : Add. on Contr., 495.
3. *Robinson* v. *Bletcher*, 15. Q. B. (U. C.), 160.
4. *Id.*
5. *Goodman* v. *Taylor*, 5. C. & P., 410.

without any want of care on the part of the driver, no *prima facie* presumption of negligence is raised when an accident does occur, so the injured one must give affirmative evidence of gross negligence on the part of his obliging friend."

"Oh, yes; that is well settled by a case where the Privy Council reversed the decision of the Supreme Court of Victoria. A gentleman was conveying the plaintiff, who was a decorator and gardener in his employ, to perform for him certain work. The defendant, the gentleman, drove, and while on the road the king-bolt broke, the horses bolted, the carriage was overturned, the plaintiff thrown out and stunned; and when the man came to himself the horses and forewheels of the buggy had vanished. There being no evidence of gross negligence the decorator had to bear his injuries and bruises unavenged.[1] One cannot fairly be expected to examine very strictly and carefully the state of the bolts and fastenings of his carriage every time he goes out with it."[2]

"By the way," said my companion, "your own right to recover is perfectly clear, for I am sure that I have seen in some place or other that where a woman was jolted off a stage and had her leg fractured by some luggage that was thrown on it, she was successful in a suit against the owners of the vehicle."[3]

"Thanks for the information," I replied, "I did not know that there was a case so exactly on all fours with my own."

"A little research nowadays will enable one to find a decision on almost every possible point the mind of man can conceive, so great is the number of the reports now accumulating with fearful rapidity upon the shelves of law libraries. Verily of the making of many law-books there is no end. Do you smoke?"

And he added to the effect of his question by handing me a well filled case of choice cheroots. Soon we were both lazily puffing at our cigars and dreamily enjoying ourselves as we drove

---

1. *Moffatt App.* v. *Bateman Resp.* L. R. 3 P. C. App., 115.
2. *Ibid.*
    Curtis v. *Drinkwater*, 2 B. & Ad., 169.

along past woodland and meadow, up hill and down, over sparkling, bubbling streamlets, beside fields of waving grain.

The day was charming; the heat of the July sun was tempered by a cooling breeze which blew softly upon us as we journeyed; the dust had been laid to rest by the sprinkling of an early shower; the birds carolled gaily amid their leafy bowers; here and there the squirrel peeped forth from his hiding-place and chattered at us as we passed or raced ahead along the zig-zag fence; at one moment fluttered by a

> Butterfly ranging on his yellow wings
> A primrose gone alive with joy, to dance with living things;

then came large white ones "which looked as if the May-flower had caught life, and palpitated forth upon the winds."

And my friend dreamily muttered, "Would that I were an insect! Fancy the fun of tucking one's-self up for a night in the leaves of a rose and being rocked to sleep by the gentle sighs of summer air; and having nothing to do when you awake but to wash yourself in a dewdrop and then eat your bed-clothes."

Ever and anon we heard the truly rural sounds of the whetstone against the sythe and the lowing of the kine, or the plaintive cry of some wandering lamb; all these arcadian sights and sounds acted as a gentle lullaby upon our senses already soothed by nicotine. And we slept.

CHAPTER II.

NEARLY DRIVEN TO DEATH, AND HOW TO PASS.

Narrow escape—Look out for the locomotive when the bell rings—Railway not liable when driver in fault—On the wrong side—The laws of the road—Fatal indecision—Lien on trunks—Reflections on lawyers.

WE had a sharp awakening from our calm repose; a shrill cry of "Stop," a jerk that nearly threw us to the ground as the driver reined in his horses, the wild fierce screech of an engine, the rumbling roar of a train as it dashed by, recalled us effectually from our wanderings in Dream-land to the fact that we had been near a sudden and a fearful death. The driver had been nodding sleepily on his box and had not noticed that we were so near a railway crossing, and so had not looked out for the train: and when aroused the horses' feet were actually upon the track and the cars but some seventy yards distant; the train as it rushed past almost scraped the horses' noses, so little had he been able to back them. On looking round I saw that the track must have been visible for some time before we came upon it, and one of the ladies said that she had heard a whistle a few seconds previously.

Of course, as might be expected, we all launched forth against Master Coachee, who was too frightened to reply. I said:

"Don't you know that you are bound to keep your eyes open? It is your duty, and a duty dictated by common sense and prudence, on approaching a crossing, to do so carefully and cautiously, both for the sake of your own passengers and those travelling by rail."[1]

---

1. *Nicholls* v. *Gt. Western Rw.*, 27 U. C., Q B., 393; *Boggs* v. *Great Western Rw. Co.*, 23 U. C., C. P., 573; *Ellis* v. *Gt. Western Rw. Co.*, L. R., 9 C. P., 551; *Johnston* v. *Northern Rw. Co.*, 34 U.C., Q.B., 432; *Penn. Rw. Co.* v. *Beale*, 9 Can. L.J., N.S., 298.

"Yes," chimed in my friend; "Chief Baron Pollock says, that a railway track *per se* is a warning of danger to those about to go upon it, and cautions them to see whether a train is coming."[1]

"One must judge and act reasonably in crossing a track," I continued. "One must not blindly and wilfully drive upon it whether there is danger to be apprehended from his doing so or not. If one wilfully goes upon the line of rails, as you were about to do, when danger is imminent and obvious, and sustains damage, he must bear the consequences of his own rashness and folly.[2] In fact, of late it seems to have been held that a man crossing a railway where there are no gates or flag-men must stop, listen and keep a sharp look out for the trains."[3]

"And," quoth my new friend, "a traveller is not exonerated from the duty of looking up and down the rails before going upon them, by reason of the engineer omitting to ring the bell or blow the whistle; nor is the company in such a case liable for injuries,[4] unless it is shown that the engineer's omission had a tendency to produce the loss or damage."[5]

"The late Sir J. B. Robinson, however, thought that where the proper signals were neglected, the company could not excuse themselves by showing that the injured one did not manage so well as he might have done, or that his horse was restive or unsteady;[6] and —"

Here a low wailing cry of "Oh, we might have all been killed—been killed—been killed"—uttered by one of the old maids, the

---

1 *Stubley* v. *London and North-Western Rw.*, L.R., 1 Ex., 16; questioning *Bilbec* v. *London, B. & S. C. Rw. Co.*, 18 C. B., N. S., 584.

2. *Winckler* v. *Gt. Western Rw.*, 18 U.C., C.P., 261; *Dascomb* v. *Buffalo & State Line Rw.*, 27 Barb., 221; *Mackay* v. *N. Y. C.*, 27 Barb., 528.

3. *Pittsburgh & H. W. Rw.* v. *Dunn*, 56 Penn. St., 280; *Balt. & Ohio Rw.* v. *Breing*, 25 Md., 378; *Skelton* v. *L. & N. W. Rw.*, L.R., 2 C.P., 631; *Johnston* v. *Northern Rw.*, 34 U.C., Q.B., 439.

4. *Havens* v. *Erie Rw.*, 41 N. Y., 296; *Grippen* v. *N. Y. C.*, 40 N. Y., 34; *Parker* v. *Adams*, 12 Met., 415; *Johnston* v. *Northern Rw.*, supra.

5. *Galena & Ch. Rw.* v. *Loomis*, 13 Ill., 548.

6. *Tyson* v. *Grand Trunk Rw.*, 20 U.C., Q.B., 256: see also *Ernst* v. *Hudson R. Rw.*, 35 N. Y., 9.

others joining in the chorus, struck upon our ears : I chimed in with

"And if we had, allow me to inform you, ladies, that neither we ourselves nor those who come after us could recover damages against the company therefor, because it would have been owing to the gross carelessness of our driver,[1] and we would be considered as being in the same position as he is and partakers with him in his sins."[2]

"That's so," said my friend ; "every traveller in a conveyance is so far identified with the man who drives or directs it that if any injury is sustained by him from collision with another vehicle, through the joint negligence of the drivers of the two traps, so that his driver could not maintain an action against the other driver, the passenger is himself equally prevented suing."[3]

"What a shame!" chorused the Graces, plus one. "And is there nobody you can punish ?" they querulously queried.

"Oh, yes ; you can sue your own driver, or his employer. You have a clear and undoubted remedy against them."[4]

"Much good it would do you to sue me," growled the man. "You can't take the breeks off a Heelander."

"It has always seemed to me," I remarked to the legal gentleman beside me, "to be highly unreasonable that by a legal fiction the passenger should be so identified with the driver. What do you think on that point ?"

"I quite agree with you," he returned, "and with my celebrated namesake, Mr. Smith, and I think that the question why both the wrong doers should not be considered liable to a person free from all blame—not answerable for the acts of either of them—and whom

---

1. *Winckler* v. *Great Western Rw.*, supra ; *Nicholls* v. *Ib.*, 17 Q. B., U. C., 382.
2. *Stubley* v. *London & N. W. Rw.*, L. R., 1 Ex., 13.
3. *Thorogood* v. *Bryan*, 8 C. B., 131 ; *Rigby* v. *Hewitt*, 5 Ex., 240 ; *Greenland* v. *Chaplain*, *Ib.*, 247.
4. Maule J., in *Thorogood* v. *Bryan*, 8 C. B., 131.

they have both injured, should be more seriously considered than it has ever yet been."[1]

Just then we passed a heavy waggon; it was on the wrong side of the road, and we narrowly escaped collision. I sung out to the farmer driving it:

"If you want to drive on the wrong side, old fellow, you should take more care and keep a better look out,[2] for if an accident had happened, as we had not ample room to avoid your wheels, you would have been liable for the injury, being on the wrong side of the road."[3]

"Fine day, sir," was the only response that came, and our driver, with a grin, told me that the old man was as deaf as a door-nail.

My companion turned and said to me, "I have often wondered why the rules of the road should be so different in England from what they are in America. In the old country the three laws are —first, on meeting, each party shall bear to the left; second, in passing, the passer shall do so on the right hand; and, third, in crossing, the driver shall bear to the left and pass behind the other carriage.[4] In America, the rule is the reverse—that is, each party must keep to the right;[5] in passing, the foremost person bears to the left, and the other passes on the off side, and in crossing, the driver bears to the left hand and passes behind the other carriage —at least so says Story."[6]

"'Tis singular that there should be the difference. It is fortunate, however, that these rules are not inflexible, like the laws of the Medes and Persians, but may be departed from."[7]

1. Note to *Ashby* v. *White*, 1 Smith's Leading Cases, 6th ed., 227.
2. *Pluckwell* v. *Wilson*, 5 C. & P., 375.
3. *Chaplin* v. *Haines*, 3 C. & P., 554.
4. *Wayde* v. *Carr*, 2 Dowl. & Ry., 255.
5. *Kenard* v. *Benton*, 25 Maine, 39; and in Ontario, by Con. St. U. C., ch. 46, in meeting, conveyances must turn to right, and so when one is overtaken by another.
6. Story on Bail. s. 599.
7. *Wayde* v. *Carr*, supra.

"Yes, in the crowded streets of a city situations and circumstances may frequently arise where a deviation from the rules of the road will not only be justifiable, but absolutely necessary."

"In fact," I added, "if there was sufficient room for a defendant to pass without inconvenience, it will not assist him when sued to say that the plaintiff was on the wrong side."[1]

"Well," said Mr. Smith, "we have had a very pleasant drive together, and a very interesting conversation. I have enjoyed myself very much, for it is not very often that one can meet on the top of a coach, in this Ultima Thule of civilization, with a man who can discourse so learnedly on the law of carriers as you have done. But I regret to say that I must leave you at this little tavern, where the stage stops for dinner."

"I share your regret fully; and I, too, have thoroughly enjoyed myself, and even my bruised toe has forgotten to twinge and throb during our converse."

"By the way," added Smith, "I find I have forgotten, or lost, my purse; could you kindly lend me a V, for I have my fare to pay."

"Oh certainly," I replied, with apparent pleasure, but with inward heaviness, for alas

> "I could plead, expound and argue,
>   Fire with wit, with wisdom glow;
> But one word for ever failed me,
>   Source of all my pain and woe;
> Luckless man! I could not say it,
>   Could not—dare not—answer: No!"

The transfer of the Five was speedily made, and at that moment the driver reined in his old horses and drew up at the door of a country inn. Quickly my debtor jumped off the coach, with his bag swinging in his hand, a nod to me and a low salaam to the ladies, he was walking away when the driver called after him,—

"I say, mister, where's that ere fare?"

---

1. *Clay* v. *Wood*, 4 Esp., 44 : *Parker* v. *Adam*, 12 Metc., 415 : *Kennard* v. *Burton*, 12 Shepley (Maine), 39.

"Ah! that's a trifle that quite escaped my memory," responded my quondam comrade. "Never mind, however, you will have a lien upon my trunk in the meantime."[1]

"Where's your box?" queried Jehu.

"Oh! that's a question more easily asked than answered. It is where many a more valuable thing is, *in nubibus*, or *in partibus infidelium*. However, it matters little, because you could not detain me for the paltry fare, nor the clothes that I have on, nor even this bag that I have in my manual possession. So by-by to you."

And away he went, leaving coachee pouring forth his vials of wrath in epithets and expletives strong, if not polite.

"Alas," thought I to myself, "it is such sharp and improper conduct that makes men wish, like Shakespeare's Dick, 'to kill all the lawyers;' makes them abuse those who are (or should be) the counsellors, secretaries, interpreters and servants of justice—the lady and queen of all moral virtues—and apply to the members of our profession the language of Congreve of old: 'There's many a cranny and leak unstopped in your conscience. If so be one had a pump in your bosom, we should discover a foul hold. They say a witch will sail in a sieve, but the devil could not venture aboard your conscience.' But I can flatter myself that an honest lawyer, like myself, 'is the life-guard of people's fortunes; the best collateral security for their estate; a trusty pilot to steer one through the dangerous and, oftentimes, inevitable ocean of contention; a true priest of justice, that neither sacrifices to fraud or covetousness; and one who can make people honest that are sermon proof.' He is one who can

> Make the cunning artless, tame the rude,
> Subdue the haughty, shake the undaunted soul;
> Yea, put a bridle in the lion's mouth,
> And lead him forth as a domestic cur."

1. *Wolf* v. *Summers*, 2 Camp., 631.
2. *Sunbolf* v. *Alford*, 3 M. & W., 248.

CHAPTER III.

DINING, RAINING, LOSING AND ENDING.

Must wait at stopping places—Place booked taken at any time—Falling in ascending—Drenched with rain—Coachmen are common carriers and liable as such—Loss of money—Loss of luggage—Dangerous short cut—Safe arrival.

THE driver, annoyed at the loss of his fare, said he would drive ahead at once and not wait, as he usually did at this place, for his passengers to take refreshments, but as my wife was hungry and the old maids thirsty, I insisted upon his remaining; for a carrier has no right to deviate from established usages to gratify his own whims and fancies.[1] While we were partaking of a cold collation, portions of which, doubtless, had done duty on several former occasions, a gentleman arrived at the inn, and from his conversation with the driver I quickly perceived that he had paid his fare for the whole way from town to our journey's end, and that he now intended to take his seat, as he clearly had a right to do.[2] He, too, was booked for an inside place and protested strongly because sufficient room had not been left for him, saying that as more than the legal number were already on board he would not get on but would sue the proprietor for all expenses he might be put to in performing the remainder of his journey by another conveyance.[3] The son of Nimshi tried to smooth down matters, but in vain; and the irascible gent. went off in high dudgeon; whereat I rejoiced.

Just as we were starting, an old woman approached, and after some chaffering agreed with the driver as to the sum for which he would carry her to the next village and began to mount. Before

---

1. Chitty on Carriers, 253; Story on Bailments, s. 597.
2 *Ker* v. *Mountain*, 1 Esp. 27.
3. Chitty on Carriers, 252.

she was up the horses started, and she was thrown to the ground and injured so much that she could not come with us. I endeavoured to apply some balm by informing her that she had better sue the owner of the stage; for, she, being a passenger as soon as the contract was made, he was liable to her for the negligence of his man.[1]

We had not gone far after our refreshments, before the sky grew overcast, the wind arose, heavy clouds began to scud across the sky, distant mutterings of thunder grew more and more audible, rolling, rumbling, rattling nearer and nearer, the heavens were wrapt in gloom, through which, ever and anon, the lightning flashed vividly. Quickly the thunderstorm was upon us, the rain descended first in large heavy drops, then in a perfect deluge; the sky seemed on fire with electric flashes darting hither and thither like fiery, flying serpents. In vain the coachee whipt up his wearied horses and made their very bones to rattle, striving to gain shelter from the pitiless storm: before protection could be gained we were all drenched to the epidermis; even those within did not escape, for the old stage leaked like a sieve and let in the flood in every part. (My wife declared afterwards that she had read that in the days of Henry II., of France, there were three, and only three, coaches in existence, one belonging to Catherine de Medicis, another to the fair, but frail, Diana of Poictiers, and the third to René de Laval, a noble seigneur, and that she verily believed that this was the one owned by the fat old René—so weak, so frail, so rickety, was the old antediluvian monster; in fact, she remarked, there was nothing strong about the entire concern except the smell!)

But, after all, it was only a thunderstorm, and ere very long its fury was over-passed, the sun emerged from behind the murky clouds, and we all steamed away beneath its fiery rays like small portable steam-engines. Far worse, however, than being thoroughly

---

1. *Brien v. Bennett,* 8 C. & P.; *Lygo v. Newbold,* 9 Ex., 302.

damped ourselves, the heavy down-pour had penetrated our trunks and bags, playing the mischief with the things therein, for the carrier had not provided tarpaulins, or cart clothes and such necessary coverings to protect the baggage from the rain, as he was bound to do.[1] The thoughts of the damages which I might recover, alone kept me from pouring forth my ire upon the coachman's devoted head.

Of course, proprietors of stage-coaches,[2] or mail coaches,[3] who hold themselves out as carriers of goods, as well as of passengers, are liable as common carriers, and responsible at common law for all damage and loss to goods during the carriage from what cause soever arising, save only the act of God; and this liability extends to the luggage of passengers, as well as to the goods of strangers, although no specific charge be made for the luggage.[4] In England (by the Railway Clauses Act) railways, stage coach proprietors, and other common carriers of passengers, their baggage and freight, are put upon precisely the same ground, both as to liability and as to any protection, privilege or exemption; and the same rule obtains in the great Republic, except, perhaps, that inasmuch as transportation by rail is infinitely more perilous, a proportionate degree of watchfulness is demanded of carriers thereby. Care and diligence are relative terms, and the degree of care and watchfulness is to be increased in proportion to the hazard of the business.[5]

The thorough damping which he had received seemed to have had a mollifying effect upon our knight of the reins, and when I ventured to address him on the subject of his master's liability for loss or damage to luggage, I found him quite thawed out, in fact, communicative.

---

1. *Webb* v. *Page*, 6 M. & G., 204; *Walker* v. *Jackson*, 10 M. & W., 168; *Philleo* v. *Sandford*, 17 Texas, 227.
2. *Clark* v. *Gray*, 4 Esp., 177; *Lovett* v. *Hobbs*, 2 Shower, 127; *Hutton* v. *Bolton*, 1 H. Bla., 299; *Dwight* v. *Brewster*, 1 Pickering, (Mass.) 750; *Jones* v. *Voorhes*, 10 Ohio, 145.
3. *White* v. *Bolton*, Peake, N. P., 113.
4. *Robinson* v. *Dunmore*, 2 B. & P., 419.
5. *Commonwealth* v. *Power*, 7 Met., 601; *Jencks* v. *Coleman*, 2 Summer, 221.

"Wal," said he, "I knows summat about that; but I rather guess you'd find yourself mistook if you thought him liable for all losses, and put a lot of money in your trunk, and didn't tell on it, and had it lost."

"Why," queried I, "what about that?"

"Not much, only this: a chap one time thought so as how he'd come a sharp dodge on a coachman, so he just put $11,250 in his old trunk and said nothink about it; and when they got to their journey's end the box was nowheres, the man tried to make the owner of the stage pay, but the judge decided he could not."

"Who told you all that?"

"Wal, stranger, I heerd it in rather a round-about way, my master told me, another man told him, and an angel told the other man."[1]

"Ah, indeed!" I exclaimed. "That is undoubted authority."

"Another time there was a *long fellow* put a £50 note in his bag among his old duds, in getting on the stage he gave his bag to the driver, who lost it; he sued the master to court, but the jury only paid him for his old clothes."[2]

"There must have been some stage-coachman on that jury," I said.

"Like enough, there's a deal of them scattered around every civilized country."

"I suppose you know," I added, "that if you were to carry parcels for your own particular profit, your master would not be liable for the loss of them,[3] unless, indeed, he paid you less wages, because of the opportunity thus afforded you of making small sums."[4]

"I guess there's no chance of my makin' a fortun', along this ere road that ere way; folks think I ought to carry their traps

---

1. Angell on Corporations, 262.
2. *Miles* v. *Cottle*, 4 M. & P., 630; 6 Bing.; and on this point see notes pages 28 & 29.
3. *Butter* v. *Basing*, 2 C. & P., 614.
4. *Dwight* v. *Brewster*, 1 Pick. (Mass.), 50.

for nothink. Look ye here, mister, how would it be 'sposing a man took his portmantee with him, and kept his own eye on til it, and it was lost after all."

"Oh, it's clear the owner of the coach would be liable.[1] But if a gentleman keep, for instance, his overcoat wholly in his own custody and possession, and does not actually deliver it to the carrier, the latter cannot reasonably be held liable for the loss[2] if it disappears."

(P.S. & N.B. Any person or persons desirous of becoming thoroughly posted upon the all important question of the liability of carriers for the loss of baggage, will find it to their advantage to consult chapter XI. of Part First, of this my Book.)

"I say, mister, had I better take a short cut over that ere bridge which is so rotten that I calkerlate it will go down mighty soon with a tremendous whack into the water below ; or go away round a couple of miles to the stone bridge ?" queried the driver.

"Well," I replied, "I think you had better go round, for the law saith, if a common carrier—which you decidedly are in every sense of the word—goes by ways that be dangerous, or drive by night, or in other inconvenient times, or if he overcharge a horse, whereby he falleth into water or otherwise, so that the stuff is hurt or impaired, then he shall be charged for his misdemeanor."[3]

The man grinned a ghastly grin, but said not a word, and I, seeing that we were rapidly approaching our journey's end, leaned over the side and informed the ladies of the fact, whereat they expressed not the slightest dissatisfaction, regret or annoyance.

Quickly now we drove along the bank of a little babbling, bubbling river, which 'like a silver thread with sunsets strung upon it thick like pearls' wound in and out, and round about, doubling the distance we had to travel ; but I was quite content and sought not to descend from my high perch, for the breeze was

---

1. *Robinson* v. *Dunmore*, 2 B. & P. 419 ; *Brooke* v. *Pickwick*, 4 Bing., 218.
2. *Tower* v. *Utica & Sch. Rw.*, 7 Hill, 47.
3. Doct. & Stud., Dial. 2 ch. 38.

"Sweet as Sabæan odours from the shores,
Of Araby the blest;"

and the woods near by had many verdurous glooms, and winding mossy ways, to charm the eye, and I had ever loved to gaze upon

"groups of lovely elm-trees bending
Languidly their leaf-crowned heads,
Like youthful maids, when sleep descending,
Warns them to their silken beds."

On and on we clattered along the rough and stony road, rattling and jolting, till a loud " Toot-toot-toot " from the driver's horn announced the fact that that day's work was done—that our journey was complete, and we were safe in the little village of Ayr.

BOOK THIRD.—BY BOAT.

CHAPTER I.

HOTEL EXPERIENCES.

A common inn-keeper and his duties—Choice of rooms—Limitation of liability—Act of Parliament—The view—The tea—Mine host responsible for losses—Kicking horses—Ferries and ferrymen—Lien on travellers—A midnight hunt—Entomological—A man pummelled.

"WELL, my Elizabeth, here we are at the hotel wherein we are to stow our wearied limbs until the morrow's morn, when we will take ship and go on our way rejoicing along the trackless main." Thus spake this autobiographer.

"Is this pokey little place the best hotel in the village?" was queried.

"Yes! and I might almost say, the only one. Come, I can already smell 'am and heggs,' as the Cockneys would say."

"I hate pork. But, are you sure this is an inn. There's no sign up, and no name."

"That's of no moment," I replied. "Every one who makes it his business to entertain travellers and passengers, and provide lodgings and necessaries for them and their horses and attendants, is a common innkeeper, whether he has a sign before his door or not."[1]

"A common enough innkeeper he looks, in all conscience," remarked my wife, as Boniface appeared, burly, beery and beardy, hot-looking, clad in genuine homespun, and with arms akimbo, bestrid the narrow doorway like a Colossus.

---

1. Bac. Abr., Innkeeper, B: *Parker* v. *Flint*, 12 Mod., 255.

At sight of me a scowl came over his face, for he was a man whom I had lately been forced to sue, and the remembrance of the costs and damages paid, doubtless rankled in his bosom.

"You are not agoing to cross threshold of mine, mister!" he said, surlily.

"Indeed!" I replied. "How's that? Do you know that every man who opens an inn by the wayside, and professes to exercise the business and employment of a common innkeeper, is bound to afford such shelter and accommodation as he possesses to all travellers who apply therefor, and tender, or are able to pay the customary charges;[1] for an actual tender is not always requisite now-a-days.[2] You have no right to refuse to receive us, as we are neither drunken or disorderly, nor afflicted with any infectious or contagious disease. And it would not matter if the would-be guests are travelling on Sunday, or the inn-keeper's family are in bed."

"An Englishman's house is his castle, and so is a Canuck's; therefore I refuse you admission;" growled the landlord.

"Well you render yourself liable to an action for any damages I may sustain by reason of your unaccountable refusal, and to what would, perhaps, suit you better, to be indicted for your conduct."

"I am not an innkeeper: I only sell provisions and refreshments and don't furnish beds or lodgings for the night."

"If that were true" I calmly answered, "the case would be different;[4] but I know for a fact that your house is a place of public entertainment and lodging, both for man and beast."

"Well, you can't stay here, for I am sick and have to go away to see the doctor, and there is no one to look after you."

"Neither your sickness nor pretended intended absence is any

---

1. *Taylor* v. *Humphreys*, 30 Law J., 242. See *Copley* v. *Burton*, L. R., 5 C. P., 489.
2. *Rex* v. *Jones*, 7 C. & P., 213, Abinger C. J.; *Fell* v. *Knight*, 8. M. & W., 268.
3. *Hawthorn* v. *Hammond*, 1 C. & K., 404 : '*Howell* v. *Jackson*, 6 C. & P., 725 : *Rex* v. *Jones* 7 C. & P., 219.
4. *Doe* v. *Laming*, 4 Camp., 77.

excuse,[1] so let us in you must;" I spoke dogmatically. He might have excused himself, however, if his servants were ill or had deserted him and he had not been able to replace them.

"What's all this hubbub about, John?" asked a buxom female, who, attracted by the voices, now appeared on the scene. "Out of the way, man, and let the lady and gentleman in," she continued, hurriedly shouldering her husband out of the way. Seeing that the mistress of the establishment was on our side, and eager for our entrance, we walked calmly in and were ushered into the little sitting-room.

A description of this sanctum with its rag-carpet, its antique sampler and brilliantly coloured pictures on the wall, its festoons of gorgeous paper on the ceiling, the mats with wondrous mosaic monsters on the floor, and the little table islanded in the middle of the room supporting a bouquet of wax-flowers, is beside the subject of this work, and is it not written in the book of the chronicles contained in half a score of yellow-covered novels?

Shortly afterwards we were led up to our bedroom by the landlord, who had not yet recovered his temper, but was apparently in the sulks. *En route* for our apartment we passed the open door of a very neatly-furnished room. When my wife cast her eyes upon the little den (not big enough to swing a cat round in, unless the tail was short and pussy kept her claws well in), wherein we were to pass the night, her nose was lifted heavenward most evidently ; (P. S. Perhaps it will be the more honourable course to confess at once that my lady's was a regular and decided case of *nez retrousse*), and she asked the landlord if he had not a better room for us ; if he could not give us the one we had just passed?

Boniface now found once again his tongue, and quickly he wagged it, as he said : "All I have got to do is to find you reasonable and proper accommodation, and this is good enough for the likes of you. You can take it or leave it, just as you like,

1. Bac. Abr., Inns. c 4.
2. *Rex* v. *Jones*, 7 C. & P., 213.

only if you leave it I'll make you leave my house, and hunt for board and lodging elsewhere."

"There is no help for it, my dear," I said. "The landlord is quite correct; so make the best of it."[1]

"Well," said my wife, "we will not go to bed. I'll sit up all night sooner than get between those dirty sheets."

"If you intend to sit up all night you must sit downstairs, for I won't have people awake up here and listening to my old woman a-blowing of me up," growled the landlord; the thought of the curtain lecture *in futuro* giving a peculiar shake to his usually gruff tones.

"Not so fast, my dear sir," I said in mollifying accents, "we have taken this room and so will keep it, and as Baron Alderson (whom perhaps you knew) once said: 'Travellers are not bound to go to bed, and an innkeeper can't turn out his guests because they refuse to go to sleep.' Though I admit, that if we had not taken the bedroom, you might have objected to giving us one if we informed you that we were going to sit up all night.[2] When will supper be ready?" I queried, anxious to change the subject.

"In half an hour," responded mine host, as he departed, taking the door with him as far as it would go in a violent manner.

As I gazed around our dormitory, I noticed on the wall a paper announcing that, in consequence of the "numerous robberies that had taken place in hotels in the neighbourhood, the landlord would not be responsible for money, jewellery, or articles of value, unless left at the bar." On my wife's asking me if I was going to hand over my valuables, I told her that Pollock, C. B. was of the opinion that such a notice did not apply to such articles of jewellery as a person usually carries with him, as his watch, which would be of little service if left at the bar—unless it was a jewelled one, set in valuable diamonds.[3]

---

1. *Fell* v. *Knight*, 8 M. & W., 276.
2. *Fell* v. *Knight*, 8 M. & W., 276.
3. In argument, *Morgan* v. *Ravey*, 6 H. & N., 265.

" I don't see that card that one generally finds in hotels, about the owner not being liable for the loss of things over a certain sum," remarked my wife.

"No; our sweet lamb of a landlord has not got up the notice which the statute requires[1] he should have printed in plain type, and conspicuously posted up in his office, the public rooms and every bed-room of his inn. Well, it is all the better for the guests if they are robbed or lose anything; for he cannot now claim the benefit of the provision that he shall not be liable to make good to any guest any loss of or injuries to, goods or property in his inn to a greater amount that $40 (the English law says £30), unless it be a horse, or other live animal, or any gear appertaining thereto; and except where such goods or property shall have been stolen, lost or injured, through the wilful act, neglect or default of such innkeeper, or any servant in his employ; or where such goods or property shall have been deposited expressly for safe keeping with the innkeeper, who, in such case, may require them to be placed in a box or other receptacle fastened and sealed by the guest.[2] And if the innkeeper refuses to receive such goods and chattels for safe-keeping, or through his neglect a guest is unable to make such deposit, then he will not be entitled to any of the privileges of the Act."

While my wife, who had speedily tired of my harangue, was deep in the mysteries of the toilet (which, like those of the *Bona Dea*, must not be detailed to the *profanum vulgus*), tittivating herself for supper, I took a general survey from the window, of the surrounding country.

The view was charming, if nothing else about the place was. The pebbly shore of the lake was but a few yards off, and there the little wavelets babbled pleasantly, as gently and joyously they kissed the sands and laughingly tossed their tiny heads in the golden light of the evening sun; some kine were lazily quaff-

---

1. 37 Vict. (Ont.), c. 11. s. 4.
2. 37 Vict. (Ont.), c. 11. s. 2: Imp. Stat. 26 & 27 Vict. c. 41, s. 1.

ing the sparkling waters and then, lifting their heads, were gazing out into the west; and away off some half a mile or so clustered a group of little islets looking in their summer's verdure like emeralds in a setting of silver.

Near by was the village wharf, and on it a crowd of *gamins*, ragamuffins and tatterdemalions, inspecting a little boat—a veritable cockle-shell propelled by that magic agent steam. One juvenile mounted on a post was trying to gaze down the little steamer's funnel, as if anxious to behold the doings of the fire-fiend down below. The affair reminded me of when the *Gleniffer*, the first steamer from Paisley to Largs, on the *Clyde*, lay at Greenock one day, the tide was out and the funnel was almost on a level with the quay: a smart boy sang out,

"Capten, capten, there is a laddie a-spitting down your chimley, and he will put your fire out."

Who shall attempt to depict with preraphaelite art the tea? Words of mine would fail were I to attempt the task. I must quote from that refined and elegant writer, Josh Billings—who seems to have had experience, extensive and varied, in hotels. "Tea tew kold tew melt butter, fride potatoze which resembled the chips a two-inch auger makes in its journey thru an oak log. Bread solid: biefstake about az thick az blister plaster, and az tuff az a hound's ear. Table kovered with plates, a few scared to death pickles on one of them, and 6 fly-indorsed crackers on another. A pewterunktoon caster with 3 bottles in it—one without any musterd, and one with two inches of drowned flies and vinegar in it." Such was the bill of fare as sketched by a master hand.

At the table I got into a discussion with one of the other guests as to the liability of a publican for the goods of his patrons. I said, "The fact of goods being stolen from an inn is *prima facie* evidence of negligence on the part of the innkeeper."[1]

---

1. *Dawson* v. *Chauncey*, 5 Q.B., 164.

"Yes; but they are not responsible to the same extent as common carriers. Though the loss of a guest's goods will be presumptive evidence of the negligence of the innkeeper or his servants; still he may, if he can, repel the presumption by shewing that there was no negligence whatever, or that the loss is attributable to the personal negligence of the guest himself;"[1] quoth my companion.

I replied, "An innkeeper though he has not only not been negligent, but has been even diligent in his endeavours to preserve the goods of his guests, is still—at common law—liable for any loss or injury that may happen to them which does not arise from negligence on the part of the guest, the act of God, or the Queen's enemies."[2] But a restaurant is not an inn, nor is the keeper of such a place liable as an innkeeper"[3]

"What would you consider negligence on the part of a guest?" queried my friend. "Would neglect to lock a bed-room door be such?"

"The mere delivery of the key of his room to a guest will not exonerate the landlord from liability; but if the key is taken it becomes a proper question for a jury to decide whether the guest took it for the purpose of protecting himself and freeing the landlord, or because the host desired it, or for the sake of securing greater privacy and keeping clear of Paul Prys and peeping Toms.[4] Neglect to use a key whereby a thief comes in at the door and steals one's goods is, or is not, evidence of contributory negligence as the case may be. The question is whether he would or would not have lost his things if he had used the ordinary care that a prudent man might reasonably have been expected to take under the circumstances; and what would be prudent in a small country

---

1. Story on Bailments, sec. 472, p. 498, 5th Ed.
2. *Morgan* v. *Ravey*, 6 H. & N., 265.
3. *Carpenter* v. *Taylor*, 1 Hilton, 193.
4. *Burgess* v. *Clements*, 4 M. & S., 310; 1 Stark, 252 n.; *Cayle's case*, 8 Co. 32; 1 Smith's L.C., 6 Ed., 105.

hotel, might be the extreme of imprudence in a large hotel in a large city."[1]

"Can one take such exclusive charge of one's own goods as to absolve the hotel-keeper?"

"Oh yes! that is quite clear.[2] Where a lady left a reticule containing money on her bed, and went into the next room for about five minutes, and during that time the bag disappeared and could never again be found, for

> "In vain she searched each cranny of the house,
> Each gaping chink impervious to a mouse,"

the innkeeper was held bound to make good the loss;[3] and so where pieces of silk were stolen out of the commercial room.[4] But, on the other hand, where a guest opened a box in a public room, and exposed money and bank notes therein to the bystanders, and then left the box in that room and it was robbed, the proprietor of the establishment was considered not chargeable with the loss.[5] If a guest takes a room for the purpose of business distinct from his accommodation as guest, the host is not responsible as an innkeeper for goods lost or stolen therefrom."[6]

"I remember that the servant of a friend of mine once asked permission to leave a parcel at a tavern, but the innkeeper's dame refused to receive it; the man, however, being a thirsty soul sat down, called for something to drink, putting the parcel on the floor behind him while he was imbibing. When he was thus keeping his spirits up by pouring spirits down, the parcel disappeared and never was seen again, and the innkeeper was held res-

---

1. *Oppenheim* v. *White Lion Hotel Co.*, L.R., 6 C.P., 515; *Cashill* v. *Wright*, 6 Ell. & Bl. 900.
2. *Farnworth* v. *Packwood*, 1 Stark. 249; Bayley, J., in *Richmond* v. *Smith*, 8 B. & C., 9.
3. *Kent* v. *Shuckard*, 2 B. & Ad., 803.
4. *Richmond* v. *Smith*, 8 B. & C., 9.
5. *Armistead* v. *White*, 20 Law J., Q.B., 524; 17, Q.B., 261.
6. *Burgess* v. *Clements*, 4 M. & S., 306; *Farnsworth* v. *Packard*, 1 Holt W.P., 209.

ponsible for the loss.[1] But the damage must be received while one is in the position of a guest; where there was a ball at an inn and a guest thereat lost his coat, though he had given it to the clerk of the hotel to keep, the innkeeper was held not liable."[2]

"It is settled," I said, "that the proprietor is liable even if he is on the sick list and unable to attend to the business of his establishment, or if he is *non compos mentis*.[3] But he can free himself by shewing that he is an infant under age."[4]

"Does it make any difference to a man's rights as a traveller how long he remains at the inn? or does the length of his visit vary or qualify the liability of the host?"

"No.[5] But if he takes rooms for any definite length of time, or makes a special contract for his bed and board, he ceases to be a traveller, and becomes a lodger in a private boarding house; and if he is then robbed, the proprietor will not be liable."[6]

"I noticed the other day that, under the old law, on the first day at an hotel, a man was called a traveller, on the second a hogenhind, and on the third he was called, and considered, a menial for whom the host was bound to answer in the leet as for a domestic.[7] By the way, when you have finished your tea, will you come out and see my horses, I calculate I have as pretty a span of black ponies as you would care to own."

"Certainly. I will be most happy," I replied.

Soon we were wending our way across the yard to the stables. To the great rage of my friend he found that one of his horses had been kicked by another equine—not seriously, however.

"Ah! it's well it's no worse, for the innkeeper is not responsible for injuries inflicted by the horses of his guests on each other, if

---

1. *Bennet* v. *Mellor*, 5 T. R., 276.
2. *Carter* v. *Hobbs*, 2 Mich. 52.
3. Bac. Abr., Innkeeper, C., 4; *Cross* v. *Andrews*, Cro. Eliz., 622.
4. Rolls Abr., Infancy and Age, II.
5. Add. Torts, 501.
6. *Watbroke* v. *Griffith*, Moore, 877; *Grimston* v. *Innkeeper*, Hetl. 49.
7. Per Latch, 88.

he takes due care to exclude vicious and kicking animals."[1] I remarked, coolly, calmly and collectively, for a man can generally philosophically hear the wrongs of his neighbours.

"I have the worst luck in the world with my horses," he said. "It was only the other day that I was crossing the Mersey on a steam-ferry, and the hand rail to the landing stage was so bad that it broke, and a sharp iron rod so severely wounded a fine mare I was leading on board, that I had to kill her."

"But why did you not sue the ferrymen? They are common carriers and bound to provide safe and secure boats, slips and landing stages, and all proper means and appliances for the safe transit of all who may choose to use the ferry for themselves, or for their horses and carriages, luggage and merchandise."[2] I hurriedly exclaimed, anxious to show off my deep reading and extensive knowledge: and then breathlessly I added, "In America ferrymen must have their flats so made that all drivers and carriages may enter them with ease:[3] and as soon as a carriage is fairly on the drop or slip of the flat, though it be driven by the owner, still it is considered to be in the ferryman's possession, and he is liable for any damage that happens to it or the horses."[4]

"I did sue them, and recovered £31 10s damages,"[5] he quietly replied. "But some of the American cases take a somewhat different view from the one you suggest. In one case, the ferryman was held not to be liable for injury received unless the owner of the team surrendered its custody to the carrier or his servants: in another, not to be liable for injury arising from want of care in the owner.[7] Although in a case away down in Mississippi it was

---

1. *Dawson* v. *Chauncey*, 5 Q.B., 105; explained and qualified by *Morgan* v. *Ravey*, 30 Law J. Ex. 134.
2. Add. on Torts, 493.
3. *Miles* v. *James*, 1 McCord, 157.
4. *Cohen* v. *Hume*, 1 McCord, 439.
5. *Willoughby* v. *Horridge*, 12 C.B., 751.
6. *White* v. *Winniesiniek Co.*, 7 Cush., 155.
7. *Wilsons* v. *Hamilton*, 4 Ohio, N. S., 722.

decided that as soon as property is put on board their boat, ferrymen have it *prima facie* in their charge, and are responsible for it, unless the owner consents to take exclusive charge; and they were held liable where two stage horses jumped overboard."[1]

In the stable we met a dilapidated looking specimen of the *genus* seedy, who, upon investigation, appeared to have compartments to let in his upper story. His pants had quarrelled with his boots and had crawled up his legs as if to avoid a kick : here and there patches of bare-skin peeped out through his tattered sit-upons, as if pleased to see daylight and have a little fresh air : his coat in colours would have rivalled Joseph's; his hat might have been for generations the breeding place of barn-door fowls. He was engaged in yard duty, and told us in most piteous tones that the landlord would not let him go on his travels because he was not able to pay for the first meals he had got at the place.[2]

"It is perfectly absurd; he has no right to keep you, or any other man, against your will for such a reason. A judge once said it could be done, but that idea was knocked on the head long since,"[3] I said.

"Oh! thank you!" exclaimed the poor wretch; "but"— he added in saddening tones, "can he keep my clothes?"

"He may detain whatever you have, except the clothes you are wearing, or anything in your hand.[4] So you had better cut off at once."

Having thus made a fellow mortal happy by sound advice and friendly counsel, I returned to the inn and sought the company of my spouse, bearing with me a *mens conscia recti*.

Time waits for none. Night came quickly on, and the myriad creatures which seem born on every summer night uplifted in joy their stridulous voices, piping the whole chromatic scale with

---

1. *Powell* v. *Mills*, 37 Miss., 691.
2. Bac Abr., Inns, D.
3. *Sunbolf* v. *Alford*, 3 M. & W., 254 :
4. *Sunbolf* v. *Alford*, sup. : *Smith* v. *Dearlove*, 6 C.B., 132.

infinite self-satisfaction. Innumerable crickets sent forth what, perhaps, were gratulations on our arrival; a colony of tree-toads asked in the key of C. sharp major after their relatives in the back country : while the swell bass of the bull frogs seemed to be, with deep and hearty utterances, thanking heaven that their dwelling places were beside pastures green in cooling streams. For a while we listened to the concert of lilliputians rising higher and higher as nature hushed to sleep her children of larger growth. Ere long the village bell tolled the hour for retiring, I told the landlady to call us betimes, and my wife and self shut ourselves up in our little room for the night.

Very weariness induced the partner of my joys and sorrows to commit her tender frame to the coarse bedclothes; but, before "tired nature's sweet restorer, balmy sleep" arrived and with sweet repose our eyelids closed, an entomological hunt began. First a host of little black bandits found us out, and attacked us right vigorously, skirmishing bravely; then came a detachment of heavy foot—of aldermanic proportions—pressing slowing on. A light was quickly struck. Faugh! what a time we had pursuing and capturing, crushing and decapitating hosts of ——(shall I use words offensive to ears polite? no I will say)—F sharps and B flats! I am an ardent entomologist, but I solemnly avow I grew tired that night of my favourite science. At length we arose in despair, donned our apparel and sat down beside the window to gaze upon the moonbeams glinting on the water.

Mrs. L. asked, "Must we pay for such wretched accommodation?" Mournfully I shook my head, and replied :

"I fear me so. It was once decided that where a furnished house is let there is an implied condition that it is necessarily fit for habitation, and not so infested with creeping things as to make it uninhabitable:[1] but Woodfall, who is well up in such matters, says, that that decision is not to be relied upon: that it has been

---

1. *Smith* v. *Marrable*, 11 M. & W., 5.

greatly shaken, if not over-ruled, by subsequent cases.[1] Still Abinger, C. B., thinks that if a house is infested with vermin : if *cimeces lectularii* be found in the beds, even after entering into possession of the house, the lodger is not bound to stay in it.[2] So perhaps, we may escape payment: however I don't want to have a row about a bill in a dollar house."

When morning came, with joyful hearts we descended to the lower regions. Here we found a man in high dudgeon : he had been asked by mine host the night before, to take a friendly supper at the house : the supper being good or the man's taste very bad (most probably the latter), festivities were prolonged late into the sma' wee hours, and when they were over the guest was " unsteady on his pins," so he was pressed to remain all night. While he slept he was robbed of his watch, and now he was demanding satisfaction from his boon companion of the previous evening. The latter refused to compensate him for his loss, and in this position he was sustained by the law because the man was not a traveller. He was, however, persistent in his demands, grew demonstrative and excited. This drew forth smiles and sallies of country wit from some loiterers around the bar: number one retaliated : words were soon followed by blows, and the *ci-devant* reveller was pretty well pummelled.

When he saw me he eagerly asked if the landlord was not responsible for the assault upon him : although I would have dearly liked to have punched or punished the host myself, still my inner man compelled me to say :

" No: even if you were a traveller you would have no action against the innkeeper for being beaten in his house : for his charge extends not to the person of his guests, but to their movables only."[4]

1. *Hart* v. *Windsor*, 12 M. & W., 68, 87 : *Sutton* v. *Temple, Ib.*, 52, 60.
2. *Sutton* v. *Temple*, supra.
3. Bacon's Abr., Inns., c. 5.
4. *Cayle's Case*, 8 Co., 32.

When at length the hour came for our departure, and we had summoned the lady of the house to settle with her, my wife spoke strongly about the occupants of our bed.

The woman hotly exclaimed, "You are mistaken, marm: I am sure there is not a single flea in the whole house."

"A *single* flea," returned my wife with withering scorn; "a *single* flea: I should think not, for I am sure that they are all married, and have large families too."

"Yes" I added:

> "The little fleas have lesser fleas
> Upon their backs to bite them:
> The lesser fleas have other fleas,
> And so ad infinitum."

CHAPTER II.

LIFE ON THE ROLLING DEEP.

Primitive steamers—Hole in the wharf—Passenger injured—Curiosity hunters hurt—Breaking of fender—A grievous case—Steamboats must carry all—Unless disreputable, disobedient or disgusting—Not up to time—Time the essence of contract—Behaviour at table—Ungentlemanly conduct—Sea sickness.

WE stood patiently on the wharf awaiting the arrival of the fire-driven barque that was to carry us along the broad waters of the St. Lawrence and its wide-spreading inland seas; until, like Mariana in the moated grange, my wife

> She only said, "It is very dreary,
> She cometh not," she said;
> She said, "I am aweary, aweary,"
> *I see her not ahead.*

At length, somewhat after her appointed hour, we espied our steamer rounding a point in the far distance; with steady stroke of paddle she approached, walking o'er the waters like a thing of life. What a contrast did she present to the frail birchen cockleshells that some hundred years ago were the only craft upon what was then a waste, a wilderness of waters, but what is now the highway for two mighty nations. Yea, what a contrast did she present to the crudities which, dignified under the name of steamboats, first ploughed up the waters of the Hudson and the St. Lawrence. The "Clermont," on 17th August, 1807, set sail with Fulton, a few friends and half a dozen passengers, leaving behind at New York an incredulous and jeering crowd, and travelled up to Albany at the rate "of near five miles an hour." The first Canadian steamer was the "Accommodation," concerning which the Quebec *Mercury* of 1809, in a transport of joy and excitement, said, "Her passage from Montreal to Quebec was sixty-six hours, thirty of which she was at anchor. No wind or tide can stop her." But I must not dive too deeply into the forgotten memories of the past.

The wharf on which we stood was in a very dilapidated state, and as we moved to avoid the rope swung from the deck of the steamer, to be fastened to a post, my wife fell into a hole covered only by a rotten board which gave way like pie-crust, and she hurt herself considerably. Of course we had the satisfaction (but it was only a slight one) of knowing that the steamboat proprietors were answerable for the injury; for they had invited my wife into a trap of which they must have been aware, and which was in a place of which they had the use, if not the entire control; and then, again, by selling tickets they had contracted to carry us safely, and therefore, independently of any occupation of the wharf, they were responsible for an injury arising from want of due care.

The contract made by the ticket was to carry us from the shore at Ayr to our journey's end, the wharf was part of the means of transport, and the steamboat company were responsible for accidents arising from the improper state of the wharf, whether such state was caused by the negligence of their own servants, or of other persons.[1] Or at least, this is how I would apply the late English decisions. In one case[2] a man called Bacon agreed to carry one John from Milford Haven to Liverpool. John went in the usual way on board a hulk lying in the harbour, and waited there till the steamer came alongside and took him on board. On the hulk, close to the ladder down which poor John had to pass to reach the steamer, was a large hatchway—unguarded and badly lighted— down this he fell and was injured. The hulk belonged to a third party, but Bacon had a right to use it for embarking and disembarking his passengers: so in an action brought by John, the

---

1. *Indemaur* v. *Dames*, L. R., 2 C. P., 311.
2. *John* v. *Bacon*, L. R., 5 C. P., 437.

court held that Bacon was answerable for all injury occurring through the means of transit being improper, and that whether it arose from the negligence of his own servants, or of others who helped to provide the means of transportation; and also that Mr. B., having invited Mr. J. on to the hulk, was bound to protect him from concealed dangers.[1]

Of course the rule is not so rigid where a person comes into a dangerous place merely as a visitor, influenced by the motive that led Eve to eat the forbidden fruit, instead of being on lawful business; under the latter circumstances one may be entitled to recover for injuries received, when under the former he would not be.[2]

But hark! I hear the whistle of the boat!—or, is it only the snort of impatience from my reader? It is time to be off.

As our steamer was backing out from the wharf she broke the fasteners of one of her fenders on the starboard side, abaft the wheel-house, and the fender as it fell struck a man who was standing on the wharf on the shoulder and injured him severely; the Captain had called out, "Keep clear of the fenders," and some persons standing near jumped safely beyond harm's reach.

(P.S.—To preserve the continuity of my tale—as the dog tried to do when his was getting cut short—I may here state what, however, I did not learn until some time afterwards, namely, that the poor man, a Mr. Grieve, lost the use of his arm by this accident, so he sued the boat owners and recovered £387 10s. damages against them. However, the court, Macaulay, C. J., dissenting, set aside the verdict and granted a new trial, considering that the action might have been avoided by the exercise of reasonable care on Grieve's part.[3] They said that the occurrence of such a catastrophe cannot be regarded as conclusive proof of negligence. If

---

1. See, also, *Great Western Rw. Co.* v. *Blake*, 7 H. & N., 987; *Brexton* v. *North Eastern Rw. Co.*, L. R., 32 Q.B., 549.
2. Add. on Torts, p. 189.
3. *Grieve* v. *Ontario and St. Lawrence Steamboat Co.*, 4 C. P. (Ont.) 387.

the injury had been received by a passenger on the boat the company would have been liable, but in this case there was no contract between Grieve and the company, although the contact was *grievous*. While they are bound to use all reasonable precautions to prevent accidents to persons standing on the wharves, yet steamboat companies cannot be regarded as insuring them against the occurrence of such misfortunes.[1])

Just before we started, a man had stepped on the gangway with the evident intention of coming on board, but the Captain in stentorian tones forbade him; the man expostulated, but in vain. When we were fairly off, as I chanced to know the commander, I spoke to him on the subject, and told him that in England, on one occasion, a man applied to be carried by a regular passenger steamer to Gibraltar, but in consequence of information received from the Portuguese consul, the agent of the ship refused to carry him, although there was plenty of room. The rejected sued and recovered a verdict with which the court refused to interfere;[2] and in the United States, Mr. Justice Story said that without doubt a steamboat is a common carrier of passengers for hire, and therefore the commander is bound to take a person on board if he has suitable accommodation, and there is no reasonable objection to the character or conduct of the would-be passenger.[3] And above all, our Dominion Parliament has enacted that carriers by water shall at all times, for the manner and on the terms of which they have given public notice, receive and convey, according to such notice, all persons applying for passage, as well as all goods offered for conveyance, unless there is a reasonable and sufficient cause for not doing so.[4]

"Ah! there's the rub; I have a most reasonable objection to that rascal's character—he is a notoriously bad man, and a very light-fingered individual," replied the Captain.

1. Per McLean, J., *Id.* p. 397.
2. *Bennett* v. *P. and O. Steamboat Co.*, 6 C. B., 775.
3. Story on Contracts, s. 474; Story on Bailments, s. 591.
4. 37 Vict. (Ont.), c. 25, s. 1.

"That, doubtless, is quite a sufficient reason," I replied, "for a carrier may rightfully exclude all persons of bad habits or character; all whose objects are in any way to interfere with their interests, or to disturb their line of patronage; and all who refuse to obey the reasonable regulations which are made for the government of the boat; and the carrier may rightfully inquire into the habits or motives of passengers who offer themselves."[1]

"When I was running a steamer between New York and Providence, I refused to carry a touter for a line of stages between Providence and Boston, which ran in opposition to the one in connection with our boat; he was in the habit of coming on our steamers to obtain passengers for the rival line. The court held that I had a good reason for my refusal;"[2] said the captain.

"The passenger must be in a proper state, as to sobriety, health and conduct, to associate with other passengers.[3] So you need never carry one who is so diseased that his presence would be dangerous, or it would seem even annoying, to the rest of your live-stock; or one that is drunk, or who persists in the filthy habit of smoking when told not to do so."[4]

Here the captain was suddenly called away by the mate, or, as an Irishman would say, by the man who cooks the mate, or by the man who does stern duty at the tiller, or by some other one of the ship's company. I know not who, so I was left alone.

As I was walking up and down the deck, feasting my eyes on the beauties of the surrounding scenery, the green fields, the forest-clad hills, the bold cliffs, the pebbly beach, the sparkling waters, the cloudless sky, and drinking in the fresh air as the wind gently blew over the sun-lit lake, I got into a conversation with an elderly man who was amusing himself by gazing intently at the prismatic colours of the pearly drops dashed up by the vessel's prow.

---

1. *Jencks* v. *Coleman*, 2 Sumner, U. S. C. C., 221.
2. *Jencks* v. *Coleman*, supra.
3. Story on Bailments, ss. 591, 591a.
4. Chitty on Carriers, s. 246.

After a few general remarks on that topic, which, if not exactly novel, is frequently referred to, the weather, my new acquaintance began to complain that the steamboat company did not always keep their engagements, that they had not called at the village where he lived on their previous trip, whereby he was considerably delayed and put to much trouble and inconvenience.

"It is very wrong of them," I said, "not to stop and take in passengers as they advertise to do; and in fact, if they do not they are liable to those who suffer loss and damage as for a wrongful violation of a general duty, and not upon any breach of a special contract; they are guilty of a breach of public duty, and any one suffering injury thereby may have an action."[1]

"Indeed! I am glad to hear that. These captains and companies are so independent now-a-days, and assume such lofty airs that they require to be taught a little common courtesy occasionally, by being made to pay damages for their neglects and mistakes. It seems a matter of the most supreme indifference to them whether they start on time or not."

"If," I replied, "the time of sailing form an essential part of the contract, it must be complied with; but if it does not, then the boat need only sail within a reasonable time, and the question in such case is, whether there was any understanding at the time of making the agreement, *i. e.* taking a ticket, that the ship was to sail positively at a particular time; or whether the time was only a matter of representation, while the making of the contract was going on."[2]

"Suppose that a man had urgent business in some other place, and had taken his passage thither by a steamer, and—females being always uncertain animals—she did not arrive in due time, and he took a ticket by another boat going to the desired place,

---

1. *Heirn* v. *McCaughan*, 32 Miss., 17; *New Orleans, &c., Rw.* v. *Hurls*, 36 *Id.* 660; see chapter III. Book I.
2. *Yates* v. *Duff*, 5 C. & P., 269.

could he recover the price of his ticket from the proprietors of the first boat ?" questioned my companion.

I answered by saying, "Where a circular stated that ships would be despatched on the appointed days (wind and weather permitting) to Australia, for which written guarantees would be given, and on the list attached it was said that the *Asiatic* would sail from London, August the 15th, and from Plymouth on the 25th of the month, and it was further stated that passengers from Ireland could readily join the vessel at Plymouth. One Cranston, a dweller on the Green Isle, engaged a berth on the *Asiatic*, and paid the deposit required, but got no guarantee as to he time of sailing. In due time he went to Plymouth and waited here possessing his soul in patience—a veritable Job—until the third of September ; and the vessel not having even then arrived, although wind and weather were favourable, Cranston took passage by another ship and sued for a return of his deposit and his expenses incurred at Plymouth. It was decided that the statement in the circular was not a mere representation, but a warranty that the *Asiatic* would sail on the day appointed ; and that as she did not, C. was justified in doing as he did, and that he was entitled to recover the deposit that he had paid, and his expenses at Plymouth.[1] And it was held in the United States, that where a man sold tickets to convey passengers from Panama to San Francisco, and stipulated that the ship should set sail in the month of April, it was considered that he must run all hazards of wind and weather, and could not excuse himself for the non-departure of the ship on account of any accidental or providential occurrence of foul weather, stormy wind, or tempestuous seas, having made no such exception in his contract."[2]

My new-found friend grew fidgetty during my somewhat protracted remarks, and seemed delighted—so little are the words of

1. *Cranston* v. *Marshall*, 5 Ex., 395.
2. 19 Law Rep. Am., 379.

instruction and wisdom heeded—when just at that moment the sound of the prandial bell called us into dinner.

Without delay the travellers assembled round the board. Without grace they attacked the viands. The meal was not so bountiful or so well served as one is wont to see on board of our floating palaces; some of my neighbours growled surlily over the badly-cooked edibles, the oleagenous pork, the sausages that required a large supply of condiments, and the chickens which never would have been killed by one having the slightest veneration for old age in his constitution.

I told the grumblers that they must grin and bear it, for Lord Denman once told a jury, who were trying an action against a captain for not providing good and fresh provisions, that although he was satisfied that the captain did not supply as large a quantity of good and fresh eatables as was usual under the circumstances, "still there was no real ground of complaint, no right of action unless the plaintiff had really been a sufferer. For it is not because a man does not get so good a dinner as he might have had, that he is therefore to have a right of action against the captain, who did not provide all he ought." His lordship said that the jury must be satisfied that there was a real grievance sustained by the complainant.[1]

One charitable old gent, who seemed inclined to find excuses for the short-comings and negligences of others, said: "Perhaps one reason of the poorness of the fare is that the boat is late: she ought to have arrived at K. before this, where, doubtless, a fresh supply of comestibles would have been obtained."

"That is a very good reason," I returned. "Indeed it has been expressly decided that the unusual length of a voyage is a sufficient defence to an action for the breach of a covenant to keep up a supply of necessaries, and the usual quantity of water for the use of the passengers."[2]

1. *Young v. Fewson*, 8 Car. & P., 56.
. *Corbin v. Leader*, 6 C. & P., 32.

One of the company near by eat as if he had never eaten in any place but a shanty or hovel all the days of his life: to quote the words of another, 'he tore his dinner like a famished wolf with the veins swelling in his forehead, and the perspiration running down his cheeks,' à la Dr. Johnson.

"Such a savage ought not to be permitted to take his meals in the saloon," said one of my near neighbours.

"I don't know how he could be prevented, if he has got his ticket," said another, who was shovelling peas with a knife into his mouth, which could not have been much broader unless Dame Nature had placed his auricular appendages an inch or two further back.

"I think he could not be excluded," remarked a third. "I remember once when coming from Madras to London, around the Cape of Storms, there was a man on board who was in the habit of reaching across the other passengers at table, and of taking potatoes and broiled bones in his fingers and devouring them *au naturel*. The captain, offended at his ungentlemanly conduct, refused to treat him as a cuddy passenger, excluded him from the cabin, and would not allow him to walk on the weather side of the ship. The man, when we arrived in England, sued the captain for the breach of his agreement to carry him as a cuddy passenger; and the officer pleaded that the conduct of the plaintiff was vulgar, offensive, indecorous and unbecoming. The man, however, got a verdict for £25."

"By the way," I said, "did he not threaten to cane the captain, and was not that threat one of the grounds of defence?"

"You are right, Sir, he did, and I believe the judge said something about it."

"Yes," I said, "Chief Justice Tindal observed, 'It would be difficult to say what degree want of polish would, in point of law, warrant a captain in excluding one from the cuddy. Conduct unbecoming a gentleman, in the strict sense of the word, might justify him; but in this case there was no imputation of the want of gentlemanly principle. With respect to the threat "that he would cane the defendant," if it operated on the mind of the captain at the time of the exclusion, I cannot conceive that such conduct would not justify such exclusion. A man who has threatened the commanding officer of a ship with personal violence would not be a fit person to remain at the table at which the officer presided.'[1] The defendant, in that case, unfortunately was not able to prove his pleas. What I have seen on this boat induces me to remark, that carriers of passengers are bound to see that their servants treat all those on board with kindness and respect."[2]

The dinner and the conversation both came to an end, as all things here below must, and the passengers soon dispersed fore and aft, aloft and below.

Before the bell rang again to summon the travellers to the evening meal, a heavy breeze had made its appearance, and its effect upon the vessel,

> With wave on wave succeeding,

was decidedly unpleasant to most of the passengers. No longer did the good ship preserve a level deck, but 'at one moment the bowsprit was taking a deadly aim at the sun high up in heaven, and in the next it was trying to harpoon a sturgeon at the bottom of the lake.' It mattered very little now to most of those on board what there had been for dinner; however *recherché* that meal had been, now it would have been wasted—thrown away. The gentlemen were to be seen intently gazing over the rail at the troubled waters; the fairer and frailer part of the company had disappeared into their state rooms,

> The world forgetting, by the world forgot.

" By some happy fortune I was not sea-sick. That was a thing to be proud of. I had not always escaped before. If there is one

---

[1]. *Prendergast* v. *Compton*, 8 Car. & P., 454.
[2]. *Bryant* v. *Rich*, 106 Mass., 180; *Godderd* v. *Railroad Co.*, 57 Me., 202.

thing in the world that will make a man peculiarly and insufferably self-conceited, it is to have his stomach behave itself the first day at sea, when nearly all his comrades are seasick." At least so writeth Mark Twain, and to his sentiments, from personal experience, I can say: "Amen!"

CHAPTER III.

THE AUTOCRAT ON BOARD SHIP.

Calm after storm—Disreputable people on board—Landing passengers *nolens volens*—Carriers responsible for effects of gravitation—Protection against fellow travellers—Lost by fire, Imperial, American and Dominion statutes—Rocks and snags—Running on Anchor—Authority of captain—Imprisonment—Compelling passengers to fight or work—Too far—The Devil's Invincibles—Charge—Tennysonian stanzas.

THE storm passed over during the watches of the night—anything but silent while the tempest lasted—and when betimes in the morning my wife, who had by this time well nigh recovered from the effect of the fall (I mean the one on the wharf, not Adam's), and myself issued from our state-room, wherein we had been cramped, cabined and confined—although it was large enough to swing a cat in, provided the tail was a bob, and the motion vertical not horizontal—and appeared on deck, all nature seemed to smile (although there was nothing peculiar about our personal appearance), all the passengers appeared in the best of spirits, and the steamer was merrily plying on her way towards the city that was gradually opening up in the distance.

As we drew near the wharf, I observed the captain in angry converse with a low-browed, heavily-bejewelled, vicious looking man, and as he caught my eye, he beckoned me over to where they were standing. When I went up to them, the captain told me that the man, 'who had the hanging mark upon him,' was a pickpocket, and that he was going to turn him off the boat, that the man said that he would not go willingly, and that the captain had no right to force him off.

I asked if he had been practising his tricks, or been guilty of any impropriety, while on board.

The irate commander said " No."

" Well then," I replied, " although, as you know, you need not have let him, or any one of notoriously bad repute and character on board ; still you cannot, after having received his fare and admitted him as a passenger, turn him off when he has done nothing wrong while here."[1]

" But I did not know who or what he was until this a.m."

" That makes no difference. Once in England, the captain of a vessel turned a man off at a place where he did not want to land, and conducted the affair—as the declaration alleged—in a scandalous, disgraceful and improper manner, whereby, and also by the contemptuous usage and insulting language of the captain, the poor man sustained damage. The jury gave him a verdict, and the court held that he was entitled thereto, and that the judge was right in receiving evidence of the captain having called him a 'pickpocket and a member of the swell-mob,' and in telling the jury that the owners were responsible for any injury naturally resulting from the acts of their captain, and bound to fairly recompense the man for the damage done to him by putting him ashore at a haven where he would not be, so far any injury arose from his being put on shore."[2]

" Then it can't be helped: the fellow must be allowed to stay among gentlemen for once in his life. But look ye here, sirrah, see that you behave yourself," said the captain, emphatically.

The man grinned, for those may laugh who win.

" Of course," I added as the trio parted, " he, as well as all others on board, is bound to submit to all reasonable regulations which are adopted for the convenience, comfort and safety of the passengers."[3]

1. Chitty on Carriers, 247.
2. *Coppin* v. *Braithwaite*, 8 Jur. 875.
3. *Cheney* v *Boston & Maine Rw.* 11 Met., 121 ; *Commonwealth* v *Power*, 7 Met., 596 ; *Hall* v. *Power*, 12 Met., 482.

As the vessel glided up to the wharf she hit against it in a way that caused all the travellers to experience a decided jerk; and one of the ropes that supported a small boat hanging over the deck gave way, and let the boat down with an unpleasant momemtum upon the toe of an unfortunate passenger, who forthwith began to dance around the deck on one leg with the injured member clasped between his hands.

I at once told the captain that he ought to settle with the man, for such an accident is evidence of negligence, as carriers are bound to see that such small boats and things hanging up aloft are so fastened that they will not fall from any cause reasonably to be anticipated or from the ordinary carelessness or misconduct of other passengers.[1]

The captain growled a little, but I went on talking to him as a friend, and telling him that passenger carriers for hire are bound to exercise the utmost vigilance and care, not only in saving their patrons from injuries from inanimate things but also in maintaining order and guarding them against violence, from whatever source arising, which might be reasonably anticipated or naturally expected to occur in view of the circumstances, and the number and character of people on board. That they are bound to protect one passenger from the violence of another. And that in one case where there was a company of soldiers on board and two of them got into a fight, and one dropped his musket on the deck and it went off and injured a passenger who was a civilian, it was held that the proprietors were liable for the damage.[2] But I did not tell him of Mr. Greenland's experience; he was standing at the bow of a steamer when she was struck by another steamer, and the concussion caused the fall of an anchor which broke Mr. G.'s leg: he sued the colliding steamer and recovered.[3]

For some reason or other the captain got huffy, and told me not

---

1. *Simmons* v. *New Bedfordshire* &c., *Steamboat Co.* 97 Mass., 361.
2. *Flint* v. *Norwich and New York Transp. Co.*, 34 Conn., 554, Circuit Ct. of U. S.
3. *Greenland* v. *Chaplin*, 5 Ex., 243.

to bother him, as he had something else to do beside standing talking with me all day, and, as he shouted "out with your gangway there," I turned away aggrieved and walked off to see that my dear wife was not in any mischief.

I found Mrs. L. talking with another lady and her husband (who had sat near us at table) on the agreeable subjects of steamboats catching fire. It appeared that my wife's companions had been on board the ill-starred *Kingston* (once patronized by H. R. H. the Prince of Wales), when she was burnt among the Thousand Islands, and they had on that occasion lost all their baggage.

"But did you not get paid by the company for your loss?" I asked the gentleman.

"Oh, dear no!" was the reply. "One lady who lost all her clothes sued the company in one of the inferior courts; but the judge decided that she could recover nothing for her loss; that an old statute of George III[1] was in force here; and by it it is enacted that no owner of any ship or vessel shall be liable to answer for any loss or damage which may happen to any goods or merchandise whatever, which shall be shipped, taken in or put on board such ship or vessel, by means of any fire happening to, or on board, the said ship or vessel."[2]

"I had an idea that there was an English case which decided that statute not to be in force in regard to ships on the tidal waters of the river Clyde, a river wholly within the territory of Great Britain?"

"Yes, there is such a case.[3] But Sir James Macaulay, in a case where a vessel was burnt while sailing from Port Credit to Oswego, decided that it was in force with respect to vessels sailing upon the great lakes of this continent, and carrying goods between ports in Upper Canada, and ports in the United States, and he

---

1. 26 Geo. III. ch. 86, s. 2.
2. *Leslie* v. *Canadian Inl. Trans. Nav. Co.*, C. C. of Frontenac, 1872.
3. *Hunter* v. *McGowan*, 1 Bli. Rep., 573.

thought that the doctrines of the Scotch case ought not to be extended."[1]

"And in the case of the loss of the *Kingston*, was the statute held to be in force on the river St. Lawrence?"

"Yes. The judge gave quite a geographical disquisition, remarking that the surface of the river, between the City of Kingston and the sea, measured 8,600 square miles, being considerably larger than Lake Ontario; that ships of more than a thousand tons burthen, built at Kingston have carried the British flag all over the world; that the river—like the sea—is the highway of nations, and carries a commerce which forms no inconsiderable portion of the trade of Great Britain; and his conclusion was that the statute was in force on the St. Lawrence as much as on the sea, or on the Great Lakes."[2]

"Upon reflection," I said, "I remember that south of the line 45°, there is an Act of Congress exempting carriers of goods and merchandise by water from responsibility for losses by accidental fire occurring without their neglect, and that such Act extends to the baggage of passengers.[3] But that Act does not apply to any boats used in inland or river navigation. And the Imperial Act to the same effect is also limited in its operations to ocean-going ships.[4] Yet it is enacted by a Canadian statute[5] that carriers by water (without any limitation), shall not be liable to any extent whatever to make good any loss or damage happening without their actual fault or privity, or the fault or neglect of their agents, servants or employees, to any goods on board any such vessel, or delivered to them for conveyance therein, by reason of fire or the dangers of navigation; but other carriers are liable for loss by fire, except where the fire is occasioned by lightning."[6]

---

1. *Torrance* v. *Smith*, 3 U. C., C.P., 419; *Hearle* v. *Ross*, 15 U. C., C.P., 259.
2. Burrows, J., in *Leslie* v. *Canadian Inl. Nav. Co.* Supra.
3. *Chamberlain* v. *Western Trans. Co.*, 44 N. Y., 305.
4. 17 & 18 Vic. c. 104, s. 503.
5. 37 Vic. (Can.) c. 25, s. 1.
6. *Mershon* v. *Hobensack*, 2 Zab., 372; *Forward* v. *Pittard*, 1 T. R. 27, ; *Hyde* v. *Tren & Mersey Nav. Co.*, 5 T. R., 389.

" Special favour seems to be shown to those who navigate in ships: for instance, where a vessel foundered on a rock not known to the master, and not generally known to navigators, it was held to be a loss from the act of God.[1] And where a vessel, in a river, ran upon a snag brought down by a recent freshet, the captain was considered excused.[2] And a carrier by water is freed from liability for damage accruing to goods under his charge through a hurricane, or a tempest, or lightning, or any unexpected and sudden interruption to navigation by frost."[3]

" I think, however," I replied, " that the cases you alluded to as to snags and rocks are all American ones, and they have been questioned, and perhaps have not been generally followed even in the United States."[4]

" Indeed. I was not aware of that, but it may be so."

" Yes," I continued, " long ago in England, it was decided that carriers could not excuse themselves from loss occasioned by their running against an anchor that was not buoyed.[5] And then, in cases of collision, even where the fault is solely on the part of the other vessel, the carrier is still responsible."[6]

" The first duty of the carrier is, of course, to provide a vessel tight and staunch, and furnished with all the tackle, sails and furniture necessary for the voyage.[7] And there must also be a crew adequate in number, and sufficient and competent for the voyage ; a competent and skilful master, of sound judgment and discretion, and some one qualified to take his place in case of illness,[8] for the

1. *Williams* v. *Grant*, 1 Conn., 487 ; *Pennewill* v. *Cullen*, 5 Harring, Del., 238.
2. *Smyrl* v. *Molin*, 2 Barber, 421; *Faulkner* v. *Wright*, 1 Rice, 108; *Redpath* v. *Vaughan*, 48 N. Y., 655.
3. *Bowman* v. *Teall*, 23 Wend, 306 ; *Parsons* v. *Hardy*, 14 Id., 25 ; *Harris* v. *Rand*, 4 N. H., 259 ; *Crosby* v. *Fitch*, 12 Conn, 410.
4. Red. on Rw. vol. 2, p. 9.
5. *Trent Navigation Co.* v. *Wood*, 3 Esp., 127.
6. *Oakley* v. *Portsmouth and Ryde Steam Packet Co.*, 11 Exch., 618 ; *Converse* v. *Brainard*, 27 Conn., 607.
7. *Lyon* v. *Mills*, 5 East, 428 ; Story on Bailments, sec 509.
8. *Forshaw* v. *Chabert*, 3 B. & B., 168 ; *Ewbank* v. *Nutting*, 7 C.B., 810.

owners are responsible not only for damage arising from want of care and attention on the part of the persons in charge, but also for lack of proper knowledge and skill."[1]

"But," I replied, "it is sufficient if the vessel and her equipments are such that she will probably—in the absence of any extraordinary accident—perform the journey in safety.[2] If any sudden gust of wind,[3] or any unexpected lull in the breeze,[4] bring a ship to grief, the master and all will be excused."

"We were talking at table last night, my dear sir, about the authority of captains over the passengers on their boats; they seem to be as despotic as the Czar of Russia or the Shah of Persia. In fact, when on their quarter-deck they seem to be able to say:—

> 'I am monarch of all I survey,
> My right there is none to dispute;
> From the centre all round to the sea.
> I am lord of the fowl and the brute.'"

"Yes," was the rejoinder, "the grave responsibility of the person to whose skill and conduct, life and property are entrusted on the deep, and the situations of unforeseen emergency to which he may be reduced, render it necessary that he should be invested with large and, for the time at least, unfettered authority. And obedience to this authority, in all matters within its scope, is a duty which should be cheerfully yielded by every passenger. Yet even a captain's powers have a limit, and the owners are liable for any injury naturally resulting from his unlawful deeds when acting as their servant.[5] I have had occasion to look pretty fully into the rights and powers of these Vikings, for I have oft-times crossed the raging main."

"Indeed! I should be pleased to hear some of the points that

---

1. *St. John* v. *Pardee*, 10 Howard, (U. S. Sup. Ct.) 557.
2. Chitty on Carriers, 155.
3. *Amies* v. *Stevens*, 1 Stra., 128; *Sharp* v. *Gray*, 9 Bing., 457.
4. *Colt* v. *McMechan*, 6 Johnson, 160.
5. *Coppin* v. *Braithwaite*, 8 Jur., 875. Ex.

have been decided," I replied. " If it would not be too great a tax on your good nature."

"Sir, I am always delighted to impart information to those who can appreciate and value it. So to begin at random, I may say that a captain has absolute control over the passengers in all that is necessary to the safe and proper conduct of the ship; still the exercise of his power must ever be defined and limited by the necessity of the case.[1] He has a right to use force when required for the safety of the vessel.[2] Necessity must ever be his excuse; and that tyrant's plea will justify conduct that would otherwise expose him to censure, to civil liabilities and to punishment. A captain was held to have exceeded his power when he imprisoned a man in his cabin for a week for alleged insolence.[3] But whatever is requisite for the security of the craft, the discipline of the crew, or the safety of those on board, he may lawfully require from those whom he has engaged to carry.[4] In fact, if the vessel be attacked by a hostile force he may compel the passengers to fight in its defence, and for the preservation of those on board."[5]

"Would a man get pay for this compulsory work?" I asked.

"Yes, as one may lawfully (except under peculiar circumstances) leave the ship, if he voluntarily remains to assist her in distress, he will be entitled to remuneration for his services."[6]

"That would be a small consolation, however, to a member of the Peace Society compelled to shoot at pirates, or to a dainty swell obliged to man the pumps."

"I remember one case," continued the gentleman, "where the captain went a little too far, and in consequence got into hot water and burnt his fingers. A Mr. Boyce was a passenger in the gunner's mess on board an East Indiaman; when near the Cape

1. *King* v. *Franklin*, 1 F. & F., 360.
2. *Aldworth* v. *Stewart*, 14 L. T., N. S., S. C. 4 F. & F., 957.
3. *Aldworth* v. *Stewart*, supra.
4. *Boyce* v. *Bayliffe*, 1 Camp., 58.
5. *Newman* v. *Walters*, 3 Bos. & Pull., 612.
6. *Newman* v. *Walters*, supra.; *The Two Friends*, 1 Rob. Rep., 285.

of Good Hope two strange sail were discovered in the offing, supposed to be enemies. The captain piped to arms, and assigned to every man his post. Boyce and other passengers were ordered on the poop where they were to fight with small arms. All mounted except B., who, because he had shortly before been forbidden by the captain to walk on the poop, now refused to go there, but expressed his willingness to fight for the honour of the old flag in any other part of the ship. For this contumacy the captain had him carried up whither he refused to walk, and kept him there in irons during the whole night. No foeman came to try their courage. When the vessel reached St. Helena, B. (not relishing the way in which he had been treated) left her, and on arriving in England sued the commander for assault and false imprisonment. Lord Ellenborough, who tried the case, at first said that he did not know but what the confinement of Boyce was necessary, and therefore justifiable; but when it came out that he had been kept all night in irons on the deck, he clearly held that the captain had exceeded the limits of his authority."[1]

"And I quite agree with his lordship," I said; "though he was such a ninny that when in 'the Devil's Invincibles' (a famous volunteer corps) he was ever in the awkward squad; and Eldon used to say that he thought Ellenborough more awkward than himself, but others thought it was difficult to determine which of the two was entitled to bear the palm."

"Ah, yes! 'the Devil's Invincibles' was the corps in which there were some attorneys, and when Lieutenant-Colonel Cox, Master in Chancery, who commanded, gave the word 'Charge,' two-thirds of the rank and file took out their note-books and wrote 6s. 8d."

"Ha! ha! that is as good as the story of the volunteer company of lawyers, who, when the drill-sergeant gave the command 'Right about, face,' all stood still, and cried 'Why?'"

"Unlike the six hundred,

---

1. *Boyce* v. *Bayliffe*, 1 Camp., 58.

> ' Theirs was to make reply,
> Theirs but to reason why,
> Theirs not to do, nor die.' "

"You might add the concluding lines of that noble poem," I said.

> ' When can their glory fade?
> O the huge charge they made !
> All the world wondered.
> Pay them the charge they made !
> Pay them the bill they made !
> Noble attorneys.' "

CHAPTER IV.

LOST! AND LAST!

Petty larcenies—Statutory exceptions to liability—Valuables—American rule—Lien on luggage—None on person—Pranks of rats and mice—Acts of God, of the Queen's enemies—No fare for newly born babes—Dead men must pay—Horse overboard—Vessel overladen—Trunk given to wrong man—Owner retaining possession of baggage—Limiting liability of carrier—Delivery to passenger—roof of age—Pedestrians—Colliding—Telegrams after missing baggage—The King's town—The resting place.

"MY dear sir," exclaimed one of my new made friends, coming hastily out of his state-room; "are steamboat people iable for all losses occurring upon their vessel?"

"Oh, dear, no!" I replied; "*modus in rebus*, as Lord Kenyon would say, there must be a limit to everything."

"I thought that common carriers were liable for all damage except that arising from the act of God or the Queen's enemies?"

"So they are as a rule. But there are exceptions to every rule; and there are statutory exceptions with regard to carriers by water," I returned.

"What are they?" was anxiously queried, as if the questioner had a personal interest in the matter.

"Well shortly. In Canada they are not liable for the loss of, or damage to, goods received on board their vessels or entrusted to them for conveyance, unless arising from fire or the perils of navigation, or from robbery or irresistible force, happening without their actual fault or privity, or the fault or neglect of their agents or servants. They are not responsible for any robbery, theft, embezzlement, removal or secreting of any gold, silver, diamonds, watches jewels or precious stones, money or valuable securities, or articles of great value (not being ordinary merchandise,) unless their true nature and value has been declared in writing to the carrier or his agent at the time of shipment.[1] Carriers are liable for loss of, or damage, to personal baggage, but not to a greater extent than $500; nor are they responsible for the loss of such valuables, as I have mentioned, unless their true nature and value have been declared as I have stated."[2]

"Do you mean to tell me that if my watch and purse are taken away out of my state-room the steamboat owners are not liable?" my friend asked.

"I would not, in the absence of any decisions, like to speak positively; but the Act of Parliament seems to be against you, unless you had made a declaration concerning them to the carrier. And in England (where the Carrier Act applies only to common carriers by land), if a trunk containing wearing apparel, jewellery and trinkets, exceeding £10 in value, be taken by a passenger with him and the trunk is lost, the carrier is not responsible for the jewellery and trinkets, unless the declaration has been made, but he remains responsible for the value of the trunk and the wearing apparel.[3] Where the trunk, is entirely full of these excepted articles, and is lost, the owner cannot even recover the value of the trunk.[4] Of course a carrier is responsible for the felonious acts of his servants;[5] but the grossest carelessness will not render him liable for things not duly declared.[6] However, in Massachusetts, it has been decided that the Act of Congress limiting the responsibility of sea-going vessels for the loss of valuables, shipped without notice to them, does not apply to passengers and their baggage.[7] But that

1. 37 Vict. (Can.), chap. 25, s. 1. Similar provisions (but applying only to sea-going vessels) are in Imp. Stat., 17 and 18 Vict., chap. 104, s. 503, and Act of Congress, March 3, 1857.
2. Sec. 2 of 37 Vict. (Can.), chap. 25.
3. *Bernstein* v. *Baxendale*, 6 C. B., N.S., 259; *Hearn* v. *London & S. W. Rw.*, 10 Ex., 793; *Treadwin* v. *Gt. Eastern Rw.*, I. R., 3 C. P., 308.
4. *Wyld* v. *Pickford*, 8 M. & W., 462.
5. *Hearn* v. *London & S. W. Rw.*, 10 Ex., 801.
6. *Hinton* v. *Dibbin*, 2 Q.B., 646.
7. *Dunlop* v. *International Steamboat Co.*, 98 Mass., 371.

in such cases the carrier is responsible (as in other cases of passenger carriers) for such an amount of money as is requisite for the journey and ordinary contingencies (if such sum be lost). Although not for the money of one passenger in the valise of another."

"There is some comfort to be extracted from that case."

"A little : but do not try to get too much out of it, for I don't know whether that Act has the same words as ours has about non-liability for loss or damage to valuables among personal baggage."

"Then I fear it is rather a blue look out for me."

"What have you lost?" I asked.

"My watch and purse;" was the reply given in lugubrious tones.

"I fear you have not much chance of recovering their value, unless you can satisfy a jury that the loss happened through the fault or neglect of some of the servants or hands. How did they get into your state-room?"

"Well"——began the man.

"Pardon me," I said hurriedly. "Excuse me one moment; I see my wife calling me." And in obedience to a beckoning finger I rushed off to Elizabeth.

Mrs. Lawyer was anxious to consult me on behalf of a lady on board who had unfortunately run a little short of the needful sinews of war, and was afraid that the captain would not let her take away her baggage until she had satisfied all demands upon her. I quickly told this individual that the captain had a right to detain her luggage for the amount of her passage money, if she had nothing to pay it with;[1] but that if he desired to keep herself, or the clothes which she was actually wearing, he would have to call in the aid and assistance of a parson.[2]

She did not see the joke—I think she was a Scotch body, and we all know what Sydney Smith said in that connection,—but

---

1. *Wolfe* v. *Summers*, 2 Camp., 631.
2. *Id.*

went on to complain that her carpet-bag had been eaten into by rats or mice and some things therein contained had been damaged by the voracious rodents.

"That is well," I said. "You can set off the injury done to your property against the amount of your passage money."

"What do you mean ?" she inquired.

"I mean that the depredations of rats are neither the acts of God nor of the Queen's enemies, nor are they dangers and accidents of navigation, and that therefore carriers must make them good ;[1] even though they have cats and mangooses on board, and have availed themselves of the valuable services of the venerable sire of the pretty ratcatcher's daughter of Paddington Green."

"Thank you, thank you," exclaimed my fair *vis-a-vis*, and so gushing was she that ——well, I wished just then that my Elizabeth had been at the other end of the boat. "I'll make the captain let me go free. Rats are such horrid things. And he is responsible for all the mischief they did ?" she questioned.

"Doubtless." I replied. "Even where they gnawed a hole in the bottom of the boat and the water came in at the leak and damaged goods on board, the owners were held liable for the performances of these daring little creatures."[2]

My wife looked as if she now deemed it quite unnecessary that the conversation should be any further prolonged ; so I raised my hat, let the breeze play around my noble brow and ruffle my hyacinthine locks, said "Adieu," and turning on my heel was about to return to the friend I had left on deck, when Mrs. L., calling me aside said :

"There is a poor woman who, since she came on board, has introduced a little stranger into this vale of tears, and she is very much afraid that she will have to pay something for the fare of the newcomer."

1. *Kay* v. *Wheeler*, L. R., 2 C. . . 302.
2. *Dale* v. *Hall*, 1 Wils. 281.

"You may calm her troubled mind;" I replied, "no fare or freight can be charged for an infant born on board; that was decided long, long ago."[1]

"That is good," said my better half.

"Fresh arrivals are treated with more consideration than those who shuffle off the mortal coil while on board ship. The latter (or rather their friends for them,) will be charged the usual fare,[2] unless it was expressly agreed that the freight or fare was to be paid for *transporting* them."[3]

"I suppose old Charon established that rule when he ran the ferry across the Styx," said my wife, who was somewhat of a Blue, and knew (or fancied she knew) a thing or two about the heroes of days long gone by. She appeared to be poking fun at me, so I left.

Just then I heard a great stamping, and rushing, and noise, in the forward part of the boat, and hurrying on I reached the deck in time to see a splendid horse that had broken away from its fastenings, spring from the boat into the lake. Every effort was made to save the noble animal from a watery grave, but all in vain; and soon it sank beneath the waves to rise no more, and the waters flowed on as before, darkly, deeply, beautifully blue. The owner stormed away and swore that he would have satisfaction for his loss; and in my humble opinion the carriers were responsible.[4]

Shortly after this we passed a little schooner which was so heavily laden that, although there was little more than a ripple upon the water, still some of her people fearful of the effects of the swells from our paddles commenced throwing overboard part of the freight. And they were quite right in thus looking after number one, for if a barge or vessel be overladen or surcharged

---

1. Roccus, not. 79 : Abbot on Shipping, p. 366, 11th Ed.
2. Dig. 14. 2, 10 ; Roceus, not. 76 : Abbott, 366.
3. *Moffat* v. *East India Co.*, 10 East, 468.
4. *Porterfield* v. *Humphreys*, 8 Humph, 497 ; see also, *Stuart* v. *Crawley*, 2 Stark, 323 ; but see *Richardson* v. *N. E. R. W. Co.*, L. R., 7. C. P., 75.

any of the passengers may, in the time of accident and necessity, cast out the things to preserve life ; and the owners of the goods will have a right to be recouped by the carrier, for the fault was in him in overloading. But if the load was not too great, and the danger accrued, only by the act of God through stormy wind or tempest, the carrier being free from blame, every one must bear his own loss if things are tossed into the sea, for as the Latins would say, *Interest republicæ quod homines conserventur*.[1]

I spent some time looking about for the person with whom I had had the conversation related at the beginning of this chapter. I wished to tell him of a Lower Canadian case that had occurred to my mind since I left him. The case was this : A man gave a trunk containing a large sum of money to the baggage keeper on board one of the Richelieu River Navigation Company's boats, contrary to the advice and directions of the captain, who said that the office was the proper place to leave it. The trunk was lost, and the court held that the company were not liable therefor.[2]

I searched for my friend in vain, so at length I sat myself down and began ruminating concerning that important subject the liability of carriers for the baggage of their passengers, especially on the point as to when the carrier is relieved from the responsibility which ordinarily presses heavily upon him. I recalled to mind a Michigan decision, where a man intending to take passage in a steamer took his trunk on board and left it in the usual place for luggage, but without notifying anyone employed on the boat of the fact, or that he was going to embark with them. He went on shore again for a while, and during his absence the steamer left. He never again beheld his trunk. The judgment of the court was that there never had been such a delivery of the baggage as to charge the owner of the boat as a common carrier.[3] And where

1. *Mouse's Case*, 12 Co. 63.
2. *Senecal* v. *The Richelieu R. Nav. Co.* 15 L. C. Jurist, 1.
3. *Wright* v. *Caldwell*, 3 Mich., 51.

an emigrant passenger, on the way from Liverpool to New York, took his box under his own peculiar and particular care and supervision, placing it under his bed and fastening it to his berth by ropes, and yet, notwithstanding his vigilance and caution, it was stolen during the voyage, it was held that the owners of the ship were not liable.[1]

But it has been decided that where passengers on board of a ferry-boat take care of their own goods and chattels, they may be considered agents of the ferryman, who is still liable for the property as a common carrier.[2] The carrier is not excused if the goods are lost through his servants disregarding the eighth commandment of the Mosaic law.[3]

Of course the steamboat proprietors can limit their liability by special conditions made known to the traveller, and either expressly or impliedly agreed to by him. When for instance, one Wilton, took passage across the ocean in one of the steamers of the Atlantic Royal Mail Line, and received a ticket containing conditions stipulating that the company should not be responsible for loss or detention of the ship by accidents of navigation, or perils of the sea ; nor for baggage, goods or other property, unless a bill of lading was signed therefor. W's luggage—consisting of several trunks—was received on board without any questions being asked about it, and he never declared what was in his boxes, nor did he take a bill of lading, nor was he ever asked to do so. The ship was lost, and all the baggage with it, through the negligence of the captain ; yet the company was excused on the ground that no bill of lading had been signed.[4]

It would appear (though, by the way, this is a rather sudden change of the subject) that where an individual is to get a certain portion of the ship's hold wherein to stow away his traps and be-

1. *Cohen* v. *Frost*, 2 Duer, 335.
2. *Fisher* v. *Clisbee*. 12 Ill., 344.
3. *Schieffelin* v. *Harvey*, 6 Johns. 170 ; *Hearn* v. *London & S. W. Rw.* 10 Ex., 801.
4. *Wilton* v. *Atlantic R. M. S. Nav. Co.* 10 C. B. (N.S.) 453 see also *ante* page 183.

longings, he must have asked the authorities for it, before he can successfully sue for not getting it.[1]

If, after the arrival of the vessel at her port of destination, an offer is made at a proper time by the boatman to deliver the passenger's baggage, and the traveller for some whim, or fancy, or apparently solid reason, declines to receive it, the carrier is freed from all further liability as such ; and if it still remains in his custody he is only liable for the exercise of ordinary care in respect thereof as a bailee.[2]

But, as I was fortunate enough on this trip not to lose anything, I will not weary my readers with any further dilating anent the loss of baggage and the legal rules affecting the same, especially as my experience in this respect is fully reported in the earlier part of this work. Besides an amusing incident occurred just at this juncture, disturbing the train of thought on which my mind was running, and sending off my cogitations and reflections in quite another direction. An old lady, with a little boy, and a well worn carpet bag between them, had come on board at one of the stopping places. The purser now strolled up and demanded the fares ; the mother tendered a fare and a half for the two. The official demurred, saying the boy was not under ten years of age.

" You don't think that boy is under ten ? Eh ? and you won't pass him for half-fare ? " said the woman in angry accents. Bursting asunder the string that tied together her bag she delved down and rummaged about among its contents ; and, then with trembling eagerness and eyes proclaiming triumph, she drew forth a well-worn Bible.

The man asked what that was for, he did not want to read it.

"I dare say not;" replied his antagonist; "for the truth is to be found in it;" and turning quickly to the pages at the end of the volume reserved for " births, deaths and marriages," she thrust it under the purser's nose, exclaiming :

---

1. *Corbin* v. *Leader*, 6. C.&P. 32.
2. *Young* v. *Smith*, 3 Dana, 91.

"Just look at that, young man! Does that look as if I was a liar? See what it says, 'John Thomas, son of John Smith and Betsy Jane, his wife, born on the———'"

"All right, my dear madam, all right," cried the purser, completely overcome by the proof produced, and anxious to escape from the laughter of the amused spectators. The victor, with a triumphant nod, deposited the sacred volume in its former resting place.

In his haste to escape from the scene of his defeat, the discomfited official rushed against a gentleman who was coming out of the saloon, with such momentum that the latter went down on the deck like grain before the reaper's scythe. This episode and the expletives and apologies that ensued set my busy brain once more at work, and I began meditating on the amount of caution and circumspection required of persons when walking about. A passage in Addison (not, however, to be found in the *Spectator* or the *Tatler*) came into my mind, and it is to this effect: the degree of care to be exercised by foot-passengers in a public thoroughfare to prevent collision with others depends, in a great degree, upon the injury that would be likely to result to others from that want of care. Thus a man who traverses a crowded thoroughfare with edged tools, or bars of iron in his hands, must take especial care that he does not cut or bruise others with the things he carries. Such a one would be bound to keep a better look out than the man who merely carries an umbrella; and the person who carried an umbrella would be bound to take more care in walking with it' than he who had nothing at all in his hands.[1]

My reflections and meditations were cut short, as they often were, by my wife approaching me; she asked me to get our baggage ready, for we were nearing our journey's end. I raised my head which had fallen low while I communed with myself; then I saw that rounding a tree-clad island we were entering one of the loveliest bays to be found within the fair Dominion of Canada, although she has many such gems of the finest water adorning her

---

1. Addison on Torts, 390, 391.

coronet of glory. I hurried off to do all things needful, that I might quickly return to enjoy the panorama that was opening up before us.

I got my traps and belongings all safely together, and was on the point of re-ascending the stairs to the saloon, when a friend called out,

"Hulloa! come back, I say! The baggage-man has just coolly informed me that he can't find my trunks, and that he believes he must have put them out at the last stopping-place."

"Very likely. Accidents will &c.; &c.," I replied.

"Now, don't chaff. Be serious, and tell me what is to be done."

"Well, you had better telegraph back when we land," I said.

"But it is too bad that I should be put to expense through the negligence of the servant of a wealthy company," returned my friend, who always looked at both sides of a twenty-five cent piece before he parted with it.

"You need not bear the expense. According to a recent New Brunswick decision, where baggage has been lost, the owner may recover all reasonable expenses that he has been put to in the search for his goods and chattels, such as telegraphing, cab-hire, &c. Though he can get nothing for his loss of time."[1]

"Oh, thanks! that's a comfort."

When again I gazed around me from the bow of our steamer, what a striking picture did I see?—wood and water, land and and houses, islands and vessels, the works of nature and those of art, of the Creator and the creature, all harmoniously blended together. Near by, on our right (as we left the lake astern), were two islands, named in days gone by Ganounkouesnot and Kaocienesgo, but now called, the one after the brave hero who gave Canada to Britannia, the other after an early governor; and a little further off rose above the glassy waters an islet, a veritable hive of industry and thrift. To the left was a little isle, bearing a solitary but noble elm tree, which shades the crumbling ruins of a fort, a

---

1. *Morrison* v. *E. & N. A. Rw.*, 2. Pugsley's Rep., no. 3, p. 295.

momento of the Old Regime; near by, but in the azure waters, was a lighthouse, to give light to those who traverse the pathless waves; while beyond, as far as the eye could reach, in one direction stretched the winding shores of the Bay of Quinté, dotted here and there with cosy houses, capacious barns and smiling fields of herb for the service of man; and in the other still rolled away, to be divided into countless channels by the Thousand Islands, the waters that had travelled from the Far West and were destined still to gleam and glide, and foam and roar, and slip and slide, till lost in the all-absorbing bosom of hoary ocean. Straight a-head towered a lofty and capacious building, where are housed and tended those hapless ones whose light of reason has been darkened; close by came the walled and guarded home of those who have broken their country's laws; then came villas nestling mid noble trees, then clustering cottages, and then—with its churches and colleges, its schools and factories, its stately public halls and substantial home-like houses—the Limestone City. As onwards, past floating palaces and puffing little tugs, graceful yachts and deeply-laden schooners, nearer, still nearer to the pier the boat bore us, we distinguished the brave old flag of England's might flying from the fort that crowns the hill across the harbour, and which, with the batteries on Point Frederick and the round towers, keep watch and ward over the city of Kingston.

The wheels revolved for the last time, the steamer was at the wharf; then the engine stopped, and all the complicated machinery was still. My wife laid her hand gently on my shoulder, and said:

"Let us stop here awhile. The town seems so peaceful and quiet, and I am tired."

"Yes," I replied. Doubtless all are weary; so I will stop here, and will bring to an end (so far as I am concerned) THE WRONGS AND RIGHTS OF A TRAVELLER.

THE END.

INDEX.

A.

ACCIDENT,   PAGE

    horses frightened by 4
    not sufficient proof of negligence . . . 25, 71, 73
    carriers not liable for unforeseen . . . 70, 74
    nor are stage coach proprietors 131
    from dangers of navigation . . . 177, 178

ACCIDENT INSURANCE,

    what is an accident? 8, 9
    Lord Cockburn's definition 8
    Michigan definition 9
    Maryland and New York definitions 9
    one may recover for railway accident, even if there is no accident to car 9
    compensation for injuries 9, 10
    injuries from external causes 10
    while bathing 11
    caused by negligence 12
    wilful exposure 13

ACTS OF PARLIAMENT,

    not those of the Apostles 34

AGENTS. (*See* SERVANTS.)

    carrier liable for the torts of . . . 116, 117
    for wilful acts within range of employment . . 117
    a person injured must shew authority of . . 117
    persons acting as, presumed to be . . . 117
    liberal discretion allowed 117
    carrier liable if agents disobey him . . . 107
    but not when they exceed authority . . . 118

ALIGHTING AT RAILWAY STATIONS,

    cars should be drawn up at a safe place . . 50
    is calling out name an invitation to alight? . . 51, 52, 53
    depends on circumstances 54

ALIGHTING AT RAILWAY STATIONS—*continued*.

	PAGE
stopping of train an invitation	54
calling out name a mere intimation	54
jumping off the steps	52, 53
company should assist passengers at difficult places.	55
passenger should require train put in a proper place	55
alighting when warned not to	50, 108

AMERICAN CASES,
authority of 27

ANECDOTE,
Lord Kenyon and Erskine	7
The Devil's Invincibles	180
a sleeping car	87

ARRESTS,
by carrier's servants . . 63, 64

AUTHORITY, ACTS IN EXCESS OF,
arresting a man	63
arresting to prevent a crime	64
carriers not liable for acts of agents	117, 118

AUTHORITY OF MASTER OF VESSEL,
master has absolute control in all things necessary	179
may use force towards passengers	179
or make them fight or work	179
what is an excess of?	179, 180

B.

BABIES,
no fare payable for, if born on board ship . . . 155

BAGGAGE OF PASSENGERS,
falling on one's toes	36, 37, 107
checking	18, 19
what is personal baggage	57, 60, 111, 114
owner may recover for loss of, unless negligent	58
what is not personal baggage	59, 63
passenger cannot carry anything instead of	60
carrier not responsible for loss or damage beyond actual value	62
notice limiting liability	62, 110
who is liable for lost baggage	63
when liability begins	108
when it ceases	121, 122
can only recover for one's own	109
left in car by servant	109
need not be marked with name	109
carrier liable even if with owner	109, 145
loss on other lines	110

INDEX. 195

BAGGAGE OF PASSENGERS—*continued.* PAGE
  is a present baggage? 112
  what is re-delivery 110, 112, 121, 122
  hotel 'buses, loss in 112
  liability ceases when ready for re-delivery 121
  loss of by fire at station 122
  stolen from warehouse 122
  owner should take it in reasonable time 122
  should not leave it all night 122
  not properly packed 127
  carrier has lien on, for fare 140
  carrier by water liable to $500 for 183
  lost on board ship 187, 188
  carrier should pay for telegrams as to lost baggage . . . 191
BED-CLOTHING,
  is it baggage? 61
BOARDING-HOUSE KEEPER,
  not liable as an innkeeper . . 155

C.

CALLING OUT NAME OF STATION,
  duty of conductor 56
  (*See* ALIGHTING AT STATIONS.)
CARE. (*See* DUE CARE, NEGLIGENCE, PASSENGER CARRIERS.)
  should be increased according to danger 142
CARELESSNESS. (*See* NEGLIGENCE.)
  OF COMPANY,
   misplacement of switch 24
   injury not positive proof of 25
  OF INJURED PARTY,
   jumping off platform 24
   running against fixtures 24
   losing money 28
   jumping off train in motion 36
   " " " 52, 53, 108
CARRIERS' ACT 29
CARRYING PAST,
  damages for 35
CHANGE,
  right to expect or demand 38
  helping oneself to 64
CHECKING BAGGAGE,
  when must be done 18, 19
  penalty for refusing 18, 19

INDEX.

CHECKING BAGGAGE—*continued.*   PAGE

    not necessary 58
    is merely additional precaution . 59
    check is evidence of receipt of baggage . 64

CHILDREN,
    damages for injuries to . . . 81, 82, 83
    loss of leg and hand 82
    travelling without ticket 82
    misconduct of person in charge . , . 83
    wandering on railway track 83
    care required of parents . . . , . . 83
    rule as to damages in England and New York . 96
    damages for death of 96, 97
    value of limbs of 82, 99

CLOAK-ROOM,
    should be kept open . 62

COLLISION,
    in driving . . 81
    between foot passengers . 190

COLOURED PERSONS 39

COMPENSATION. (*See* ACCIDENT INSURANCE, DEATH, DAMAGES.)

CONDUCTOR,
    his hat and badge 29
    his duty when fighting in cars 38, 39
    whom he may refuse to receive 39
    when may put off passenger . 40, 41
    is the agent of company . . . 41
    carelessness of . . . 66, 67
    should call out name of stations 56

CROSSINGS. (*See* RAILWAY CROSSINGS.)

C'RUM CATOR 50

CURIOSITY SEEKERS,
    injuries to 163

D.

DAMAGES. (*See* PASSENGER CARRIERS, NEGLIGENCE.)
    trains behindhand 19, 20
    passenger carried past 35
        " bitten by dog 37
        " injured by others 39, 174
        " unlawfully ejected 41, 42
    too remote 41
    loss of baggage. (*See* BAGGAGE.)
    injury caused by *vis major* . . . 71

INDEX. 197

DAMAGES—*continued.*
PAGE
    unforeseen accidents . . 71, 72
    discoverable defects 72
    injuries to children. (*See* CHILDREN.)
    to passengers and employees . . . 88, 89
    injuries producing death. (*See* DEATH.)
    amounts recovered for 97, 98, 99
    excessive, ground for new trial . . . 98
    prospective . . . . . , . 99
    for what injuries given 99, 100

DEADHEAD. (*See* FREE PASSHOLDERS.)

DEATH PRODUCED BY INJURIES,
    remedy for, purely statutory . . . , 89, 90
    Lord Campbell's Act 90
    who may sue for damages 90
    damages for pecuniary loss . . • . . 90
    for mental anguish 90, 91, 92
    loss of wife . . . . . . • 91
    of mother 91
    death must not be instantaneous 93
    different rules as to amount of damages . 93, 94, 95, 97
    not to be perfect compensation 95
    deceased diseased, or of bad character 95
    or heavily insured 95, 96
    settlement before death 96

DELAY,
    carrier liable for damages for . . . 20, 21
    to what extent 22
    in sailing of vessels 167

DEVIL'S INVINCIBLES, THE 180

DOG,
    company responsible for acts of, at station] . . . 37
    lost dog 107

DRIVING. (*See* STAGE COACHES, ROAD.)
    negligence in 2–7, 128, 129
    owner, if driving, responsible 6
    carriage jointly hired, joint liability 6
    horses running away 132, 133
    upsetting a friend 133
    need not examine one's carriage every day . . . 133
    negligence of driver affects passenger . . . 137, 138
    in dangerous places 145

DRUNKEN PASSENGER,
    carrier may refuse to take . . . 165

DUE CARE,
                      PAGE
    what is it? 74
    carrier must exercise 70, 75
    not enough to deliver up passenger dead . . 71
    must use best precautions in practical use . . 71

E.

ENTOMOLOGICAL EXPERIENCES . . . 158
EVICTION FROM CARS,
    for not shewing ticket . 35, 46
EXCESSIVE DAMAGES,
    a ground for new trial . . . 98
EXCURSION TRAINS,
    company liable for accidents on . . 85

F.

FARE. (*See* TICKETS, PASSENGERS.)
    passenger refusing to pay on cars . . 34, 37
    tendering at last moment 38
    must be paid even if no seat 39
    prepayment in stages 125
    if paid, seat may be reserved 125
    if not prepaid, payable at end of journey . . 127
    carrier has lien on baggage for . . 140, 184
    but not on passenger 140, 184
    no fare on children born *en route* . . . 185
    but there is on people dying 186
FERRYMAN,
    must provide safe and secure boats, &c. . . 156
    liable for safety of horses, though driven by owner 156, 157
    horses jumping overboard 157
FIGHTING IN CAR 38
FINGERS, SQUEEZING, IN CAR . . . 66, 67
FIRE,
    liability for baggage burnt at station . . 122
    baggage destroyed on boat by . . . 175
    statute Geo. III. exempts carrier . . 175, 176
    but not on rivers of Great Britain . . . 175
    statute in force on lakes and rivers of America . 176
    Canadian Act as to carriers by water . . 176
    other carriers liable for loss by . . . 176
FISHING-ROD,
    is baggage 113

INDEX.

	PAGE
FOG,	
accidents arising from	131
FREE-PASS HOLDERS,	
entitled to be carried safely	84, 85
unless special agreement exempting carrier	85, 86
newsboy	86
loss of baggage of	108

G.

GETTING ON AND OFF,	
train in motion	55, 56
stage coach	142
GOOD FOR THIS DAY ONLY,	
ticket marked	31
or " for this trip only "	31
" for twenty days from date "	31, 32
GUN AND PISTOLS,	
considered personal baggage	113, 114
GUEST AT HOTELS. (*See* INNKEEPER.)	
cannot choose his room	150
need not go to bed	150
loss of baggage	153, 154

H.

HOTELKEEPER. (*See* INNKEEPER.)	
HOUSE INFESTED BY VERMIN,	
need it be paid for?	158, 159
HUSBAND AND WIFE,	
entitled to carry double baggage	26
henpecked husband's will	92, 93

I.

ICY PLATFORMS,	
railway company liable for	18
INDIAN RAILWAYS	69
INDECISION	61, 139
INJURIES INFLICTED BY STRANGERS	2
INNKEEPER. (*See* HOTELKEEPER.)	
running a 'bus—loss of baggage	112
who is an innkeeper	147
need not have a sign	147
must receive all who can pay	148
unless diseased, or disorderly	148
his own absence, or sickness, no excuse	149, 155
guest cannot choose his room	150

INNKEEPER—*continued*. PAGE
    but need not go to bed 150
    notice limiting liability for loss 150, 151
    claiming the benefit of the Act 151
    prima facie liable for things stolen 152
    negligence of guest 153, 154
    giving key does not free from liability 153
    guest taking exclusive charge 154
    things stolen from commercial room 154
    owner must be a guest 154, 155, 159
    horses of guests 156
    lien 157
    not liable for assaults on guest 159
INSURANCE AGAINST ACCIDENTS 8–13
INVITATION TO ALIGHT. (*See* ALIGHTING AT STATIONS.)
IRON HORSE,
    injuries from charge of 24

J.

JEWELLERY,
    is personal baggage . . . 111
JOSH BILLINGS,
    his description of a tea table . . . 152
JUMPING OFF,
    train in motion 36
    through fear of accidents 36
    stage coach 129
JUNCTIONS,
    liability of various companies at . 36
JURY,
    decisions of . . . 81

L.

LAWYERS 140
LEG,
    value of 98
    value of a baby's 99
LIEN OF INNKEEPERS,
    to what it extends 157
LIMITATION OF LIABILITY,
    of hotelkeepers 150, 151
    of carriers by water 182, 183
    of railway companies for baggage 62, 110
LOCOMOTIVES,
    must ring or whistle at crossings . . . 15

INDEX. 201

	PAGE
LOSS OF TIME	99
LOST BAGGAGE. (*See* BAGGAGE.)	
LOST OVERBOARD	186
LOST TICKET. (*See* TICKET.)	
loss of ticket falls on passenger	33, 34
even though previous purchase proved	34

M.

MAN RUN OVER	105
MASTER. (*See* RAILWAY COMPANY, STAGES, STEAMBOAT.)	
when liable for acts of servants	2, 3
MATRIMONIAL PROSPECTS,	
damages for injuries to	100
MEDICAL DEFINITION OF BLACK EYE	48
MERCHANDISE,	
not personal baggage	114
MICE AND RATS,	
carriers responsible for damages by	185
MONEY OF PASSENGERS,	
when carrier liable for	27, 28, 114, 144
not beyond a reasonable sum	27
negligence of passengers	28, 144
MUSICAL INSTRUMENTS,	
are they personal baggage?	114

N.

NEGLIGENCE OF PARTY. (*See* PASSENGER CARRIERS.)	
injury received in alighting	53, 54, 108
in entering car	67
on platform of car, or in baggage, wood or freight car	78, 80
no notice forbidding standing on platform	78
plaintiff in fault	78
no room inside car	78
party in express car	79
in charge of children	83
party is affected by driver's negligence	137
at inns and hotels. (*See* INNKEEPER.)	
NEGLIGENCE OF RAILWAY COMPANIES,	
injury not sufficient proof of	25
starting train too soon	36
stopping at unsafe places	50, 51, 55
defect in car window	65
unforeseen accident	70
injury *prima facie* proof of it	71, 73

INDEX.

NEGLIGENCE OF RAILWAY COMPANIES—*continued.*   PAGE

    latent defects 74
    loss of a dog . . . . , . 107
    not whistling at crossings 136
        (*See* RAILWAY COMPANY, STATIONS.)

NEGLIGENCE OF SERVANTS,

    in driving 2, 3
    towards fellow-servants 3
    baggage falling off truck 36, 37

NEGLIGENCE OF STAGE COACH PROPRIETOR,

    liable for negligence of driver 128, 129
    drivers must watch where they go 128, 129
    plaintiff guilty of negligence 130
    proprietor answerable for smallest neglect . . . 130
    or defects in coach 130
    unless hidden 130
    driver must be discreet, and all things sound . . 131
    not actual insurers 131
    real accidents 131, 132
    horses running away 132
    passenger suffers from driver's neglect . . . 137, 138
    party falling in ascending 142
    damage from rain 142
    acts of God 142
    driver charging for parcels 144
    dangerous places 145

P.

PASSENGER. (*See* FARE, TICKET.)

    BY COACH,
        negligence of driver affects passenger .   137
        driver must stop at usual places . .   141
    BY RAILWAY.
        refusing to pay fare, may be put off . . . 34, 37
        tendering fare at last moment 38
        may be excluded for bad conduct 39
        without seat, must pay 40
        when he may be put off 40, 41
        ticket mislaid 41
        damages for ejectment 42, 43
        killed in being put off 4
        better quietly submit to conductor . . . 42, 43
        getting off at intermediate stations . . . 44, 46
        not delivering or shewing ticket 44

INDEX. 203

	PAGE
PASSENGER—*continued.*	
rights at way stations	45, 46
must conform to regulations	79
in improper places	80
walking through cars	80
BY STEAMBOAT,	
must be safely embarked and carried	162
must not smoke if forbidden	165
when may complain of bad dinners	168
excuses for bad fare	168
ungentlemanly conduct	169
threats of violence	170
must obey reasonable rules	173
protection from inanimate things	174
from violence of people	174
clothes destroyed by fire	175
captain has supreme control	179, 180
lien on baggage	184
no fare for babies born *en route*	185
must ask for required space	189
PASSENGER CARRIERS,	
not insurers	73, 131
extent of liability	73, 74, 130
PEDESTRIANS,	
may walk on road	3
must look out at crossings	7, 14
collisions of	190
PROOF OF AGE	189, 190

R.

RAILWAY COMPANIES. (*See* NEGLIGENCE.)	
must take more care of passengers than strangers	16
are not insurers of passengers	73, 131
extent of liability	73, 74, 130
do not warrant that car is perfect	74
rule as to liability in England	74
in New York	74, 131
presumption when passenger injured	71, 73
responsible for utmost care and watchfulness	73, 74, 75
obligation extends to all apparatus of transportation	71, 72, 131
constant inspection required	72
perfect apparatus not expected	74, 75, 130
degree of care required	74, 75
must adopt every precaution in known use	71, 75

204   INDEX.

RAILWAY COMPANIES—*continued.*   PAGE
    contributory negligence 78
    seats must be provided 78, 79
    injuries to children. (*See* CHILDREN.)
    responsible for all lawfully aboard 84, 85
    may limit liability 85
    limitation does not extend to independent wrongs . . 86
    injuries producing death. (*See* DEATH.)
    liability for acts of agents and servants. (*See* AGENTS, SERVANTS.)
    bad construction of line 89
    different rule as to passengers and employees . . 89
    track must be kept in order 103
    wrongs done by strangers 105, 106
    when liability for baggage ceases 121
    afterwards liable as warehousemen . . . 121

RAILWAY ACT OF 1868 34

RAILWAY CROSSINGS,
    people must look out at 14, 16, 135, 136
    watchmen not always needed at . . . 15
    when crossing dangerous 15
    bell or whistle to be sounded . . . 15, 136
    leaving railway gates open 16
    rails must be level with road 16
    diligence required in crossing, though bell is not rung . . 136
    negligence of driver of carriage affects all in it . . 137

RAILWAY POLICE 64

RAILWAY STATIONS,
    company liable for dangerous access to . . . 16, 49
    dangers at 17, 24
    must be fit for occupation 23
    ferocious dogs at 37
    platforms 47–49
    hole in platform 47
    should be properly fenced 49

RESTAURANT,
    not an inn 153

ROAD, LAWS OF THE. (*See* DRIVING.)
    keeping right side 6
    greater care needed on wrong side . . . 6, 138
    rules in England, Canada, and United States . . 138
    may be departed from 139

RUNAWAY HORSES,
    injuries by 132, 133

RURAL SIGHTS AND SOUNDS . . . 134, 151, 152, 157

S.

	PAGE
SAMPLES AND PATTERNS,	
not personal baggage	63, 114
SEA SICKNESS	170, 171
SERVANTS. (*See* MASTERS, RAILWAY, STAGE COACH, STEAMBOAT.)	
when master liable for acts of	2
master in general not liable for injuries to	3
negligence of fellow-servants	3, 101, 102
improper servants or machinery	101
what is a fellow-servant?	102
servants of different grades	103
SLEEPING-CAR SCENE	87
SNAKES AND EELS	5
SNOW BLOCKADE,	
duty of company	68
on Pacific Railway	70
STAGE COACHES. (*See* NEGLIGENCE OF.)	
literature of	124
payment of fare. (*See* FARE.)	
owner warrants soundness of stage and equipments	125, 126, 130
reserving inside	125
racing	128
negligence of driver	128, 129
passenger entitled to seat as agreed	128, 141
jolted off	133
time for refreshments	141
when fare paid, seat may be taken at any time	141
owners not actual insurers	131
STATIONS. (*See* RAILWAY STATIONS.)	
STAIRWAY,	
slippery	17
STEAMBOATS. (*See* PASSENGERS.)	
in days of yore	161
how far owners liable for state of wharf	162
sale of ticket, contract to carry safely	162
injury to people on wharf	163, 164
must carry all, unless reasonable excuse	164
bad character and disobedience to rules	165
passengers must be sober, healthy, and well-behaved	165
owners liable for not keeping to advertisements	166
time of sailing essence of contract	166
when passenger may go by another vessel	167
and recover back expenses	167
bad weather, when not excepted	167

STEAMBOATS--*continued.*   PAGE

    servants must be kind and attentive 170
    disreputable characters on board 173
    captain putting off passengers 173
    passengers must be protected from all violence . . . 174
    accidents from dangers of navigation . . . 177, 178
    a vessel must be tight, staunch, and well furnished . . 177
    master must be qualified 178
    authority of captain 178, 179, 180
    exemptions from liability for loss 182, 183
    valuables must be declared 183
    extent of liability for baggage 183
    felonious acts of servants 183
    English and American rule 183
    animals not properly secured 186
    baggage should be put in office 187
    loss of baggage 187, 188
    when baggage should be delivered 189

STOPPING AT WAY STATIONS 31

STRANGERS,
    acts of 22

T.

TELEGRAMS AND TELEGRAPH COMPANIES,
    specimen telegrams 118, 119
    company responsible for negligence 118
    notice as to repeated messages 118
    effect of notice 119
    does not free from wilful mistakes 120
    or delay in delivery 120
    sender must be aware of rule 120
    company liable for their own defaults 119
    sender alone can sue in England and Canada . . 119
    otherwise in United States 119
    carrier must pay telegrams, when baggage lost . . 191

TICKET,
    not proof of contract to carry 21
    annual or season 29
    passenger not bound to buy before starting . . . 30
    must be produced when demanded 30
    good for this day only 30
    good for this trip only 31
    unmutilated, but old 31
    coupon ticket 31

INDEX.

TICKET- *continued.*

	PAGE
cannot be used twice	31
if journey interrupted, ticket useless	32
if lost, fare must be paid again	33, 34
even if previous payment proved	34
producing ticket, or eviction	35, 46
is the contract between company and passenger	35
company may insist on purchase of	38
ticket mislaid	41
discount on	44
children without	82
through ticket, company selling liable only on its own line	103, 104
is agent for the other companies	104
rule is different as to baggage	104
company running over other lines	104
injuries on other lines	104
wrongs of strangers	105
what is implied by steamboat ticket	162

TIME TABLES,

representations in	20
must be produced	21
proof of	21

TITLE-DEEDS,

not personal baggage	59

TOBACCO PERFUMED STATIONS 23

TRACK,

must be kept in order	103

TRAINS,

must be run at regular hours	19
time of starting must be advertised	19
proof of	21
excursion trains	39
starting too soon, and without notice	45, 46
running over a man	105

TRAVELLING IN CARRIAGE,

within meaning of accident ticket	11, 12

V.

VESSELS. (*See* STEAMBOATS.)

carrier liable for damage from overloading	187

W.

WHARF,   PAGE
    steamboat company liable for improper state of   162, 164
    curiosity seekers on 163
    users of wharf must take care   . 163

WINDOWS OF CAR,
    falling down . .   65
    need not be protected   66

ADDENDA ET CORRIGENDA.

Pa 20—Note 2, for "from" read "for."
" 21—To Note 2, add, "Where a train does not stop at the proper station, damages will be given for inconvenience suffered from having to walk there; but not for illness and its consequences arising from such walk. Expenses of carriage may be recovered. *Hobbs* v. *London and S. W. Rw.*, L. R., 10, 2 B., 111.
" 24—To Note 1, add "194."
" 28—To Note 6, add "*Batson* v. *Donavan*, 4 B. & Ald. 37."
" 53—Line 1, after "wherein" insert "in."
" 67—To Note 1, add "and *Jackson* v. *Metropolitan Rw.*, L. R., 10 C. P., 49."
" 78—In Note 7, insert "34" before "N. Y."
" 96—To Note 1, add, "But a sum received on an accident insurance policy cannot be taken into account in reduction of damages for injuries caused by negligence. *Bradburn* v. *Great Western Rw.*, L. R., 10, Ex. 3.
" 101—Note 2, for "*Ketgan*" read "*Keegan*."
" 105—Line 17, for "undirect" read "indirect."
" 117—Line 14, for "their" read "its."
" 183—Line 13, strike out "not."

www.ingramcontent.com/pod-product-compliance
Lightning Source LLC
Chambersburg PA
CBHW020813230426
43666CB00007B/990